THE
RISE
OF THE
MERITOCRACY

1870-203

Michael Young

PENGUIN BOOKS AND POLITICAL CHANGE

MANCHESTER
1824

Manchester University Press

PENGUIN BOOKS AND POLITICAL CHANGE

BRITAIN'S MERITOCRATIC
MOMENT, 1937–1988

DEAN BLACKBURN

Manchester University Press

Published by Manchester University Press
Altrincham Street, Manchester M1 7JA
www.manchesteruniversitypress.co.uk

British Library Cataloguing-in-Publication Data
A catalogue record for this book is available from the British Library

ISBN 978 1 5261 2928 4 hardback

First published 2020

Typeset
by Sunrise Setting Ltd, Brixham
Printed in Great Britain
by TJ Books Limited, Padstow

For my parents, Graham and Pam

CONTENTS

Acknowledgements   viii

Introduction   I
1 Why war?   30
2 Where do we go from here?   75
3 The rise of the meritocracy   104
4 The stagnant society   133
5 Matters of principle   175
6 Free to choose   210
Conclusion   238

Bibliography   253
Index   277

ACKNOWLEDGEMENTS

A large cast of colleagues and friends have made this book possible. I am especially indebted to Hugh Pemberton. Hugh has been an invaluable source of inspiration and guidance, and his ideas and observations have shaped much of my thinking. Others deserve special mention for their assistance and support. Martin Farr sparked my interest in some of the problems that the book engages with, and I am grateful for his tremendous generosity. Steven Fielding provided some excellent advice and good humour at key junctures in the writing process. Richard Hornsey helped me to think about the cultural significance of Penguin Books in new and exciting ways. And Ben Holland has been a wonderful friend who has always been willing to listen to my ideas about the project. I would also like to thank fellow members of the Penguin Books Archive Project (2008–2013): Markland Starkie, William Wootten, John Lyon, George Donaldson, Robert Crowe, Ika Willis, Rachel Hassall, Michael Richardson and Hannah Lowery.

My colleagues at the University of Nottingham ensured that the process of writing this book was not a lonely one. Special thanks are owed to Rúben Serém, Sara Andre da Costa, Justine Trombley, Onni Gust, Dan Hucker, Michael Freeden, Matt Ward, Spencer Mawby, Joe Merton, Rob Lutton, Richard Goddard, David Civil, Joseph Himsworth, Sarah Badcock, John Young, Harry Cocks, Ross Balzaretti, Nick Baron, David Laven and Maiken Umbach, all of whom offered advice and moral support. I also discussed the subject matter of the book with scholars from further afield. Lawrence Black, Richard Jobson, James Thompson, Richard Toye and Florence Sutcliffe-Braithwaite were particularly helpful.

Jörg Arnold deserves special praise for his generosity and friendship. Not only did he help me to work through my ideas for the book, but he also offered detailed feedback on earlier versions of the manuscript.

Tony Mason, Jonathan de Peyer and Lucy Burns at Manchester University Press patiently guided me through the process of publishing a book, and two anonymous readers provided me with valuable feedback on sample chapters.

I met my partner, Louise, as I finished this project, and her companionship has been invaluable.

My parents, Graham and Pam, have been a constant source of support, and this book is dedicated to them. Finally, I would like to thank Patch, who passed away shortly after I completed the manuscript. As a dog, Patch was not particularly interested in books. But by providing friendship during the writing process, he nonetheless helped to bring this one to fruition.

INTRODUCTION

On 18 August 1970, one of Britain's most prominent public intellectuals, Richard Hoggart, delivered a brief speech at the memorial service of the publisher Allen Lane, who had died a month earlier. After praising the contribution that Lane had made to the field of popular education, Hoggart paused to reflect on the wider significance of the publishing initiative that he had founded in 1934. 'The Penguin enterprise,' he remarked, 'ranks as a remarkable expression of important aspects of our recent cultural history, and an important contributor to the process of cultural change.'[1] Hoggart seemed to suggest that Penguin's history could be employed to illuminate the cultural and social changes that had taken place in twentieth-century Britain. For he invited his audience to regard the publisher as both an architect and symptom of broader historical forces that had reshaped British society in this period. This book responds to Hoggart's invitation by placing Penguin Books at the centre of a story about post-war Britain. But whereas Hoggart was concerned with establishing the cultural significance of Penguin's achievements, this book is principally about the political sphere.

---

1   Richard Hoggart, *An English Temper* (London: Chatto & Windus, 1982), p. 123. For an introduction to Hoggart's cultural thought, see Michael Bailey, Ben Clarke and John K. Walton, *Understanding Richard Hoggart* (London: Wiley-Blackwell, 2012).

Employing Penguin's texts as a way into the intellectual politics of the period, it explores the ideas that informed political thought.

Particular attention is devoted to the 'Specials', a series of paperback books published by Penguin between 1937 and 1988. Throughout this period, these inexpensive books were important vehicles for political ideas. Some generated considerable debate among the intelligentsia and political elites, while others were purchased in such quantities that they were able to frame the way in which ordinary readers understood important phenomena and events.[2] We will attend to the distinctive characteristics of these books in more detail below. For now, let us consider the way in which they can enrich our understanding of the political changes that took place in twentieth-century Britain. First, the Specials can help us to map the ideological terrain of British politics. Their authors, many of whom were journalists, politicians and intellectuals, attempted to understand and shape the contexts that they occupied. By evaluating the narratives and ideas that informed their writings, we can develop a more sophisticated understanding of post-war intellectual politics. The Specials reveal the contours of political debate and help uncover the meanings of particular phenomena and concepts.

Second, the Specials can help us to expose the conditions from which political change emerged. In recent decades, social scientists have developed innovative approaches to thinking about change. Particular attention has been devoted to the causal role of ideas and the way in which they can shape moments of perceived crisis.[3]

2   Several scholars have noted the significance of Penguin Specials. See, for instance, Peter Clarke, 'The Keynesian Consensus and Its Enemies' in David Marquand and Anthony Seldon (eds), *The Ideas That Shaped Post-War Britain* (London: Fontana, 1996), pp. 79–80; Kenneth O. Morgan, *The People's Peace* (Oxford: Oxford University Press, 1999), p. 199; Kevin Jefferys, *Retreat from New Jerusalem: British Politics, 1951–64* (Basingstoke: Macmillan, 1997), p. 111.

3   Mark Blyth, *Great Transformations: Economic Ideas and Institutional Change in the Twentieth Century* (Cambridge: Cambridge University Press, 2002). Paul Pierson, *Politics in Time: History, Institutions, and Social Analysis* (Princeton: Princeton University Press, 2004).

But, as yet, little historical work has been done to test some of these approaches.[4] The Specials provide one means of doing so. During periods of turbulence, their authors were often more willing to challenge ideas that had previously been excluded from mainstream political thought, and the meanings of political concepts were increasingly contested. Conversely, during periods of relative political stability, the Specials often revealed a more rigid intellectual environment. Authors were more willing to operate within prevailing systems of thought, and those that did oppose the status quo found it more difficult to bring about change. By situating the books within their respective historical contexts, it thus becomes possible to identify what conditions permitted, and constrained, the opportunities for ideological innovation.

Finally, the Specials can help us to trace the relationship between Britain's political elite and the wider social milieu in which they operated. While most of their authors were members of the intelligentsia or political elite, they wrote for ordinary readers, and their arguments were often informed by particular understandings of social change. It is thus possible to use the books to explore the ways in which intellectuals and politicians conceptualised the world in which they lived.[5] They can be used, for instance, to expose changing understandings of social class. And they can be employed to trace the ways in which emergent disciplines like sociology influenced the political thinking of both ordinary readers and policy-makers.

Penguin Specials thus provide a particularly useful lens through which to view the history of British politics. Studying them can illuminate features of post-war politics concealed within existing narratives, and it can do much to expose the way in which ideas framed understandings of the political landscape.

---

4   One exception is Matthias Matthijs, *Ideas and Economic Crises in Britain from Attlee to Blair* (London: Routledge, 2011).
5   Peter Mandler, '"Good Reading for the Million": The "Paperback Revolution" and the Diffusion of Academic Knowledge in Mid-20th Century Britain and America', Eugene Lunn Memorial Lecture, 3 April 2015.

This book does not attempt to tell a comprehensive story about post-war British politics. Nor does it draw upon the full range of Penguin's political publishing. Instead, it constructs a distinctive argument about the period that follows from a selective reading of Penguin's texts. This argument cuts across many of the orthodoxies of the existing historiography, and it is thus instructive to begin by discussing the ways in which historians have described the nature of post-war British politics.

Rethinking post-war politics: The rise and fall of Britain's 'meritocratic moment'

The quarter of a century that succeeded the 1945 election is often described as a distinctive epoch in British political history. One of the first accounts to advance this notion was Paul Addison's seminal study of Britain's wartime politics. In response to the demands of total war, Addison argued, politicians and elites constructed a new governing consensus. This consensus did not emerge from an ideological accord between the Labour and Conservative parties but was instead a product of a shared commitment to creating a 'reformed style of capitalism'.[6] Addison did not offer a detailed commentary on post-war politics, but he did suggest that the consensus he described had endured until the mid-1970s. Addison's thesis has been the subject of considerable debate.[7] At the centre of the controversy has been a dispute about the ideas that informed post-war political conduct. Some accounts suggest that the policy framework of the period was shaped by social democratic ideas. According to their authors, the leaderships of Britain's main parties shared a common commitment to removing inequalities of

---

6   Paul Addison, *The Road to 1945: British Politics and the Second World War* (London: Cape, 1975).

7   For a description of this controversy, see Duncan Fraser, 'The Postwar Consensus: A Debate Not Long Enough?', *Parliamentary Affairs*, Vol. 53, No. 2 (2000), pp. 347–362.

wealth and status and were both sympathetic to the notion that full employment was desirable.[8] Others have identified conflict, rather than agreement, as the principal feature of post-war intellectual politics. Harriet Jones has suggested that Conservatives continued to articulate ideas and values that were incompatible with social democratic principles.[9] Elsewhere, Kevin Hickson has argued that continuities at the level of policy did not follow from ideological agreement. While the Labour party sought to use the Beveridgean welfare state to achieve egalitarian objectives, its Conservative opponents employed it to foster social cohesion.[10]

This book offers an alternative narrative of post-war intellectual politics.[11] By locating Penguin's political texts within their historical contexts, it suggests that the end of the Second World War did initiate a period of relative stability and consensus. But this consensus is best understood as one feature of what Guy Ortolano has

8   Dennis Kavanagh and Peter Morris, *Consensus Politics from Attlee to Thatcher* (London: Blackwell, 1994).

9   Harriet Jones, 'A Bloodless Counter-Revolution: The Conservative Party and the Defence of Inequality, 1945–51' in Harriet Jones and Michael Kandiah (eds), *The Myth of Consensus: New Views on British History, 1945–64* (Basingstoke: Palgrave, 1996), pp. 1–17. In what follows, 'Conservative' denotes a member of the Conservative party, while 'conservative' denotes an individual who is sympathetic to conservative ideas.

10   Kevin Hickson, 'The Post-War Consensus Revisited', *The Political Quarterly*, Vol. 75, No. 2 (2004), pp. 142–154. For other critiques of the consensus thesis, see Peter Kerr, 'The Postwar Consensus: A Woozle that Wasn't?' in David Marsh et al. (eds), *Postwar British Politics in Perspective* (Cambridge: Polity Press, 1999), p. 84; Ben Pimlott, 'The Myth of Consensus' in L. M. Smith (ed.), *The Making of Britain: Echoes of Greatness* (London: Macmillan, 1988).

11   In recent years, a number of scholars have sought to construct new metanarratives of the period. See Emily Robinson, Camilla Schofield, Florence Sutcliffe-Braithwaite and Natalie Thomlinson, 'Telling Stories about Post-war Britain: Popular Individualism and the "Crisis" of the 1970s', *Twentieth Century British History*, Vol. 28, No. 2 (2017), pp. 268–304; Jim Tomlinson, 'Deindustrialization not Decline: A New Metanarrative for Post-war British History', *Twentieth Century British History*, Vol. 27, No. 1 (2016), pp. 76–99.

helpfully described as Britain's 'meritocratic moment'.[12] Under the influence of Harold Perkin's seminal history of modern Britain, Ortolano claims that in the three decades after 1945, the principle of reward according to merit achieved dominance. Ability and expertise, not inherited social status or entrepreneurship, were the principal criteria employed to determine social status, and the notion that all individuals should have an equal opportunity to develop their abilities was accepted across the political spectrum. That is not to say that Britain became a meritocratic society or that meritocratic values dissolved older ideological conflicts. In many ways, the notion that post-war educational and social reforms equalised opportunity is a myth.[13] Nor did all policy-makers and commentators regard a meritocracy as a desirable destination. Those on the left tended to see meritocratic arrangements as a basis for more meaningful egalitarian change, while those on the right were often concerned that they would disturb traditional social relationships. Nonetheless, the idea that equal opportunity was desirable and that professional expertise was an engine of social and economic progress was at the centre of the ideology that legitimised the post-war political settlement. By referring to a 'meritocratic moment' that was eclipsed in the 1970s, Ortolano gestured towards an alternative narrative of post-war intellectual politics that places questions of distribution at its core. But his study, which is concerned with the careers of two prominent intellectuals, does not explore the way in which meritocratic ideas took root within the

---

12 Guy Ortolano, *The Two Cultures Controversy: Science, Literature and Cultural Politics in Postwar Britain* (Cambridge: Cambridge University Press, 2011), pp. 16–18. Harold Perkin, *The Rise of Professional Society: England since 1880* (London: Routledge, 1989).

13 Spyros Themelis, 'Meritocracy through Education and Social Mobility in Post-war Britain: A Critical Examination', *British Journal of Sociology of Education*, Vol. 29, No. 5 (2007), pp. 427–438. John Goldthorpe, 'Social Class Mobility in Modern Britain: Changing Structure, Constant Process', *Journal of the British Academy*, Vol. 4 (2018), pp. 89–111.

ideological traditions that shaped post-war Britain. This book uses the history of Penguin Books to do that work.

When we study the Specials, we can identify a narrative arc similar to that Ortolano sketched. At the moment of Penguin's inception, the political and economic crises of the late inter-war period were compelling policy-makers and intellectuals to cast around for new ideas. Those that prevailed were often those which cut across Britain's major ideological traditions, and many of them were compatible with a certain kind of meritocratic logic that was at the root of the political settlement that was forged during the Second World War. This settlement was premised on the notion that an individual's status and rewards should be determined by their talents and skills. This distributive logic was never uncontested, and it was modified in response to changing social, economic and political conditions. Nonetheless, it set the parameters of political debate. Its ability to do so followed, in part, from the way in which key historical phenomena were discussed and understood. Here, Penguin's publishing was important. Many of the books that Penguin commissioned advanced arguments and ideas that were compatible with meritocratic ideas. They often endorsed, for instance, the idea that equal educational opportunity and the development of a politics of expertise were both desirable and the inexorable products of technological change.

From the late 1960s, the meritocratic moment was eclipsed. Ideas gained currency that broke decisively with the notion of meritocracy, and many of the stories that had sustained the fragile post-war political settlement were brought under scrutiny. This ideological counter-revolution can in part be explained by considering the aspirations that meritocratic ideas had been anchored to. It had been hoped that greater social mobility and the extension of professional expertise into new spheres of human experience would generate social harmony and increased economic growth. But by the late 1960s, it appeared that meritocratic arrangements had failed to fulfil these objectives. Not only did new currents of thought point to forms of injustice and inequality that meritocratic logic could not account for, but phenomena such as student protest and industrial conflict suggested that a new intellectual settlement would be needed if social stability and capitalist growth were to be reconciled. In turn, the intellectual climate became increasingly polarised and alternative systems of ideas began to obtain greater resonance. In some respects, Margaret Thatcher and others on the right contributed to this polarisation. They revived the entrepreneurial ideal that characterised a certain kind of Victorian social thought, and they challenged the authority of professional expertise, particularly that which was embedded within the institutions of the state.[14] Merit was not entirely displaced as a criterion for distributing rewards and status. In a wide range of policy areas, politicians and commentators continued to draw upon ideas about ability when they were determining the value of policies and distributive arrangements. But, as Ortolano has noted, merit was no longer a cultural ideal that underwrote hegemonic ideas about politics and society.[15]

Placing the concept of merit at the centre of Britain's post-war history is, of course, a choice that threatens to conceal some important aspects of the political change that took place in this period. There are, however, a number of reasons why we might see it as an appropriate starting point. First, the idea of merit relates to some key political questions that cut across the ideological divide. As well as being bound up with debates about the appropriate distribution of status and rewards, it also informed changing understandings of social class, economic efficiency and technological change.

Second, merit is a concept that can help to clarify the relationship between social and political change. On the one hand, its

14 Raphael Samuel, 'Mrs. Thatcher's Return to Victorian Values', *Proceedings of the British Academy*, Vol. 78 (1992), pp. 9–29.
15 Ortolano, *Two Cultures*, p. 253.

meanings changed according to economic and social developments, such as the emergence of new industries and occupational
groups that made claims to status and rewards. On the other, it
was a concept that political elites could employ to shape particular understandings of these transformations. By exploring the different ways in which ideas about ability and merit changed over
time, we can thus trace the complex relationship between social
phenomena and the discourses that were employed to narrate and
understand them.

Finally, placing the concept of merit at the centre of our discussion helps us to expose patterns and tendencies that are concealed by a preoccupation with 'high' politics. Most accounts of
British intellectual history devote special attention to the realm
of parliamentary politics and are concerned, above all else, with
the thought and practices of the Labour and Conservative parties. But if we are to understand the way in which concepts like
merit acquired political significance, we must look beyond West-
minster and the temporal frame of electoral politics. This study
reaches beyond some of the common points of reference
employed to trace the circulation of political ideas. It does reflect
upon parliamentary politics, but it is also concerned with the
broader systems of thought that informed political thinking, and
it demonstrates that if we want to understand the relationship
between ideas and politics, we need to look beyond the weighty
tomes written by celebrated political thinkers. The popular
paperbacks authored by the economic journalist or the obscure
backbench MP may not have reached the level of logical consis-
tency that we find in the landmark works of J. M. Keynes, Friedrich Hayek or Anthony Crosland, yet it was these kinds of texts
that reached large audiences and spoke to immediate social and
political problems.

This book also differs from most discussions of post-war politics
by drawing attention to the concepts that informed political thinking. As Michael Freeden has demonstrated, political ideologies can

be thought of as groups of concepts.[16] Because these concepts do not possess fixed meanings, it is necessary to understand the way in which they are given meaning at particular historical moments. We cannot assume that a concept had the same meaning in 1983 that it had in 1945. Nor can we assume that particular concepts were the exclusive property of certain political groups. This means that we must acknowledge the blurred boundaries that separated different ideologies and be attentive to the way in which certain concepts were able to cut across ideological divides.

Merit was one such concept.[17] Like many of the concepts that formed the basis for political thinking, its meanings were contested. That was, in part, because it is an ambiguous word. At the most general level, it merely delineates a quality that is worthy of a certain kind of reward. It does not articulate a sense of what this quality might be. Nor does it necessarily distinguish merit as being good or just. But at any point in time it is a concept that has held certain overarching meanings in relation to the ethical and social values held by those who refer to it. In the period that this book is concerned with, it tended to be associated with positive human qualities that served the common good. It is telling that when the sociologist Michael Young coined the term 'meritocracy' in a seminal work of dystopian fiction, he defined merit as a combination of intelligence and effort. Both of these attributes, Young argued, had come to be seen as desirable human qualities that could provide the basis for social progress.[18] Not all in this period associated merit with these attributes, but Young's book, published by Penguin in 1961, does

---

16 Michael Freeden, *Ideologies and Political Theory* (Oxford: Clarendon Press, 1996).

17 Chris Renwick has made a similar observation regarding the concept of social mobility. See Chris Renwick, 'Movement, Space and Social Mobility in Early and Mid-Twentieth-Century Britain', *Cultural and Social History*, Vol. 16, No. 1 (2019), p. 24.

18 Michael Young, *The Rise of the Meritocracy* (Penguin, 1961), back cover. Unless otherwise stated, the place of publication for cited Penguin publications is Harmondsworth.

demonstrate the way in which intelligence and effort came to be associated with a certain kind of logic that was available to policy-makers and political elites.

When I make reference to meritocratic reasoning, I am refer-ring to a way of thinking about how rewards should be allocated among members of a society. Advocates of meritocratic reasoning tend to claim that an individual's merits should determine the rewards they receive for their labour. That is not to say that all advocates of meritocratic ideas agree with each other. They often define merit in different terms and arrive at different arguments about how it should be rewarded. But they do share a common enthusiasm for the idea that rewards should be earned on the basis of ability. In turn, they tend to be critical of alternative ideas about distributing wealth and status. They are critical, for instance, of the entrepreneurial argument that rewards should be allocated according to an individual's possession of, and willingness to manipulate, economic capital.[19]

Having sketched the book's narrative, it is now necessary to locate Penguin Books within it by exploring the publisher's cultural and political significance. We can begin this task by demonstrating the role that it played in transforming the British publishing industry.

Penguin's 'paperback revolution'

Penguin Books was founded in 1934 by Allen Lane, a young pub-lisher who had served as the director of one of Britain's most pres-tigious hardback imprints, The Bodley Head.[20] The project emerged from Lane's disillusionment with many of the assump-tions that governed the inter-war publishing trade. These assump-tions were, to a large extent, rooted in class-based prejudices about the reading habits and tastes of the British public. Most publishers

---

19 Perkin, *Professional Society*, p. xiii.
20 For a discussion of Allen Lane's character, see W. E. Williams, *Allen Lane: A Personal Portrait* (London: The Bodley Head, 1973).

assumed that working-class readers were satisfied by 'lower' forms of cultural production, and they were therefore reluctant to publish their titles in cheap editions that might undermine the sales of their expensive hardbacks. For his part, Stanley Unwin lamented the common reader's reluctance to purchase works of literature. 'The average Englishman's idea,' he wrote, 'is that the book is a thing that one begs, borrows, sometimes steals, but never buys except under compulsion.'[21] Similar views were expressed by the director of Chatto & Windus, Harold Raymond, who warned that the 'steady cheapening of books is in my opinion a great danger in the trade at present'.[22] Nor did publishers believe that paperback books were appropriate vehicles for the most valuable forms of human knowledge. Their flimsy covers and small print, it was argued, were only suitable for the ephemeral 'low-brow' fiction that was sold at railway stations and other non-specialist retailers. When they produced cheap reprints of their popular titles in soft-cover editions, they thus did so out of expediency rather than enthusiasm.

Booksellers did little to disturb publishers' hostility to quality paperback books. Because they assumed that their middle-class clientele was unlikely to be seduced by perishable reprints, many feared that they would be unable to sell them in sufficient quantities to return a worthwhile profit.[23] Accordingly, they ordered them in small numbers and placed them on lower shelves that were less visible to patrons.

Allen Lane challenged the economic and cultural assumptions that informed the inter-war book trade. Having observed the limited

---

21 Stanley Unwin, *The Truth about Publishing* (London: Allen & Unwin, 1976), p. 160.

22 Cited in Jeremy Lewis, *Penguin Special: The Life and Times of Allen Lane* (London: Penguin, 2005), p. 93. In July 1936, Raymond wrote 'my general attitude to that series [Penguin] is one of grave doubt and I have not yet come to the conclusion whether my friend Lane is a public benefactor to the book trade or a public enemy No. 1'. Penguin Books Archive, University of Bristol (subsequently cited as 'PA'): DM1294/3/1/1–9.

23 A. C. Hanney, 'Making the Public Book-Conscious', *The Publisher's Circular*, 29 December 1934.

success of earlier interventions in the field of paperback publishing, he suggested that there was a vast audience of readers who would be prepared to buy quality literature if it were made available to them at an affordable price. The expansion of formal education, combined with the steady increase in leisure time, had, he argued, generated a new reading public with an appetite for quality literature:

> It seems really true that people are becoming more and more curious about the variety and fascination of life in all its aspects. Their interests are passing beyond the immediate necessities of their own lives to an awareness of man's past and a concern with the possibilities of his future.[24]

Lane's critique of publishing orthodoxy was not only rooted in a sociological argument; it was also based on a belief in the ability of all readers to enjoy the highest forms of cultural production. As Penguin's first production manager, Edward Young, later noted, Lane believed that 'it was time to get rid of the idea that the only people who wanted cheap editions belonged to a lower order of intelligence and that therefore cheap editions must have gaudy and sensational covers'.[25]

At the core of Penguin's publishing ethos, then, was an egalitarian aspiration. Lane and his colleagues believed that all readers should have access to the most valuable forms of knowledge, and they were committed to removing the material and social barriers that stood between the reader and good literature. This aspect of Penguin's publishing philosophy has cast a long shadow over popular understandings of the publisher's cultural, and indeed political, significance. Richard Hoggart's evaluation was emblematic. 'Penguins,' he wrote, 'will go down as one of the last expressions

---

24 Allen Lane, 'Penguins and Pelicans', *The Penrose Annual* (1938), p. 42.
25 Edward Young, 'The Early Days of Penguins', *Book Collector*, Vol. 1, No. 4 (1952), p. 210. For a discussion of Edward Young's contribution to Penguin's development, see Dean Blackburn, 'Young, Edward Preston', *Oxford Dictionary of National Biography* (Oxford: Oxford University Press, 2012).

of the liberal dream, the dream which made men think that if they tried to speak honestly and clearly they might indeed reach one another.'[26] He identified two principal features of the publisher's character. First, he drew attention to its 'sense of caring about the mind and its disciplines'. Lane and his editors, he observed, believed that all readers possessed an intellectual curiosity that, if satisfied, would be conducive to social, cultural and political progress. Implicit here was the notion that Penguin was a vehicle for a liberal humanist conception of knowledge. Hoggart seemed to suggest that the publisher placed faith in both the attainability of authentic meanings and the ability of human societies to communicate them.

Second, Hoggart identified Penguin as a serious enterprise that served the 'responsible needs of [its] audience'.[27] By making choices about the books it made available, and by presenting them in certain forms, editors encouraged readers to develop a taste for 'higher' forms of culture. This, Hoggart argued, placed Penguin in opposition to the attitudes and assumptions that were associated with 'mass' culture. Whereas crime novels and popular magazines distracted and debased their readers, the Penguin book was a noble object that cultivated co-operative and moral sensibilities.

Scholarship on Penguin has tended to replicate Hoggart's ideas about its nature and significance. In his perceptive biography of Allen Lane, Jeremy Lewis identified the publisher as one manifestation of a broader progressive project that dominated post-war British politics.[28] Rick Rylance has suggested that Penguin 'extended cultural and intellectual literacy and broke down the restrictive

26 Hoggart, *An English Temper*, p. 122.
27 Richard Hoggart, 'The Reader' in *Penguins Progress, 1935–60* (Penguin, 1960), p. 28.
28 Lewis, *Penguin Special*, p. 4. Also see Malcolm Bradbury, 'Foreword' in Linda Lloyd-Jones (ed.), *Fifty Penguin Years* (London: Penguin, 1985), p. 7; Ken Worpole, 'Penguin's Progress', *Marxism Today*, September 1985, p. 41; Brooke Crutchley, 'The Penguin Achievement', *Book Collector*, Vol. 1, No. 4 (1952), p. 211.

practices in taste and ideas that "the trade" and the cultural mandarins contrived to defend through much of Allen Lane's career'.[29] And Nicholas Joicey, in his study of the publisher's cultural significance, described it as the 'literary companion to the 1944 Education Act, the Keynesian Arts Council, and the 1951 Festival of Britain'.[30] In different ways, all of these accounts suggest that Penguin was an egalitarian enterprise that was one component of a social, cultural and political consensus that emerged in the 1940s and which dissolved in the 1970s. They do little, however, to consider the nature of this consensus or the way in which the publisher contributed to the intellectual politics of the post-war period. By locating Penguin's political publishing within a story about changing attitudes towards social status and distributive justice, this book reaches beyond the 'consensus' narrative and reveals a more complex story about Penguin's cultural politics.

Penguin was not a static enterprise. In response to change, its managers and editors adopted new practices and revised their understanding of the world in which they lived. This fact presents both a challenge and an opportunity. It requires us to be attentive to the complex ways in which change shaped non-fiction publishing, but it also offers an opportunity to understand the forces that helped to bring about social, cultural and political change in the post-war period. In order to do this, we might heed the advice of Quentin Skinner, who once wrote that 'The rise within a given society of new forms of social behaviour will generally be reflected in the development of corresponding vocabularies.'[31] Skinner was, in

---

29 Rick Rylance, 'Reading with a Mission: The Public Sphere of Penguin Books', *Critical Quarterly*, Vol. 47, No. 4 (2005), p. 64. Also see Richard Hornsey, '"The Penguins Are Coming": Brand Mascots and Utopian Mass Consumption in Interwar Britain', *Journal of British Studies*, Vol. 57 (October 2018), p. 815.

30 Nicholas Joicey, 'A Paperback Guide to Progress: Penguin Books, 1935– c.1951', *Twentieth Century British History*, Vol. 4, No. 1 (1993), p. 26.

31 Quentin Skinner, *Visions of Politics: Volume One* (Cambridge: Cambridge University Press, 2010), p. 179.

essence, claiming that new social practices and ways of thinking are often registered in a society's language. If we endorse such a claim, it has implications for how we might interpret Penguin's texts. It invites us to use the conceptual architecture of these books to tell a broader story about social and political change. When authors used concepts in innovative ways, they were often responding to underlying changes. We can thus use their books to identify the moments when change was being registered in political vocabulary. But if we are to read Penguin's books in this way, we need to consider the audiences that they reached. As they completed their work, authors and editors did not operate in a social vacuum. They imagined a body of readers whose needs they were attempting to serve. And unless we know something about these imagined communities, it is difficult to know what their books can tell us about social and cultural change.

'Cleansing the doors of perception'? Penguin and its imagined publics

Penguin privileged certain forms of cultural production over others. Its editors, despite being committed to the democratisation of Britain's cultural life, were not willing to sanction all forms of reading. Rather, they sought to encourage kinds of literature that were deemed to be conducive to cultural enlightenment. This did much to shape Penguin's engagement with its audiences and the wider social context in which it operated. Most importantly, it led the publisher to question the idea that its audience was an anonymous mass whose qualities were indeterminate. Indeed Lane and his senior editors did not want their product identified as a commodity to be consumed by all readers. On some occasions, this led Lane to celebrate the demands that his books placed upon their readers. Commenting on the early Pelican list, he remarked: 'There was no pandering to an imagined "popular taste" in the selection of [the] books; it was all very serious stuff; much of it heavy going.'[32] Similarly, W. E. Williams, who served as Penguin's chief editor from 1936 until 1965, conceived of the non-fiction Pelican list as the literary equivalent to the BBC's Third Programme.[33] Writing in 1953, he suggested that Penguin's principal motive was to 'provide good reading for people who have acquired a sound taste for books'. The publisher, he continued, 'does not deal in those products which aim to excite and contaminate the mind with sensation and which could be more aptly listed in a register of poisons than a library catalogue'.[34] When a junior editor suggested that Penguin should produce shorter and more digestible introductions than the blue-covered Pelicans, Williams firmly rejected the proposal. Drawing upon Gresham's Law, he suggested that 'the increase of the second-rate tends to diminish the market for the first-rate ... Our policy at present is to make a large number of readers reach upward until they get into the Pelican class. If an easier option were offered them, they might not reach so avidly.'[35]

Williams admitted that Penguin's emphasis on maintaining intellectual standards served to restrict the size of its audience:

> I am not convinced that outside our present range of readership there is a large untapped reservoir of potential customers. I don't believe we have reached saturation point in Pelicans – indeed I think we may get double the size of that audience – but I don't believe that, beyond these confines, there is a large number of people who can be persuaded into buying a cheaper literary commodity. Their mental wants, if any, are satisfied by the lower class periodicals, and their social habit will not be coaxed towards 'serious pleasure' of any kind.[36]

---

32 Lane, 'Penguin and Pelicans'.
33 Sander Meredeen, *The Man Who Made Penguins: The Life of William Emrys Williams* (Stroud: Darrien-Jones, 2007), pp. 77–110.
34 W. E. Williams, *The Penguin Story* (Penguin, 1956), p. 22.
35 W. E. Williams to Allen Lane, 21 July 1949. PA: DM1819/22/3/1/20.
36 W. E. Williams to Allen Lane, 21 July 1949. PA: DM1819/22/3/1/20.

An educated society, Williams argued, was 'among the few things in this world which cannot be created by mass production'. Defending the rigorous tutorial classes administered by the Workers' Educational Association, he declared that the most effective means of promoting cultural improvement was to create a 'student aristocracy'. This small minority would, by 'impressing itself on those among which it lives and works and plays', help to create an 'enlightened community'.[37] These ideas came to inform Penguin's approaches to non-fiction publishing, and it is perhaps unsurprising that when the journalist Marghanita Laski assessed the publisher's cultural significance in 1956, she claimed that it was helping to 'cleanse the doors of perception'.[38]

By endorsing these ideas about the function of literature, Lane and his editors situated themselves within a broader cultural formation that took root in the inter-war period. This formation was once described by Alan Sinfield as 'left-culturism', and while a full description of its character cannot be offered here, its principal assumptions and beliefs can be briefly outlined.[39] At the core of its ideology was a belief in the essential virtues of 'high' culture. Following Matthew Arnold and F. R. Leavis, its proponents argued that canonical works were of eternal value and their appropriation by members of the working class would generate a more harmonious social order.[40] Their privileging of 'high' culture followed from a set of moral and aesthetic judgements. High culture, it was

---

37 Cited in Meredeen, *The Man Who Made Penguins*, p. 62.
38 Marghanita Laski, 'Penguin Public', *Sunday Observer*, 29 July 1956.
39 For Sinfield's discussion of 'left-culturism', see *Literature, Politics and Culture in Postwar Britain* (London: Continuum, 2004), pp. 273–278.
40 Raymond Williams, *Culture and Society* (London: Penguin 1985), pp. 285–323. A number of writers who located themselves in the Leavisite tradition, including Malcolm Bradbury and Boris Ford, had close relations with Penguin. See Malcolm Bradbury, 'Foreword' in *Fifty Penguin Years* (London: Penguin, 1985), pp. 7–11; Boris Ford, 'Round and about the *Pelican Guide to English Literature*' in Denys Thompson (ed.), *The Leavises* (Cambridge: Cambridge University Press, 1984), pp. 103–112.

claimed, was virtuous because it encouraged its audience to actively engage with moral and social questions.

Left-culturists were also suspicious of cultural activity that served commercial objectives. In their view, the profit motive led cultural producers to marginalise moral and aesthetic concerns. Despite being a capitalist enterprise, Penguin was rarely accused of being a publisher that was preoccupied with its profits. Hoggart, in his aforementioned essay, positioned Penguin in opposition to the commercial impulse: 'Of course, Penguins are in business and aim at a profit. But you do not usually feel that "It's your money they're after"; that choices are made solely, or even pre-eminently, on commercial grounds.'[41]

Finally, left-culturists gave weight to the idea that disseminating serious works of literature could build communal ties between different social groups. Such a commitment was not particularly novel. Its basic impulse, namely that education could foster a common sense of humanity, had been embedded within Britain's liberal tradition. But in the discourses of left-culturists, it acquired a different hue, whereby culture was conceived as an instrument that could expand social citizenship.[42]

Penguin's publishing philosophy was rooted in a set of liberal concerns about the autonomy and potential of the individual. Lane and his editors believed that the individual conscience was paramount, and they were hostile to the idea of a 'mass' culture that would obscure the individual's needs.[43] It is perhaps unsurprising that when they attempted to describe their audience, Penguin's editors were reluctant to construct sociological abstractions that would implicate the reader within a wider social

---

41 Hoggart, 'Allen Lane', p. 122.
42 The clearest exposition of this argument can be found in Raymond Williams' *The Long Revolution*, which was published by Penguin in 1961. Raymond Williams, *The Long Revolution* (Penguin, 1961), pp. 363–383.
43 Christopher Hilliard, *To Exercise Our Talents: The Democratisation of Writing in Britain* (Harvard: Harvard University Press, 2006), p. 142.

milieu. Instead, they placed emphasis on the diversity of their audience, and they frequently invited individual readers to recall their distinctive reading experiences.[44] It is telling that one such individual, Richard Hoggart, resisted the temptation to identify his own experience as being synonymous with those of other readers: 'I can't claim to be a typical reader and don't suppose anyone can.'[45]

Commentators were more willing to describe Penguin's audience in general terms. In her aforementioned essay, Marghanita Laski described the 'Penguin public' as a body of autodidactic readers who were primarily employed in lower-middle-class occupations:

> It is neither an elite nor an intelligentsia, and as yet capable of being only very roughly described in terms of some of the things it does. Thus we might say that it tends to read *The Observer*, to listen to the Third Programme, use the public libraries, join the Film Society, go to concerts and art exhibitions, look critically at architecture and watch birds.[46]

Such descriptions of Penguin's audience followed from subjective beliefs about post-war social change. But some evidence suggests that they did capture some basic features of the publisher's audience. In 1946, one of Britain's earliest opinion-polling organisations, Mass-Observation (M-O), conducted a comprehensive survey of a thousand Penguin readers and produced a report that summarised its findings. 'Middle class book readers,' it suggested, 'are very much more likely to be Penguin readers than people from any other class group.' Whereas 41 per cent of middle-class respondents had read a Penguin book, the corresponding figure for the working class was only

---

44 See, for instance, Malcolm Bradbury's foreword to *Fifty Penguin Years*.

45 Hoggart, 'The Reader', pp. 27–29. Also see Richard Hoggart, 'The New Battle of the Books', *New Society*, 7 July 1966.

46 Laski, 'Penguin Public'.

8 per cent.[47] Accordingly, the Penguin reader was also 'more intellectually and socially active than his non-Penguin reader contemporary'. As well as spending a greater proportion of their free time
reading and watching films, the Penguin reader was more likely to be
a member of organisations that catered to cultural and intellectual
interests.[48] Finally, the report concluded that 'if the voter is also a
Penguin reader, he is much more likely to vote Labour'. Among
middle-class Penguin readers, the Labour vote was five times that of
the Conservative party.[49] According to M-O's survey, then, the average Penguin reader was, in the immediate post-war period, a member of the middle class who was more intellectually engaged than the
average reader and whose political views were distinctly progressive.

No comparable survey was conducted by M-O or Penguin
between the 1950s and the 1980s. It is therefore difficult to establish
a clear picture of the way in which the publisher's readership
changed in this period. Editorial correspondence and the records of
Penguin's early interventions in the field of marketing do, however,
suggest that social change exerted a significant impact upon its composition, habits and tastes. As well as becoming more fragmented, its
audience developed a greater range of interests that corresponded
with new cultural forms. These changes are discussed in more detail
in Chapters 5 and 6. For now, it is sufficient to state that they contributed to the eclipse of some of the social identities that Penguin had
helped to construct. Attention can be drawn, for instance, to the
category of the 'intelligent layman [sic]'. For much of the post-war
period, this term had often been employed to describe the kind of
reader who was deemed to be at the centre of Penguin's democratic

---

47 Mass-Observation Archive (MOA): TC20/Box 9: *A Report on Penguin
World*, p. 40. As Mandler has suggested, M-O may have understated the
size of Penguin's working-class readership, as its surveys failed to accommodate artisans within their definition of this class. Mandler, 'Good
Reading for the Million', 2015.
48 *A Report on Penguin World*, p. 53.
49 *A Report on Penguin World*, pp. 45–46.

revolution. But by the early 1970s, it had largely disappeared from the publishing industry's cultural lexicon.[50]

Penguin's politics

Although he was an instinctive egalitarian, Allen Lane did not describe himself as a socialist.[51] His political convictions were probably best described by Penguin author and Labour politician D. N. Pritt, who remarked:

> I would have read him as what I would call an old-fashioned liberal ...
> It never occurred to me to think of him as a Socialist, I just thought he
> had the generous mind which would lead a man halfway to Socialism.[52]

Lane certainly upheld the belief that cultural democracy could be reconciled with individual liberty, and at some junctures he sought to reconcile his egalitarian impulses with a liberal concern for individual freedom. In 1938, for instance, he wrote that:

> There is an increasing realisation of the ultimately communal
> nature of human life, side by side with a demand for more opportu-
> nities of individual development.[53]

Like Lane, W. E. Williams was not an ideologue. One of the earliest editors of the Pelican imprint, H. L. Beales, once

---

50 Some Penguin authors were active in constructing a certain description
    of the 'intelligent layman'. See, for instance, Richard Hoggart, *The Uses
    of Literacy* (Penguin, 1958), pp. 9–10.
51 J. E. Morpurgo, *Allen Lane* (London: Hutchinson, 1979), pp. 269–270. Ian
    Stevenson, *Book Makers: British Publishing in the Twentieth Century* (London:
    British Library, 2010), pp. 105–106.
52 Interview with D. N. Pritt, 15 February 1971. PA: DM1294/14/1/40/2.
    Pritt has been a member of the Labour party until 1940, when he was
    expelled for supporting the Soviet Union's invasion of Finland. In this
    period he authored two Penguin Specials: *Light on Moscow* (1939) and *Must
    the War Spread* (1940).
53 Lane, 'Penguins and Pelicans', p. 42.

remarked: '[Williams] is a moderate. He knows that no one dogma contains all truth.'[54] It is perhaps unsurprising, then, that Lane and Williams were unwilling to furnish Penguin's non-fiction list with a distinct political identity.[55] Endorsing the pluralist ideas that had been embedded within Britain's progressive political tradition, they argued that intellectual and cultural progress was the product of a dialogue between competing ideas and values.[56] The Specials list contained a range of political views, and authors were 'free to express divergent and even heretical views'.[57] When George Orwell made reference to the series in 1938, he suggested that Penguin was forging 'the link between Left and Right which is absolutely necessary for the purpose of war'.[58]

Nonetheless, while Penguin did not develop a distinct partisan identity, the egalitarian and democratic values that were inscribed within its publishing philosophy did colour the composition of its non-fiction list. Books authored by H. G. Wells and G. D. H. Cole, two socialist writers whose thought had been shaped by their dialogue with Britain's liberal tradition, were among the first batch of titles to be published as Pelicans in May 1937. And the Specials list

---

54 H. L. Beales, 'W. E. Williams' in *Pelican Books: A Sixtieth Anniversary Celebration* (Chippenham: Penguin Collectors' Society, 1997), p. 21.

55 BBC *Frankly Speaking* broadcast, 1 February 1961. PA: DM1294/6/1/1. In his later life, Williams wrote that he 'had no political affiliations whatsoever, a form of virginity which remains unsullied'. W. E. Williams, 'The Truth about ABCA', *Sunday Telegraph*, 11 October 1970.

56 Michael Freeden, *Liberal Languages: Ideological Imaginations and Twentieth-Century Progressive Thought* (Princeton: Princeton University Press, 2005), p. 18.

57 Lewis, *Penguin Special*, p. 136.

58 George Orwell, 'Stalinism and the Aristocracy', *New English Weekly*, 21 July 1938. When an anxious Conservative party asked Lord Eustace Percy to enquire into Penguin's editorial policy in 1937, Percy's response was that they were 'sound political neutrals with no political or philosophical axe to grind'. Cited in Nicholas Joicey, 'The Intellectual, Political and Cultural Significance of Penguin Books, 1935–1956' (unpublished PhD thesis: University of Cambridge, 1995), p. 96.

became populated with works written by prominent progressives such as Richard Acland, Harold Laski, Tom Wintringham and Hugh Dalton.[59] By the early 1940s, Penguin was beginning to be identified as a prominent vehicle of centre-left opinion, and when the electorate awarded Labour a landslide victory in the 1945 General Election, some progressives cited Penguin as one of the cultural institutions that had shifted popular attitudes to the left. *Tribune*, for instance, wrote that 'Penguin Specials broke into a new book-reading market. Millions of people … found themselves guided daily to the left.'[60]

Although the political orientation of the Specials list was not determined by a rigid editorial policy, there were periods when editors became preoccupied with particular controversies and phenomena. And when they did so, they often commissioned books by authors who belonged to the same social and political milieu. In the early 1960s, for instance, a series of books were published that sought to explain the nature of Britain's relative economic decline. Their authors often had similar social backgrounds, and they often shared common assumptions about the political problems that they discussed in their writing. It is possible, then, to employ the Specials to trace the emergence of new political formations.

Ideas, hegemony and political change

This book explores the way in which particular ideas, and indeed ideologies, obtained and reproduced their authority within post-war Britain. Such phenomena can be conceptualised in a range of different ways, but in this study the concept of hegemony is employed to understand the way in which ideas mediate political

---

59 H. G. Wells, *A Short History of the World* (Penguin, 1937). G. D. H. Cole, *Practical Economics* (Penguin, 1937).
60 Cited in Lewis, *Penguin Special*, pp. 229–230.

activity. This concept has a long history. In the nineteenth century, it was used to describe the predominance of a particular state formation.[61] But a more recent framing was first developed by the Marxist theorist Antonio Gramsci, and it is this usage which is employed in the following chapters.[62] Its basic features were captured by Raymond Williams. Hegemony, Williams wrote, is:

> a lived system of meanings and values – constitutive and constituting – which as they are experienced as practices appear as reciprocally confirming. It thus constitutes a sense of reality for most people in the society.[63]

Some important propositions are present in this passage. Consider, for instance, the emphasis that is placed on the 'lived' nature of hegemonic relations. Far from being a system or structure that is fixed, hegemony is an unending process. It follows that hegemony is a relationship of dominance that must be renewed and whose reproduction requires concrete action that operates upon dynamic relations.

Second, hegemony is not conceived as a form of authority that is necessarily coercive in nature. Rather, it is identified as a system of meanings that comprise 'a sense of reality', or what Gramsci termed 'common sense'. A hegemonic project does not impose a set of coherent ideas upon a social formation that, by virtue of its subordinate status within the productive system, is compelled to conceptualise the relations of force in which they are situated in a 'false' manner. Instead, it determines the pressures and limits of

---

61 Raymond Williams, *Keywords: A Vocabulary of Culture and Society* (London: Fourth Estate, 2014), p. 141.

62 T. R. Bates, 'Gramsci and the Theory of Hegemony', *Journal of the History of Ideas*, Vol. 36, No. 2 (1975), pp. 351–366.

63 Raymond Williams, *Marxism and Literature* (Oxford: Oxford University Press, 1977), p. 110. Also see Robert Hewison, *Culture and Consensus: England, Art and Politics since 1940* (London: Methuen, 1995), p. xvi.

what communicative practices are able to articulate at a historical moment. Hegemony, then, describes a set of ideological meanings and values that possess a predominant character and determine the possibilities of communication. In *Marxism and Literature*, Williams outlined the injunction that the concept of hegemony can impose upon cultural analysis:

> The major theoretical problem, with immediate effect on methods of analysis, is to distinguish between alternative and oppositional initiatives and contributions which are made within or against a specific hegemony ... and other kinds of initiative and contribution which are irreducible to the terms of the original or adaptive hegemony.[64]

The following chapters make the sort of distinctions that Williams describes. They use Penguin's texts as instruments to trace the contours of political debate and to identify the character of those ideas which might be described as hegemonic. They are not, of course, perfect tools for performing such a task. But they do provide a useful means of determining which ideas were authoritative at particular moments in time.

Chapter outline

The Specials series was established at a moment when a series of economic and political crises were shaping Britain's intellectual politics. Chapter 1 explores the way in which Penguin's editors and authors responded to these crises. In doing so, it makes the claim that this period witnessed the emergence of ideas and social formations that became the foundation of a new political settlement. At the core of this settlement was the concept of planning, a notion whose success can be partly explained by its association with a certain kind of meritocratic logic.

---

64 Williams, *Marxism*, p. 114.

In response to the outbreak of the Second World War, Allen Lane redefined the role of the Specials. Readers, he argued, were demanding books that were 'discussing the possibility of a new world order when all this mess is over'.[65] He and his editors thus commissioned a series of books that contributed to debates about Britain's post-war reconstruction. Chapter 2 explores the contents and reception of these books. It claims that if we are to identify a hegemonic ideology in debates about post-war reconstruction, we might seize upon the concept of merit. Not only did this concept inform some of the ideas about citizenship that were popularised during the war, but it also reconciled some of the ideological objectives held by different political groups. Even non-progressives, who had often been suspicious of extending educational opportunity and other ideas that followed from meritocratic reasoning, came to regard ability as an appropriate criterion for determining the allocation of resources. These developments were informed by new understandings of Britain's social order that were popularised by the emergent field of social science.

In the post-war period, Penguin encountered a very different political climate. The Labour party's 'glad confident morning' of 1945 was succeeded by a decade of Conservative electoral success, and the Cold War appeared to narrow the boundaries of political contestation. In response to these developments, Penguin significantly reduced its engagement with politics. Not only was the Specials series temporarily suspended, but those political texts that it did publish garnered much less attention that their predecessors. Chapter 3 looks at these developments and locates them within a broader shift in the intellectual climate of British politics. It argues that particular narratives of the period were able to acquire a hegemonic status and that they served to restrict the efficacy of new formations that were attempting to displace the dominant values

---

65 Allen Lane to Charles Laughton, 1 February 1940. Cited in *Fifty Penguin Years*, p. 38.

and beliefs of the post-war meritocratic moment. These narratives often followed from the notion that new forms of social mobility were rendering older social antagonisms redundant. Their predominance can, in part, be attributed to the way in which meritocratic assumptions were reconciled with objectives that were shared by Britain's major ideological traditions.

From the early 1960s, it became common for intellectuals and policy-makers to argue that Britain was in a state of decline. Indeed by 1963, when Harold Wilson became the leader of the Labour party, it was possible to identify a widespread cultural unease that stemmed from anxieties about Britain's relative economic performance and the apparent decay of its social and cultural life. Penguin published a number of books that explored the phenomenon of decline, and by exploring their arguments and reception, Chapter 4 suggests that in the early 1960s the legitimising ideology of Britain's post-war settlement was renegotiated. Previously, the institutions that comprised this settlement had been conceived as egalitarian instruments that could resolve social antagonisms. In response to declinist anxieties, however, some political elites sought to redefine their function. Centre-left writers, for instance, came to regard the welfare state and other state institutions as agencies that could engineer a more rational and entrepreneurial social order. Many accounts have described the early 1960s as a moment that legitimated a meritocratic vision of the future.[66] Yet a study of Penguin's texts suggests that the fragile meritocratic consensus of the preceding decade was fracturing under the weight of Britain's perceived decline.

In the late 1960s, as the second Wilson government struggled to resolve a number of economic problems, the contradictions of Britain's meritocratic settlement were brought to the fore. The chief consequence was the emergence of a more polarised political climate. As it had done in the inter-war period, Penguin's texts

---

66 Hewison, *Culture and Consensus*, pp. 123–158.

revealed this polarisation. The publisher, which had been regarded as a benign instrument of cultural democracy in the preceding two decades, became implicated within broader patterns of ideological conflict that were driven by the collapse of the post-war consensus, and its books gave voice to ideas that were difficult to reconcile with the status quo. Chapter 5 traces these developments and suggests that they amounted to an eclipse of Britain's meritocratic moment.

The final chapter of the book discusses the social and political changes of the 1980s. By locating Penguin's books in a broader context, it challenges the notion that Thatcherism reshaped Britain's political landscape. Although some Thatcherite themes acquired a hegemonic status in this period, others often encountered considerable resistance. Indeed Penguin's books reveal that the 1979 and 1983 elections did little to resolve the social antagonisms that had been exposed in the 1970s. Not only did many of its publications expose the contradictions of Thatcherite policies and beliefs, but they also popularised ideas that were incompatible with Thatcherism's legitimising ideology. Some of these ideas would inform the New Labour project of the 1990s, and it is possible to argue that the origins of Thatcherism's demise can be traced to the early 1980s. A conclusion then relates some of the book's arguments to contemporary developments. By exploring some of the non-fiction texts that Penguin have published in the last decade, this conclusion argues that many of the distributive questions that Thatcher sought to resolve are now placing urgent demands upon political elites.

I

WHY WAR?

When Penguin published the first Special, in November 1937, Britain was in the grip of two inter-related crises. The first was economic. Although some efforts had been made to resolve the economic downturn that had followed from the global financial crisis of 1929, over 10 per cent of the adult population remained unemployed, and primary poverty continued to blight large sections of the population.[1] The second crisis was political. The Spanish Civil War had aroused considerable anxiety, and as they observed Hitler's advance, many commentators and intellectuals had begun to argue that liberal democracy was under threat. This chapter views these crises through the lens of Penguin's political texts. It begins by exploring the way in which these crises were described by Penguin's authors before tracing the ideological change that took place in response to them. The late inter-war period was a moment of rupture that witnessed the birth of a new ideological settlement. Despite being fragile and fraught with tensions, this settlement nonetheless established some hegemonic principles and assumptions that were accommodated by a wide range of policy-makers and intellectuals.

---

1   Sidney Pollard, *The Development of the British Economy, 1914–1990* (London: Edward Arnold, 1992), p. 124.

The argument that the late 1930s witnessed the emergence of a new intellectual settlement with enduring consequences is not entirely new. As early as 1964, Arthur Marwick suggested that in their attempts to resolve the economic turbulence of the period, progressive politicians and intellectuals established a policy agenda sponsored by agencies of 'middle opinion' and which laid the groundwork for the creation of the post-war welfare state.[2] But while Marwick and others were preoccupied with ideas about planning that formed the basis for political agreement, this chapter is concerned primarily with the way in which certain assumptions about reason and knowledge brought together intellectuals and policy-makers from different ideological traditions. Its central claim is that by the time war was declared, a set of ideas about rationality and the appropriate function of expertise had obtained a hegemonic status. These ideas had significant implications for the way in which many actors understood the social order and the nature of political conflict, and they provided a foundation for more substantive debates about the state and the kinds of policies that could resolve the perceived social conflict of the inter-war period.

When they constructed the intellectual basis for new kinds of political co-operation, political elites were not operating in a social vacuum. Their thinking was informed by broader social and cultural changes that disturbed older assumptions and generated new demands and aspirations. Penguin certainly played its part in these changes. Its commercial success followed, in part, from the emergence of new social groups that challenged prevailing cultural hierarchies, and many of Penguin's books popularised a nascent sociology of 'everyday life' that allowed new descriptions of Britain's social order to gain currency. One of the objectives of this chapter is to explore the implications of this regime of knowledge.

---

2   Arthur Marwick, 'Middle Opinion in the Thirties: Planning, Progress and Political Agreement', *English Historical Review*, Vol. 79, No. 311 (1964), pp. 285–298.

Penguin Books, which played an important role in disseminating new ideas, was both architect and symptom of the pre-war political settlement. In many respects, its social democratic vision of cultural democracy chimed with its legitimising ideology. As well as popularising the ideas of those progressive writers who were attempting to forge an alliance between anti-fascist forces, Penguin also supplied books to an emergent social scientific community that was forging a link between science and democracy.[3] And its own attempt to reconcile its commercial interests and cultural ideals can be mapped on to a broader agenda of reform that sought to incorporate broadly egalitarian conceptions of social citizenship within an economic system that enshrined private property relations.

Because it was comprised of assumptions and beliefs that were the lowest common denominators of different ideological formations, the emergent intellectual settlement that Penguin helped to shape was fragile and incoherent. Yet it nonetheless established a set of parameters that framed wartime discussions about post-war reconstruction. It was, in part at least, the product of shared uncertainty. In response to the crises they observed, intellectuals and policy-makers from across the political spectrum cast around for new ideas that that could provide them with an understanding of their social environment and a vision of the future. In the ensuing battle for ideas, a new regime of knowledge was established, and although this did not inhibit all forms of political disagreement, it did install some hegemonic ideas that orientated political thinking towards particular problems. Many of these problems followed from new understandings of both the social order and the nature and potential of the modern state.

This chapter traces two ideological shifts that took place in the late inter-war period. First, it explores how the crises of the period changed the way in which intellectuals and policy-makers thought

---

3   D. L. LeMahieu, *A Culture for Democracy: Mass Communication and the Cultivated Mind in Britain between the Wars* (Clarendon: Oxford, 1998).

about knowledge. In attempting to understand and resolve the crises that they observed, these actors were compelled to consider the
capacity of reason to comprehend the world, and although not
everyone arrived at the same conclusions, many began to frame political problems in relation to a particular set of assumptions. Penguin
Books facilitated this shift in a number of ways. Many of its authors
advocated the conscious organisation of society in accordance with
rationalist principles; it contributed to the establishment of new social
identities that gave legitimacy to professional expertise; and it significantly increased the availability of social scientific knowledge.

Second, the chapter explores the way in which key political concepts acquired new hegemonic meanings. As Julia Stapleton has
noted, the ideological landscape of the 1930s was complex.[4] But it
is possible to identify some ways in which the intellectual flux of
the period allowed new meanings to be attached to some key concepts. These changes can be partly attributed to the way in which
ideas about the appropriate relationship between merit and reward
were accommodated by Britain's major ideological traditions.

Making democracy social: Penguin Books and cultural democracy in inter-war Britain

We can begin by discussing the wider significance of the publishing enterprise that Allen Lane established. Doing so can not only
reveal some of the social and cultural changes that informed the
intellectual politics of the late inter-war period; it can also help us
to understand why Penguin played such an important role in disseminating new ideas. When contemporaries cast their gaze upon
Allen Lane's ambitious project, they often drew attention to its
egalitarian qualities. Margaret Cole's assessment was characteristic.
Writing in the *Listener*, Cole noted that Lane had helped to

---

4   Julia Stapleton, 'Resisting the Centre at the Extremes: "English" Liberal-
    ism in the Political Thought of Interwar Britain', *British Journal of Politics
    and International Relations*, Vol. 1, No. 3 (1999), pp. 270–292.

accelerate the 'democratisation of books'.[5] Until the Edwardian period, it had been common for publishers to assume that working-class readers lacked an appetite for quality literature. But the expansion of lending libraries and the popularity of cheap reprints had led to a slow shift in attitudes. Lane's achievement was to demonstrate that there was a sizable market of readers who were willing to buy, as well as read, serious books.[6] Similar observations were made by the authors of one of Penguin's early Specials. Charles Madge and Tom Harrison had established Mass-Observation, a social research organisation, in 1937. When invited to publish a paperback outlining its activities in 1939, they identified Penguin Books as one of the institutions that had demonstrated that 'a growing number of people want less stories and more facts'.[7] After arguing that the function of democracy required a bridging of the gap between the 'intellectual leader and the ordinary man', they invited readers of the book to actively participate in their initiative.[8]

Implicit in Madge and Harrison's commentary was an argument about the classless nature of the Penguin book. The Penguin book, it seemed, was an object that could move between the cultural boundaries that separated different social groups. Other left-leaning commentators were also sympathetic to this notion, and, in turn, they often regarded the Penguin book as a both an agent and symptom of social progress. George Orwell, for instance, drew attention to the way in which the paperback book was facilitating the emergence of a common intellectual culture. Whereas their hardback companions tended to be retained within the private home, paperbacks, he noted, might 'pass through hundreds of hands before [they go] back to the pulping mill'. And because Penguin had popularised books that would have been considered 'impossibly highbrow' only a few years prior, it had expanded the market for

5   Margaret Cole, *Listener*, 22 December 1937.
6   Margaret Cole, *Books and the People* (London: Hogarth, 1938), pp. 30–32.
7   *Britain by Mass-Observation* (Penguin, 1939), p. 10.
8   *Britain by Mass-Observation*, p. 233.

quality literature.[9] Evident in Orwell's statements about Penguin is an acknowledgement of the distinctive social function of the paperback book. Penguin's inexpensive books were the vanguards of a new social movement that was disturbing cultural hierarchies by removing the barriers to 'higher' forms of knowledge.

When writers identified Penguin as an agent of democratic advance, they often awarded the concept of democracy a distinctly social meaning. They not only employed this term to denote the notion that all citizens should have an equal opportunity to exercise their democratic will; they also used it to describe the equal status that citizens should enjoy within the social order. By increasing the availability of knowledge, Penguin, it seemed, was making democracy social. There were some tensions in Penguin's vision of cultural democracy. Because Allen Lane and his editors invited their readers to 'reach upwards' in their pursuit of good literature, they necessarily privileged some readers over others. But these tensions should not obscure the way in which Lane's 'paperback revolution' contributed to the cultural democratisation that took place in the inter-war period. According to most commentators, the Penguin book was a symbol of democratic citizenship, one which had demonstrated the redundancy of the aristocratic notion that virtuous skills and talents could only be nurtured by a hereditary elite.[10]

When describing Lane's enterprise as a democratic achievement, writers drew upon broader ideas about social citizenship that had been in circulation since at least the beginning of the decade. As Pat Thane and others have noted, the 1930s witnessed the emergence of more expansive conceptions of citizenship.[11] In response to the perceived crises of the decade, intellectuals and

---

9 Cited in Steve Hare, *Penguin Portrait: Allen Lane and the Penguin Editors 1935–1970* (London: Penguin, 1995), p. 102.
10 'Books and the Public', *Spectator*, 22 July 1938.
11 Pat Thane, 'The Impact of Mass Democracy on British Political Culture' in Julie V. Gottlieb and Richard Toye (eds), *The Aftermath of Suffrage: Women, Gender and Politics in Britain, 1918–1939* (Basingstoke: Palgrave, 2013), p. 57.

commentators from across the political spectrum began to conceive of citizenship as an active, democratic process rather than a fixed and formal relationship between the individual and the state. Greater emphasis was placed upon the interdependence of the different social groups that comprised the national community, and older individualist traditions struggled to reconcile themselves with the more interventionist state that was emerging in response to technological and economic change. Even Conservatives, who had often been suspicious of arrangements that would impinge upon the individual's private sphere, began to employ organicist language to articulate a more expansive conception of citizenship. Society, they argued, was akin to a living organism whose different components were inter-related. In turn, it was argued that each member of society had a duty to act in ways that served common ends.[12]

Penguin sat among the institutions that were circulating these novel understandings of social citizenship. Its vision of cultural democracy correlated with the notion that citizens had social responsibilities to the society in which they lived. When it encouraged the active participation of readers within a community of knowledge, it railed against the idea that individuals were atomised individuals who were only concerned with their private sphere of influence. Lane and his editors defined the members of this community in particular terms. Rather than distinguishing their readers by describing their cultural tastes or class identities, they instead identified this imagined community on the basis of their intellectual aspirations. In an early edition of the publisher's newsletter, for instance, the constituency of readers that might purchase a non-fiction 'Pelican' book was described as follows:

They want to use their brains on something different from their ordinary job, but not to embark on a hobby which is merely a way of escape. They want to think more widely along lines which have a

---

12 See, for instance, Harold Macmillan, *The Middle Way* (First edition 1938. London: Macmillan, 1966).

bearing on their everyday life; they want to base their thinking, too, on authoritative books, supplied by the leaders in different spheres of activity and thought.[13]

A Penguin reader, then, was understood as a consumer of 'serious' literature who was receptive to the authoritative knowledge of the trained expert. Evident here was a distinctive social logic. By electing to purchase a Pelican book, the reader, it seemed, was aspiring to understand a world beyond their own private sphere. The book's covers reinforced this notion. Their bold text and colour-coded bands invited potential readers to conceive of them as the bearers of objective, authoritative knowledge whose value was permanent rather than ephemeral.[14]

Allen Lane's publishing enterprise was one component of a broader intellectual movement that took root in the 1930s. This movement cut across party-political boundaries, and the alliances that it forged were often fragile and temporary. Yet it was bound together by some common assumptions about the nature of the social and economic problems that had brought fascism into being.

Narrating the crisis of civilisation

The late inter-war period is often described as a moment of crisis that demanded urgent political action. But we should be suspicious of the idea that this crisis was a self-evident fact that followed from objective material conditions. As Colin Hay and others have demonstrated, crises do not generate their own meanings.[15] The way they are understood depends upon the way in which actors locate events within stories. If we are to understand the intellectual politics of the late inter-war period, it is therefore necessary to

13 'Enter Pelicans', *Penguins Progress*, April 1937.
14 I am grateful to Richard Hornsey for his insights on this matter.
15 Colin Hay, 'Crisis and the Structural Transformation of the State: Interrogating the Process of Change', *British Journal of Politics and International Relations*, Vol. 1, No. 3 (1999), pp. 317–344.

establish the way in which the crises of the period were narrated. The Penguin Specials are a particularly useful resource in this regard. Alongside other vehicles for ideas, these books helped to determine the intellectual climate in which actors operated. By identifying their dominant assumptions and themes, we can illuminate some of the ways in which intellectuals and policy-makers understood social problems and trace the way in which the crises of the 1930s disturbed older regimes of knowledge.

Penguin's early political titles reflected the mood of crisis that had punctuated political debate for much of the decade. The first books to be published in the Pelican series are particularly instructive. Adorned with blue jackets, these books offered general introductions to 'changes in the outlook of science and thought which are affecting our everyday life'.[16] The first batch of titles were edited by Krishna Menon, a committed socialist who had been a member of the Independent Labour Party until 1931, and their authors included a number of prominent socialist intellectuals, including George Bernard Shaw, H. G. Wells, Harold Laski and G. D. H. Cole.[17] Although these authors were situated in different intellectual traditions, they shared a common hostility to the ideas that had informed the policies of successive inter-war governments. Cole's *Socialism in Evolution* argued that *laissez-faire* economics was 'dead as a practical guide to industrial or commercial, or even to financial, policy'.[18] Even those economists who continued to endorse the 'older doctrines', he argued, were coming to accept that some forms of economic regulation were necessary.

---

16 '100 Not Out', *Penguins Progress*, April 1937.
17 Russell Edwards, 'Founder's Fate', *Pelican Books: A Sixtieth Anniversary Celebration*, pp. 15–17. Krishna Menon résumé. PA: DM1819/20/3. Also see Janaki Ram, *V. K. Menon: A Personal Memoir* (Oxford: Oxford University Press, 1997); J. E. Morpurgo, *King Penguin* (London: Hutchinson, 1979), pp. 119–126. In the post-war period, Menon obtained a number of prominent diplomatic and ministerial roles within the Indian government.
18 G. D. H. Cole, *Socialism in Evolution* (Penguin, 1938), p. 197.

To support his argument, Cole noted that long-term shifts in the organisation of the economy had rendered the market inefficient. As large-scale production methods had emerged, the economy had become dominated by a small number of firms, creating monopolistic patterns of ownership that had served to restrict competition. Under such conditions, the unregulated market could secure neither high productivity nor low prices.[19] In Cole's view, only state planning could repair the defects of the capitalist order.

One of Britain's leading political theorists, Harold Laski, arrived at a similar reading of the crisis. In a new introduction to *Liberty in the Modern State* (1930), which was reprinted as a Pelican in 1937, he traced the origins of diplomatic instability to the contradictions of capitalist democracy: 'at the base of the complicated motives of national policy', he wrote, 'there will be found a drive towards profit by the owners of capital who use the sovereignty of the State to defend the purposes they have in view'.[20] Though Laski was clearly influenced by Marxism, he did not believe capitalism's dissolution to be inexorable. This notion, he argued, followed from a misreading of capitalism's historic development. Despite being fraught with contradictions, capitalism, Laski argued, was a remarkably resilient edifice. In turn, he cautioned against the notion that its imminent collapse was guaranteed.

Laski's rejection of determinism reflected a broader ideological shift that took place in inter-war Britain. Until the First World War, it remained common for commentators and intellectuals across the political spectrum to subscribe to Whiggish narratives of social progress. But the destruction of the war led many intellectuals to question the notion that social progress was intrinsic to modern societies.[21] Many writers were increasingly likely to regard the

---

19 G. D. H. Cole, *Practical Economics* (Penguin, 1937), pp. 9–15.
20 Harold Laski, *Liberty in the Modern State* (Penguin, 1937), p. 18.
21 This development reflected the eclipse of idealist thinking. See Jose Harris, 'Political Thought and the Welfare State, 1880–1940: An Intellectual Framework for British Welfare Policy', *Past and Present*, No. 135 (1992), pp. 116–141.

'civilised' social order as a fragile entity.[22] As well as placing emphasis on the threat that fascism and other ideologies posed to rationalist ideas, these writers also offered increasingly pessimistic readings of human nature.

This pessimism informed how many intellectuals understood fascism. Far from being regarded as an ideology that was unlikely to take root in Britain, fascism was viewed as a general affliction that could emerge in any social order. Sir Peter Chalmers Mitchell, a zoologist who was an advisory editor for the Pelican series, wrote that 'Fascism is a pathological condition, a disease of Society. Unfortunately it is contagious ... I fear that a very slight change in economic conditions would produce the virulent phase even in England.'[23] Many political thinkers reproduced the viral metaphors that were present in Chalmers Mitchell's description, and they often endorsed the notion that if actions were not taken to extend economic democracy, fascism could begin to infect British society. Like Germany and Italy, Britain, it was argued, possessed an economic system that was fraught with contradictions. It followed that in the last instance, the capitalist class might dissolve democratic institutions in their efforts to protect their privilege. Challenging the complacency that he identified in some sections of the left, Laski wrote that the coercive power of the state was 'wholly at the disposal of the possessing class'[24] and warned that when national traditions were 'formed by fear and hate', it was more difficult for the power of reason to determine their character.[25] Cole was less sympathetic to the Marxist assumptions that informed Laski's reading of fascism, but he nonetheless placed emphasis on the resilience of capitalism and the threat it posed to democracy.[26]

---

22 Richard Overy, *The Morbid Age: Britain and the Crisis of Civilisation, 1919–1939* (London: Penguin, 2010), pp. 9–49.
23 *Authors Take Sides on the Spanish War* (London: Left Review, 1937).
24 Laski, *Liberty*, p. 29.
25 Laski, *Liberty*, p. 31.
26 Cole, *Socialism in Evolution*, p. 196.

As they brought into question the orthodoxies of the inter-war order, Penguin's authors were often drawing upon a common set of ideas about the nature of human reason. These ideas were not always articulated in explicit terms; however, they coalesced around the concept of planning and fed into a general enthusiasm for arrangements and practices that could permit the scientific attitude to expand its sphere of influence. It is perhaps unsurprising, then, that some of the most popular Penguin books of the period explored the nature and significance of scientific knowledge. J. B. S. Haldane's *The Inequality of Man* was one of the first Penguins to discuss the social consequences of the 'scientific point of view'. Haldane was a prominent figure in the field of human biology, and he identified an imbalance in the way that modern societies understood material and social phenomena. While the economies of modern societies had been transformed by scientific attitudes, the predominant approaches to social and biological problems, he argued, remained 'emotional and ethical'. He arrived at the conclusion that:

> until the scientific point of view is generally adopted, our civilisation will continue to suffer from a fundamental disharmony. Its material basis is scientific, its intellectual framework is pre-scientific. The present state of the world suggests that unless a fairly vigorous attempt is made in the near future to remedy this disharmony, our particular type of civilization will undergo the fate of the cultures of the past.[27]

One of the striking features of this passage is its reference to the 'fate of the cultures of the past'. As Richard Overy has demonstrated, the notion that civilisation was under threat gained considerable currency in the mid-1930s.[28] It not only informed the way in which many observers understood the international crisis, but it also compelled some intellectuals to redefine those 'civilising

---

27 J. B. S. Haldane, *The Inequality of Man* (Penguin, 1937), p. 22.
28 Overy, *The Morbid Age*, p. 31.

values' that had sustained civilised life. In Haldane's view, civilisation was a scientific achievement. By expanding knowledge of the
natural world, and by revealing those techniques that humans
could employ to marshal its resources, scientists had established
the foundations of the political thinking that had been responsible
for civilisation.[29] At this juncture, Haldane intervened in the debate
about the relationship between science and ethics. Challenging the
assumption that scientific values could not be applied to moral
problems, he raised two arguments. First, he claimed that the scientist, who was concerned with the pursuit of truth, suppressed
the emotion that was the barrier to the application of reason. Second, he suggested that 'since the scientist ... is contributing to an
intellectual structure that belongs to humanity as a whole, his influence will inevitably fall in favour of ethical principles and practices
which transcend the limits of nation, colour and class'.[30] When the
scientific attitude was absent, human effort was often channelled
into conflict. But if it was fostered among ordinary individuals, it
could defeat the ignorance that was at the root of such conflict.
Haldane concluded that the scientific attitude was the enemy of
prejudice and self-interest: 'The vague conception of the mean
will be rendered exact by quantitative science, and the ideal of
self-sacrifice will perhaps be rationalized as co-operation in a real
and intelligible super-individual reality.'[31]

It was not only scientists who subscribed to these ideas. Harold
Laski, writing in the Pelican edition of *Liberty in the Modern State*,
located fascism within a crisis of reason. Freedom, he argued, could
only be valued within an atmosphere of tolerance, for tolerance
allowed reason to 'exercise its empire'. Fascism, which thrived on
'angry passions', had exposed this fact.[32] In his Special, Norman

---

29 Haldane, *The Inequality of Man*, p. 119.
30 Haldane, *Inequality of Man*, p. 102.
31 Haldane, *Inequality of Man*, p. 119.
32 Laski, *Liberty*, p. 17.

Angell, a former Liberal who had joined the Labour party after the First World War, offered a similar description of fascism. After describing the way in which 'humane and kindly civilisation' had emerged from 'the scientific spirit' and a 'desire to hear the other's point of view', he went on to identify intellectual intolerance as the source of the 'repressions and cruelties' that fascism celebrated.[33] In turn, Angell restated the case for the kind of intellectual freedom that he believed could be jettisoned to justify the war effort, and he identified Penguin Books as one of the agencies that was correcting the 'emotionalism' that fascism sought to foster.[34]

Several Penguin authors described reason and emotion as opposing forces that existed in an inverse relationship.[35] This notion was central to the pacifist argument that the philosopher C. E. M. Joad offered in *Why War?* In this book, Joad urged his readers to regard reason as being vulnerable to the erratic influence of emotion:

> Emotion and desire dominate the field while they are clamant, and the voice of reason is drowned; but while the influence of reason, though weak, is uniform and persistent, the promptings of desire, though strong, are intermittent and capricious.[36]

Likewise in the first Special, Edgar Mowrer traced the origins of German fascism to a 'revolt against reason'. Contrasting the experience of Germany with that of other European states, he suggested that as liberalism came to be associated with 'real science', its enemies fostered a world view that undermined the forces of reason. 'Thinking with one's blood,' Mowrer wrote, 'became steadily

---

33 Norman Angell, *Why Freedom Matters* (Penguin, 1940), pp. 27, 35.
34 Angell, *Why Freedom Matters*, p. 134.
35 For a discussion of the influence that human psychology exerted upon the politics of the late inter-war period, see Mathew Thompson, *Psychological Subjects: Identity, Culture, and Health in Twentieth-Century Britain* (Oxford: Oxford University Press, 2006), pp. 216–225.
36 C. E. M. Joad, *Why War* (Penguin, 1939), pp. 244–245.

more popular.' The chief consequence, he wrote, was that 'the yoke of hard fact could be lifted and subjective aspiration take wind'.[37] A similar formulation could be identified in Richard Acland's Special. Before attempting to persuade the reader of the virtues of common ownership, the Liberal MP offered the following preamble:

> This book is addressed to your mind and not to your emotions. It is a challenge to you to follow what your reason tells you is right no matter what your feelings are.[38]

For Acland, Mowrer and Joad, then, the exercise of reason required the suppression of emotion.

These ideas about emotion and reason informed the way in which many Penguin authors drew the fault lines of political contestation. Their belief that reason was the antidote to tyranny led them to be suspicious of those political forces and traditions that were sceptical of rationalist arguments. The most visible of these was conservatism. Anticipating the 'Guilty Men' thesis that would be popularised in 1940, progressive writers often described Conservatives as the 'fellow travellers' of fascism.[39] In his aforementioned Special, Norman Angell, for instance, criticised those conservative 'realists' who, despite being critical of Hitler's project, were suspicious of the ability of rational argument to bring about change. In his view, the fascist threat was, above all else, a challenge to the rationalist conception of the human will. And conservatives, by viewing such an understanding of will with scepticism, had robbed themselves of the ability to oppose it. He rested his

---

37 Mowrer, *Germany Puts the Clock Back* (Penguin, 1937), p. 26. For a discussion of the psychological ideas that informed descriptions of fascism, see Dan Stone, *Responses to Fascism in Britain, 1933–39* (Basingstoke: Palgrave, 2003), pp. 20–44.

38 Richard Acland, *Unser Kampf* (Penguin: 1940), p. 11.

39 Cato, *Guilty Men* (Gollancz, 1940).

40 Angell, *Why Freedom Matters*, pp. 71–77.

argument on a restatement of J. S. Mill's claim that intellectual freedom was a prerequisite of social progress.[40] Since no individual or group could establish the falsity of an opinion with absolute certainty, it was necessary, he argued, for its opponents to permit its circulation.

Angell's commitment to rationalist politics did not follow from an optimistic belief in the inherent rationality of human societies. On the contrary, he followed Mill in believing that human beings were naturally unreasonable. But like Mill, he saw this as a reason to defend the achievements of rational thought. Reason should be protected, he asserted, because it was such a fragile and contingent force within human societies. Unless the 'cultivated reason' that followed from the free exchange of ideas was put to use, he wrote, it would be difficult to repress the 'natural impulse to refuse to listen to the critic who has the insufferable impudence to disagree with us'.[41]

A number of Penguin's authors shared Angell's belief in the innate irrationality of human societies, and their scepticism led them to favour policies and arrangements that could facilitate the expansion of rational thought. On their part, Charles Madge and Tom Harrison, in their summary of Mass-Observation's activities, described democracy as a scientific achievement and identified its extension as an antidote to fascism: 'Fascism thrives on fantasy, while democracy has grown up with science and recognition of newly noticed facts.'[42] But rather than searching for policies that could allow the scientific attitude to inform the activities of social institutions, Britain's political elites had allowed the organs of democratic society to become 'dangerously sick'.[43] At various junctures in the book, Madge and Harrison reserved particular criticism for those individuals and institutions who were complicit in circulating false accounts of the events that were reshaping the political landscape. Implicit in

---

41 Angell, *Why Freedom Matters*, p. 72.
42 *Britain by Mass-Observation*, p. 113.
43 *Britain by Mass-Observation*, p. 227.

Madge and Harrison's analysis was a reading of Britain's political crisis. By identifying the crisis of democracy as a consequence of the 'gap between the intellectual leader and the ordinary man', they invited their readers to understand the political conflict of the time as a battle between science and superstition. The advance of democracy, their book seemed to argue, was being impaired by those who were unwilling to embrace the 'science of ourselves'. It followed that it was 'scientists' and 'democrats' who were best equipped to protect civilizing values from the forces of fascism.

As these narratives of the political crisis proliferated, other ways of understanding political conflict found it difficult to gain traction. Considerable attention has been devoted to the apparent resurgence of Marxist thought in 1930s Britain.[44] But while some Marxist beliefs and assumptions gained resonance in this period, many of the ideas that informed a certain kind of orthodox Marxism were often marginalised. That was, in part, because they ran counter to the professional ideal that informed much progressive thought. Norman Angell's dispute with those Marxists who were committed to theories of class conflict is notable here. In his aforementioned defence of Millite liberalism, he rejected the Marxist reading of class:

> Merely to abolish private property, eliminate the 'master class' [and] proclaim the class war against the *bourgeoisie* (which means most of the technicians, thus putting civil servants, civil engineers, scientists of various sorts, surgeons, doctors, architects, ships' captains, navigators, cartographers, bankers, foreign traders, foreign finance negotiators, mangers of foreign currency, all on the other side of the barricade), would of itself achieve nothing but chaos and famine.[45]

Angell was threatening to endorse the idea that because professional workers had earned their status by conducting socially

---

44 James Jupp, *The Radical Left in Britain, 1931–1941* (London: Routledge, 1982).

45 Angell, *Why Freedom Matters*, p. 68. Also see Norman Angell, *After All* (London: Hamish Hamilton, 1951), p. 256.

useful work, their disproportionate rewards could be justified. Another Penguin author, Richard Acland, was also suspicious of the Marxist reading of class conflict. Whereas Marxists tended to regard class as the central source of political conflict, Acland preferred to cast the struggle for democracy as one that cut across the class divide. 'The fight,' he wrote, 'is not between the slaves and the parasites. It is between the wise men and the fools of all classes.'[46] Even some writers who were broadly sympathetic to Marxist readings of capitalism were critical of the notion that social antagonism was the source of political progress. This was, in part, because they remained wedded to an empiricist approach to political problems they had inherited from older liberal traditions. Of equal importance, however, was progressive hostility to ideas that threatened to deny the sovereignty of the individual conscience. As Buckler noted, many writers on the left remained wedded to liberal values that informed their engagement with Marxist ideas.[47] Not only did they assume that the individual's intellectual liberty was an end in itself; they also remained sympathetic to the idealist notions that had informed a certain kind of liberal thinking. Not all socialists were satisfied with the doctrines that had been outlined by Mill in the preceding century, but many regarded liberal values as the starting points for progressive political action.

Even radical socialists were often willing to accommodate liberal objectives within their prescriptions for reform. Many, for instance, preferred to argue that the flourishing of the individual's personality could only be achieved in a classless society. Stephen Spender's *Forward from Liberalism*, which was published by Victor Gollancz's Left Book Club in 1937, advanced this argument in explicit terms. Although Spender was critical of those liberal

---

46 Cited in *Left News*, March 1937.
47 Steve Buckler, 'British Marxism and Cultural Criticism in the 1930s' in Cornelia Navari (ed.), *British Politics and the Spirit of the Age* (Keele: Keele University Press, 1996), p. 92.

individualists who defended private property relations and obstructed the advance of democracy, he did not challenge their liberal values. On the contrary, he suggested that such values could only be realised within a socialist order:

> To go forward, the masses must be given not merely political but also economic freedom, so that they may produce their own free individualists and their own culture. The future of individualism lies in the classless society.[48]

In many of these Penguin books, a particular conception of class was articulated. Far from regarding class as a simple consequence of economic relations, their authors invited the notion that class was a cultural phenomenon.[49] Once this definition was accepted, it was possible to argue that class antagonisms could be dissolved through the free exchange of rational argument and the wider distribution of opportunities. It followed that it was class co-operation and education, not class conflict, that would be the antidote to fascism. Jose Harris drew attention to the way in which mid-century ideas about social citizenship tended to negate the significance of social and economic class.[50] The above evidence suggests that this relative absence of class-based claims might have been one by-product of a putative consensus about the relationship between rational knowledge and democratic politics.

These ideas did not just inform the way in which Penguin's writers engaged with political questions; they also entered into their understandings of culture and its appropriate function. *New Writing*, a literary magazine that Penguin acquired prior to the

---

48 Stephen Spender, *Forward from Liberalism* (London: Gollancz, 1937), p. 71.

49 For a discussion of the cultural Marxism that emerged in late 1930s Britain, see Ben Harker, '"Communism is English": Edgell Rickword, Jack Lindsay and the Cultural Politics of the Popular Front', *Literature & History*, Vol. 16, No. 2 (2011), pp. 16–34.

50 Jose Harris, 'Contract and Citizenship' in Marquand and Seldon (eds), *The Ideas That Shaped Post-War Britain*, p. 132.

outbreak of war, is revealing in this regard. Edited by John Lehmann, a member of the Communist party who had worked for the
Hogarth Press, the publication had been established in 1936 to act
as a cultural bridge between different social classes.[51] By publishing
short stories and poetry by writers of all classes, Lehmann hoped
to establish an accord between different cultural traditions. It was,
however, a project fraught with tensions. Lehmann was committed
to celebrating the virtues of social realist writing that exposed the
conditions of ordinary life. Yet he was concerned that this kind of
literature could reproduce 'optimistic estimates of what "the
masses" felt'. A passage in Lehmann's Pelican, *New Writing in
Europe*, a book that surveyed the literary movements that had taken
root in the 1930s, is revealing here. In the first instance, Lehmann
celebrated the democratic character of the literature that had documented the social realities of the decade:

> A new realism began to grow up, the aim of which was to create an
> image of life as it was, not for the fortunate and protected few, but
> for the millions who had to struggle for their living and bear the
> main brunt of all economic and social disturbances.[52]

But Lehmann went on to qualify his enthusiasm for the 'realist' sensibilities of the movement he had described. Many writers, he argued,
had discovered that 'proletarian realism' was an 'ocean that concealed
wide wastes cluttered with wreckage and without a breath of wind to
stir their ardent sails'.[53] He concluded that while the literary movement of the thirties had posed a valuable challenge to the modern
'literary English' tradition, 'true creative writers' could serve political
causes most adequately by 'sticking to their imaginative tasks'.[54]

---

51 Hilliard, *To Exercise Our Talents*, p. 137; John Lehmann, *The Whispering Gal-
    lery* (London: Longmans, 1955), p. 233.
52 John Lehmann, *New Writing in Europe* (Penguin, 1940), p. 148.
53 Lehmann, *New Writing*, p. 149.
54 Lehmann, *New Writing*, p. 150.

Lehmann's privileging of 'imaginative' writing, and his hostility to what he termed 'political literature', appeared to stem from a particular reading of fascism. As he later recalled, he had come to reject the notion that fascism was a mask to conceal the rational self-interest of the capitalist class and instead arrived at the conclusion that it was marked by a non-rational impulse: 'what I had witnessed, sensed, was much more like the outburst of some tremendous force from irrational depths'.[55] This statement seemed to invite the notion that that if anti-fascist writers were to challenge undemocratic forces, they should resist the temptation to oversimplify and propagandise.

In his discussion of Lehmann's political and aesthetic views, Hilliard identifies a sensibility that was distinctly liberal. The notion that a bridge could be established between the working class and the middle class, he writes, was as much an Edwardian liberal dream as a Popular Front one.[56] Hilliard's perceptive insight exposes some broader contradictions of the cultural settlement that took shape in the late inter-war period. Ostensibly, its organising principle was democratic: it sought to construct a common culture that could dissolve social antagonisms; however, it was also wedded to a set of aesthetic values that privileged particular forms of cultural production. Not all forms of culture were to be allowed entry into the enlightened democratic community. This is the legitimising ideology that Alan Sinfield referred to as 'left-culturism', and it echoed the welfare-capitalist settlement that would be popularised during the Second World War.[57]

The 'professional ideal' and the role of the expert

The ideas and arguments that have been described above were not the exclusive property of a coherent ideological formation. Nor did they entirely displace the prevailing ideas that had informed

55 Lehmann, *The Whispering Gallery*, p. 317.
56 Hilliard, *To Exercise Our Talents*, pp. 141–42.
57 Sinfield, *Literature, Politics and Culture*, p. 263.

political thought prior to 1931. Yet they shaped the way in which certain social and political phenomena were understood by many elite actors. Their ability to do so stemmed, in part at least, from the emergence of new social groups that entered the political stage and placed new demands upon political and social institutions. Since the late nineteenth century, technical and professional workers had come to acquire an increasingly important role within the economic system, and intellectuals and policy-makers sought to incorporate them into their visions of the good society. As they did so, many came to endorse what Harold Perkin described as the 'professional ideal'.[58] At the core of this social ideal was the idea that experts were the bearers of objective knowledge that could be employed to benefit all members of the community. Socialists and New Liberals had been sympathetic to this notion since the late nineteenth century, but it gained a new resonance in the wake of the First World War, and, according to Perkin, it was an engine of mid-century political change. In part, the ascendency of the professional ideal followed from concrete economic changes. As a growing class of lower-middle-class professionals acquired greater control over an increasingly complex economic system, it became easier for its members to make claims to resources based on the social value of their work.[59] Yet the rise of a professional ethic did not follow, in a mechanical fashion, from economic change. Rather, it was a product of an ideological struggle. In order for its logic to be accepted, political elites and other powerful actors needed to challenge older understandings of both the social order and the ideas that informed them.

Perkin's account, which drew upon Max Weber's sociological work, located the rise of the professional ideal within a struggle for power and control. The 'driving force' of corporatism and professionalisation, he argued, was the 'collective self-interest of

---

58 Perkin, *Professional Society*, pp. 7–9.
59 Perkin, *Professional Society*, pp. 266–273.

professional hierarchies seeking to expand their status and span of control'.[60] We might have reason, however, to question this description of the way in which the professional ideal took root. Although the rise of professionalism did follow from competition between competing social groups, the arguments that these groups made for their unique status did not follow from their 'objective' material interests. They followed from the ideas that agents held about the world in which they lived. These ideas did, of course, make reference to concrete social conditions. But they were not determined by these conditions. Penguin's books remind us of this. These books helped to shape the way in which readers understood the world in which they lived, and their authors and editors were actively engaged in constructing that world.[61] We need to be sensitive, then, to how the professional ideal was employed to tell a story about Britain's historical development and how it became anchored to ideas about the common good.

The professional ideal ran counter to the notion that social inequalities were the inevitable by-products of biological difference. Implicit in its logic was the idea that education and training could facilitate the development of skills and talents that were not inherited, for professional skills were commonly conceived as those which could be acquired through instruction and training. It is unsurprising, then, that some of the most vociferous advocates of professionalism celebrated the role that education and training could play in fostering specialist expertise.

Nor could the professional ideal be easily reconciled with the classical liberal argument that education should be concerned, above all else, with providing opportunities for individual growth. Bertrand Russell called this a 'negative' conception of education, and while he recognised its ethical virtues, he deemed it an unfit

---

60 Perkin, *Professional Society*, p. 288.
61 Daniel Béland, *How Ideas and Institutions Shape the Politics of Public Policy* (Cambridge: Cambridge University Press, 2019), pp. 32–35.

basis for establishing modern educational systems. In his view, the complexity of modern societies required educational arrangements that could educate citizens rather than individuals.[62] Attention can also be drawn to the meritocratic impulse that often followed from the professional ideal. If talents and skills were to be adequately developed, it followed that status and rewards should be disproportionately allocated to those who possessed them. The proponents of the professional ideal did not all agree upon either the criterion for determining merit or on the appropriate allocation of rewards that might follow from its distribution. What they shared, however, was a belief in the social value of the expertise that the professional class could foster.

Penguin Books helped to popularise a certain kind of professional ideal. While it did not offer an explicit statement of the virtues of professionalisation, it sanctioned activities and arrangements that could be accommodated by its logic. First, it helped to democratise the knowledge that could facilitate social mobility. Lane's hostility to the 'gentlemanly' model of publishing was one manifestation of the publisher's broader commitment to equality of educational opportunity.[63] Regardless of their social background and cultural tastes, all readers, he argued, should be permitted access to the best forms of human knowledge. Second, the publisher presented professional expertise as a social good. Both the Penguin Specials and their Pelican counterparts celebrated the achievements of the expert. Many of the books' blurbs would appeal to their author's professional credentials to establish their authority, and in much of their publicity material editors would endorse the idea that the health of complex societies was increasingly dependent upon the activities of its experts. This was not, of

62 Bertrand Russell, *Education and the Social Order* (London: Unwin, 1932), pp. 27–28.
63 In a commentary on Lane's achievement, the *Bookseller* noted that books were 'no longer sold from gentleman to gentleman'. *Bookseller*, 3 June 1936.

course, an entirely new development. Yet there was something novel about the authority that Penguin bestowed upon the author who had acquired expertise in their field of enquiry. The expert, it seemed, was not only a repository of valuable knowledge; they were also the defenders of democratic principles and civilising values.

One consequence of professionalisation was the weakening of the class divisions that had marked the Victorian social order. The expansion of new professional groups, such as those tasked with managing the expanding infrastructure of the state, had placed existing ideas about class under considerable strain. Their members were difficult to locate within the dominant vocabulary of class, and their tastes and aspirations did not always map on to prevailing cultural hierarchies. It is perhaps unsurprising, then, that many contemporaries suggested these groups were blurring the boundaries between older social classes. J. B. Priestley, for instance, made reference to a 'third England' that was disturbing older class prejudices, while Orwell traced to the emergence of individuals who were of an 'indeterminate class'.[64] As these social formations expanded in size, they imposed new demands upon the political class. They were not entirely successful in disturbing prevailing understandings of Britain's social order, but they did encourage political elites to cast aside the idea that class was an inevitable feature of modern industrial societies.

Many progressive writers began to regard the expansion of rational, technocratic expertise as an antidote to civilisation's decay. As we have seen, such writers had arrived at the argument that the emotional excesses of fascism had followed from a weakening of the forces of reason. It followed that its defeat required the organisation of society by those institutions and individuals who were best able to harness these forces. Authors and thinkers came to advocate

---

64 J. B. Priestley, *English Journey* (London: Heinemann, 1984), p. 300. George Orwell, *The Lion and the Unicorn* (London: Secker & Warburg, 1941).

arrangements that would elevate the status and authority of the dispassionate bureaucrat, and in many cases, their enthusiasm stemmed from the assumption that modern societies required bureaucracies that were managed by experts. Laski, in *A Grammar of Politics*, admitted that a socialist system would require a class of experts to manage it:

> Any system of government, upon the modern scale, involves a body of experts working to satisfy vast populations who judge by the result and are careless of, even uninterested in, the process by which these results are attained ... A democracy in other words must, if it is to work, be an aristocracy by delegation.[65]

A similar argument was made by the philosopher Bertrand Russell. In the wake of the First World War, Russell had drawn upon the insights of 'new psychology' to explore the relationship between emotion and reason. By the 1930s, he had begun to advocate the creation of a 'scientific state' that would permit the conscious organisation of social life in accordance with scientific principles. One of his central claims concerned the demands that technological change had placed upon modern societies:

> It is clear that as society grows more organic – which is an effect of modern inventions and technique – the importance of the bureaucrat continually increases ... The education of the bureaucrat will be an education for a special type of citizenship.[66]

It is now common for bureaucrats to be regarded as undemocratic officials. But Russell had the opposite view. Bureaucrats, he argued, owed their power to the forces of democracy, such that their authority was both just and responsible. To support this argument, he developed an argument that complemented Penguin's cultural vision:

> Genuine culture consists of being a citizen of the universe, not only of one or two arbitrary fragments of space-time; it helps men [*sic*]

---

65 Cited in Perkin, *Professional Society*, p. 393.
66 Russell, *Education and the Social Order*, pp. 43–44, 86.

to understand human society as a whole, to estimate wisely the ends that communities should pursue, and to see the present in relation to past and future ... The way to make men useful is to make them wise, and an essential part of wisdom is a comprehensive mind.[67]

In a revised Pelican edition of *The Economics of Inheritance*, Josiah Wedgwood, a master potter who dedicated the book to R. H. Tawney, endorsed Russell's critique of aristocratic principles and called for a significant reduction in economic inequality:

> in the searching light of recent events, can we say that Russell was wrong when he ascribed to the existence of a leisured class of inactive inheritors a timidity of thought which infects the cultural life of the society that surrounds it? And is not this timidity of thought about social problems one of the chief weaknesses that betrays democracy to dictatorship?[68]

Even those liberals who remained convinced that a leisured elite was necessary were willing to oppose the aristocratic defence of inequality. In *Civilization* (1928), Clive Bell, an art critic who was closely connected with the Bloomsbury group. Bell argued that civilised values tended to be fostered by leisured elites whose concerns were moral and aesthetic. Yet he was anxious to assert that such an elite could not be aristocratic:

> The only question would be how that class should be chosen. At present it is chosen by inheritance, a grossly extravagant system ... we may suppose that the future could devise some method which would exclude from the leisured class at least two-thirds of those whose names now swell the peerage.[69]

Bell, like Russell, justified his preference for an intellectual clerisy of experts on the grounds that rational individuals were less likely to

---

67 Russell, *Education and the Social Order*, p. 87.
68 Josiah Wedgwood, *The Economics of Inheritance* (Penguin, 1939), p. 9.
69 Clive Bell, *Civilisation* (Penguin, 1938), pp. 131–132.

be encumbered by superstition and prejudice. Whereas the reasonable individual was likely to practice 'enlightened generosity', the uncivilised, he argued, were more susceptible to the materialistic and utilitarian impulses that he associated with human misery. Bell threatened to endorse a benign meritocracy. A benevolent elite that was chosen on the basis of merit, he seemed to argue, would be a source of 'civilising' values that were the antidote to unkindness.[70]

Bell's vision, which was informed by a particular reading of Athenian democracy, was difficult to reconcile with the social democratic conceptions of citizenship that had been espoused by many progressives in the late inter-war period. His idealist and individualist assumptions ran counter to the emphasis that Tawney and others had placed upon the importance of communitarian values. But the basic notion that aristocratic principles hampered the realisation of civilising values punctuated the thinking of many intellectual formations that were responding to the perceived crisis of civilisation. We can return, for instance, to the thought of Haldane, who, as we have seen, advocated the extension of the 'scientific attitude' to social problems. 'Biology,' he wrote, 'does not support the idea that the hereditary principle is a satisfactory method of choosing men or women to fill a post.'[71] He then went on to explore the potential consequences of vocational selection. Although he acknowledged that selection by ability could lead to the reproduction of inequalities, he introduced the notion that if the social value of all talents and attributes was recognised, such selection would reconcile equality and diversity.[72]

As Philip Ironside has noted, Haldane and Russell shared a common enthusiasm for the establishment of a benevolent elite within a democratic state. Their interest in popularising scientific knowledge was not only a product of a pedagogical concern for the extension of scientific understanding; it also followed from the

---

70 Bell, *Civilisation*, pp. 85, 127.
71 Haldane, *The Inequality of Man*, p. 28.
72 Haldane, *The Inequality of Man*, p. 33.

assumption that this understanding would facilitate the emergence of a class of experts who could construct a more rational social and political order.[73] But while these thinkers were anxious to promote the development of a bureaucratic elite, they did not endorse ruthless competition between the talented for material rewards. On the contrary, they believed that co-operation was the foundation of a good society. The emotions associated with competition, Russell argued, were those that fostered hostility. In turn, he concluded that for both ethical and economic reasons, it was undesirable to teach children to be competitive.[74]

We may question how progressive writers were able to reconcile their commitment to social justice with meritocratic arrangements. After all, the latter tend to sanction inequalities of reward. Yet many progressives did not believe that the beneficiaries of meritocracy would use their status to entrench inequality, since they assumed that the professional class were immune to the kinds of acquisitive values that were the source of inequality. Josiah Wedgwood, in his study of inherited wealth, urged readers to absolve themselves of the notion that individuals were principally motivated by material desires. 'Once the struggle for bare existence is over,' he wrote, 'a sense of personal importance to the world, a sense of fellowship, and a sense of freedom provide ... the most powerful incentives to productive effort.'[75] In the inter-war period, then, the professional ideal was not anchored to a logic of competition. Writers like Russell, far from endorsing a ruthless competition for material rewards, envisaged a society in which the celebration of the skilled and talented created a harmonious social order in which power was exercised responsibly. A more meritocratic order, it was assumed, would necessarily be one that was rational and civilised.

---

73 Philip Ironside, *The Social and Political Thought of Bertrand Russell: The Development of an Aristocratic Liberalism* (Cambridge: Cambridge University Press, 1996), p. 213.
74 Russell, *Education and the Social Order*, p. 177.
75 Wedgwood, *The Economics of Inheritance*, p. 9.

These ideas about expertise and its appropriate function were not produced in a social vacuum. When they advanced them, members of the intelligentsia were responding to perceived changes in Britain's social structure, changes which implicated Penguin's own constituency of readers. According to evidence collected by organisations like Mass-Observation, many of Penguin's readers were located within an emergent class of technocratic professionals who might have been the vanguard of the intellectual elite that Russell and others had imagined.[76] Until at least the late 1940s, most of the readers who purchased its books were members of the middle class who had acquired some form of further education and who often bought books to furnish themselves with a better knowledge of social and scientific problems. And while it is difficult to trace their ideological preferences, they were more likely to vote for the Labour party and were hostile to certain kinds of class prejudice.[77] Moreover, the non-fiction Penguin book, with its unpretentious and functional design, seemed to become associated with the social identities of a class of 'technical' workers that began to emerge in the inter-war period.[78] An individual's possession of Penguin books came to be understood as a symbol of their membership of this emergent social formation, which could not be located within orthodox categories of class. When M-O surveyed reading habits in July 1942, its report described a number of readers who made explicit mention of Penguin's books and who privileged works of non-fiction. It recorded, for instance, the following statement by a draughtsman:

> Usually I buy only Penguins and books of that price class. I never buy fiction books. I pass a station bookstall nearly every night and if

76 For an account of these shifts, see Mike Savage, James Barlow, Peter Dickens and Tom Fielding, *Property, Bureaucracy and Culture: Middle-Class Formation in Contemporary Britain* (London: Routledge, 1992), pp. 36–57.

77 *A Report on Penguin World*, pp. 45–46.

78 Mike Savage, *Identities and Social Change in Britain since 1940: The Politics of Method* (Oxford: Oxford University Press, 2010), p. 66.

I see any Penguin that I think I might like I glance through it and buy it if I do.[79]

Commentators were also willing to make reference to 'technical' identities when they described the kinds of readers who purchased non-fiction paperbacks. In an article about the economic changes of the inter-war period, Margaret Cole wrote of a 'public of hundreds of thousands annually turned out by polytechnics, evening classes, and technical institutes which has never been and is never likely to go near a university, but which is no less eager to learn'. That this emergent class were buying Victor Gollancz's Left Book Club titles in large quantities was, she claimed, evidence of its hunger 'for information and guidance'.[80] As Savage has noted, it is likely that this popular interest in social science was a new development.[81] Studies of reading habits in the early decades of the twentieth century have not detected a significant interest in scientific enquiry, and before Lane published the first Pelicans, most social scientific texts were only available in hardback editions.[82] By sponsoring and disseminating the work of social scientists, Penguin helped to popularise ideas that had profound political consequences.

It is difficult to determine the political impact of the social changes that had allowed this class of professionals to develop a distinctive identity. But the rise of the professional ethos certainly increased the appeal of certain assumptions and arrangements. Chief among them was the idea that experts should play a greater role in political affairs.[83] In some instances, this manifested as a belief that expertise could resolve the need for the kinds of political contestation that had

---

79 MOA: 'Books and the Public', July 1942, f. 25.
80 Margaret Cole, 'The New Economic Revolution', *FACT*, April 1937.
81 Savage, *Identities and Social Change*, pp. 65–66.
82 Jonathan Rose, *The Intellectual Life of the British Working Classes* (New Haven: Yale University Press, 2010), p. 248.
83 Chris Renwick, *Bread for All: The Origins of the Welfare State* (London: Penguin, 2017), p. 191.

developed in modern democracies. Once objective, scientific knowledge was employed to manage the apparatus of the state, many forms of political activity, it was assumed, would be rendered redundant. Traces of this argument can be found in W. B. Curry's *The Case for Federal Union*, a Special that advocated a 'sanely organised world order'. Curry, who was the head teacher of the progressive Dartington Hall School, identified education as a prerequisite of internationalism, concluding that existing political loyalties were motivated by emotionalism rather than reason:

> Partisanship is a very good example of the type of emotional attitude now almost universally accepted as a virtue, but standing in need of modification and correction if a stable world order is to be created.[84]

As professional expertise came to be understood as a vital resource that could repair the defects of the political system, policy-makers came under pressure to take measures that would foster it. They were encouraged to regard the extension of educational opportunity as an urgent political objective, an idea that had circulated long before the crises of the 1930s imposed themselves upon Britain's political landscape. But once it was acknowledged that the preservation of liberal and democratic values was dependent upon productive efficiency, it acquired greater purchase among a greater range of elite actors. Even those who were critical of egalitarian objectives could sympathise with the notion that the most talented and able individuals should have access to positions of authority.

The success of the professional ethos is clear when we explore the way that Penguin's pre-war books discussed the concept of planning. This was a central point of reference for many of Penguin's authors, and although it was a contested concept, the frequency with which it appeared in the discourses of different

---

84 W. B. Curry, *The Case for Federal Union* (Penguin, 1939), p. 205. For a discussion of Dartington Hall's history, see Victor Bonham-Carter, *Dartington Hall: The Formative Years, 1927–1957* (Clarendon: Oxford University Press, 1970).

ideological formations was indicative of a significant shift.[85] Its apparent ubiquity followed from the widespread acceptance of fundamental assumptions about the nature of the social order and the capacity of political action to bring about social and economic change. As Michael Freeden noted, planning became a conceptual link between different intellectual traditions in the late 1930s.[86] And policy-makers from across the political spectrum often found the common denominators of their thought in their attempts to define a programme of planning.

One Pelican that devoted attention to planning was *Our Food Problem*, co-authored by the prominent social reformers Frederick Le Gros Clark and Richard Titmuss. Published in 1939, the book considered Britain's ability to sustain an adequate food supply in the event of another war. Its authors concluded that an improvement in the national diet would require a radical transformation of the productive system. As well as advocating the creation of a state agency that could rationalise the distribution and marketing of food, they envisaged the communalisation of meals that would be prepared by 'a staff of trained cooks and caterers'.[87] Another Special, *Britain's Health*, summarised a report produced by Political and Economic Planning, a social research organisation that had been established in 1931.[88] In the foreword, Lord Horder, a leading clinician, threatened to associate the shortcomings of Britain's healthcare system with the dominance of individualist assumptions:

> We are bad planners by temperament ... This is the price we pay for being a highly individualised society.[89]

85 Daniel Ritschel, *The Politics of Planning* (Oxford: Clarendon, 1997), p. 5.
86 Michael Freeden, *Liberalism Divided* (Oxford: Clarendon Press, 1986), p. 356.
87 F. Le Gros Clark and R. M. Titmuss, *Our Food Problem* (Penguin, 1939), p. 173.
88 Abigail Beach, 'Forging a "Nation of Participants": Political and Economic Planning in Labour's Britain' in Richard Weight and Abigail Beach (eds), *The Right to Belong: Citizenship and National Identity in Britain, 1930–1960* (London: I.B. Tauris, 1998), p. 89.
89 Mervyn Herbert, *Britain's Health* (Penguin, 1939), p. xiv.

The book also argued that the absence of professional expertise was one cause of poor healthcare: 'many of the new health problems', it was claimed, 'demand wider views and a fuller range of techniques than most men can acquire during a training which fails to bring them in touch with social and economic problems'.[90]

Some of the most important policy statements of the late interwar period justified planning by making reference to the politics of expertise. One such document was *The Next Five Years*, a statement of progressive policy prescriptions that was signed by a number of Penguin authors. After outlining the need for some forms of central planning to combat the insecurity that followed from unbridled capitalism, its authors noted that:

> The democratic system of government is on its trial. It will only survive if it can produce a policy equal to the problems of our time and a leadership capable of evoking the co-operation and enthusiasm necessary to carry it through.[91]

In order for the professional ideal to gain hegemony, it needed to be aligned with narratives of social and political progress. These narratives were, in many cases, informed by the idea that society could be understood in the same way as the natural world. Once it was accepted that there were laws that governed social behaviour that were akin to the laws that governed natural phenomena, it became possible to argue that the experts who could uncover that knowledge were agents of progress who could resolve the problems that political action sought to resolve. Penguin's non-fiction books played an important role in propagating this argument.

---

90 Herbert, *Britain's Health*, p. 200.

91 *The Next Five Years: An Essay in Political Agreement* (London: Macmillan, 1935), p. 7. The following signatories authored books for Penguin: Norman Angell, W. B. Curry, Eleanor Rathbone, Wickham Steed and H. G. Wells.

Penguin Books and the 'science of ourselves'

Scientific thought did not only become implicated with broader political controversies in the late 1930s; it also expanded its sphere of influence. By the time Penguin had established itself as an original publisher of non-fiction, the 'scientific attitude' was being applied to understand phenomena that had once been conceptualised through different modes of thought. The expansion of social science reflected this shift. As Halsey, Savage and others have demonstrated, sociology was, until at least the inter-war period, an undeveloped and marginal discipline.[92] Most practitioners coalesced around a small number of institutions, and much sociological analysis continued to be incorporated into other forms of enquiry. But the two decades that succeeded the First World War represented something of a critical juncture. As a modernist aesthetic took root and the professional middle class expanded, new aspirations and ideas began to challenge those 'gentlemanly' traditions of social observations that had dominated British sociology in preceding decades.[93] Among them was the notion that social science could uncover the laws that governed everyday social conduct. In the same way that biologists and scientists had brought certain natural phenomena under control, policy-makers, it was argued, could employ rational enquiry to understand ordinary human behaviour and, in turn, construct political solutions to social problems. A prerequisite for such a politics of expertise was a comprehensive knowledge of social relations. To this end, a number of institutions and initiatives were founded in the years preceding the Second World War. Of particular significance was Mass-Observation, which sought to establish a 'Science of Ourselves' by creating a network of amateur social observers who

---

92 Savage, *Identities and Social Change*, p. 93. A. H. Halsey, *A History of Sociology in Britain: Science, Literature and Society* (Oxford: Oxford University Press, 2004), pp. 48–70.

93 Savage, *Identities and Social Change*, pp. 51–66.

could establish the 'facts' of everyday life. By 1939, it had enlisted over 1,500 individuals to assist in the production of survey data and reports that explored different kinds of social, cultural and political activity, some of which were summarised in the *Britain by Mass-Observation* Special. The introductory chapter explored the social function of scientific knowledge and lamented the failure of the scientific community to disseminate its knowledge to ordinary citizens. 'The gap between science and everyman,' Charles Madge and Tom Harrison observed, 'is … one of the main problems of the survival of our civilisation.'[94] Their argument reproduced the familiar distinction between science and superstition; identifying a widespread enthusiasm for horoscopes, they suggested that individuals turning to the 'borderland of superstition' was one of the symptoms of political and social crisis.[95]

Madge and Harrison proposed a kind of scientific enquiry that was concerned with the routine practices that that shaped the social life of ordinary citizens. This enquiry was anchored to a particular understanding of democracy, of which science was the prerequisite. 'On democracy plus science,' they argued, 'our industrial civilisation is now inescapably founded.'[96] A distinctive understanding of knowledge informed this proposition.[97] It took the form of a challenge to a more liberal conception of knowledge that privileged the autonomy of individual consciousness:

> [Mass-Observation] will encourage people to look more closely at their social environment than ever before and will place before them facts about other social environments of which they know little or nothing. This will effectively contribute to an increase in the general social consciousness. It will counteract the tendency so

94 *Britain by Mass-Observation*, p. 12.
95 *Britain by Mass-Observation*, p. 22.
96 *Britain by Mass-Observation*, pp. 226.
97 Rodney Harrison, 'Observing, Collecting and Governing "Ourselves" and "Others": Mass-Observation's Fieldwork *Agencements*', *History and Anthropology*, Vol. 25, No. 2(2014), pp. 227–245.

universal in modern life to perform all our actions through sheer habit, with as little consciousness of our surroundings as though we were walking in our sleep.[98]

These aspirations corresponded with Allen Lane's ideas about non-fiction publishing. Like Lane, Madge and Harrison sought to foster a community of observation that could subvert the distance that separated different social groups. The Mass-Observation observer and the paperback book were thus implicated within a common logic: both were envisaged as mobile receptacles of knowledge that could traverse social boundaries, and both were described as democratic agents that could facilitate the expansion of scientific knowledge into spheres of social and cultural life. It is revealing that in *Britain by Mass-Observation*, M-O observers were often described as recording instruments:

> Through Mass Observation you can already listen-in to the movements of popular habit and opinion. The receiving set is there, and every month makes it more effective.[99]

The Penguin book was understood in similar terms. But while the Mass-Observation volunteer was conceived as a recording instrument, the non-fiction paperback was described as a device that disseminated information.[100] By passing within and between communities of readers, it could help individuals navigate the world in which they lived and aid their understanding of their own behaviour. The material qualities of the books helped to foster this idea that Penguins were tools of enlightenment: their dimensions allowed them to be carried and easily stored, and some of Mass-Observation's survey data suggests that Penguin's readers felt

---

98 Charles Madge and T. H. Harrison, *Mass-Observation* (London: Frederick Muller Ltd, 1937).

99 *Britain by Mass-Observation*, p. 10.

100 Attention can be drawn, for instance, to the recollections of the novelist Malcolm Bradbury. See Bradbury, 'Foreword' in *Fifty Penguin Years*, p. 8.

compelled to distribute the books beyond the sphere of the private home. In response to a survey on book-buying habits, one reader noted how they donated their Penguins once they had read them:

> [I b]uy practically every Penguin and Pelican I see ... This is a habit. Anyway you don't borrow 6d books (even now they are 9d). You buy them and give them to Toc. H. [Talbot House] or the boys home unless someone has pinched them first.[101]

Penguin and Mass-Observation can be situated within a broader social movement that was emergent in the inter-war period.[102] This movement might have been described by some contemporaries as 'middlebrow' in character, yet this term does not capture the novelty of the ideas and assumptions that it fostered, for it actively disturbed the cultural and aesthetic values that had allowed such a category to obtain legitimacy. It was primarily comprised of those workers occupying technical occupations, and its members challenged the aesthetic hierarchies that had informed modernism. Mike Savage has observed that the middle-class technocrat often preferred 'explicit' forms of knowledge and railed against the cultural snobbery of 'highbrow' literary culture.[103] In part, this was because technocrats often relegated aesthetic questions to functional ones. The non-fiction Penguin was a vital tool in the construction of this sensibility. Lane once described his books as 'straightforward and unpretentious', and in doing so, he threatened to expose a distinctive feature of both the 'Penguin public' who read them and the social formation that it was situated within.[104]

It would be problematic to claim that Penguin and Mass-Observation constructed a binary opposition between the 'literary' and the 'scientific', as both attempted to reconcile these different

---

101 MOA, File Report 1332 (July 1942), p. 38.
102 Savage, *Identities and Social Change*, p. 64.
103 Savage, *Identities and Social Change*, p. 79.
104 Lane, 'Penguins and Pelicans'.

forms of knowledge. In an early statement of Mass-Observation's research agenda, Madge offered a formulation that attempted to reconcile the functional with the aesthetic. The project, he wrote, was '(i) Scientific (ii) human, and therefore, by extension (iii) poetic'.[105] But by helping to foster social identities that were based on an 'ethic of expertise', they nonetheless subverted the cultural hierarchies associated with Britain's class system.

The emergent formation of middle-class technocrats privileged, and helped to encourage, a certain kind of meritocratic logic. Its members often accepted that distinctions of status were, for the time being, immutable. Yet they believed that these distinctions could be rendered functional and harmonious if rewards and status were determined on the basis of merit. This notion should not be taken too far, for there was no agreed criterion that could be employed to determine an individual's merits. Nonetheless, the principle that rewards should be distributed to incentivise socially useful work was central to this formation's ideological repertoire. Unsurprisingly, we can find traces of this logic in many of Penguin's texts, including Josiah Wedgwood's *The Economics of Inheritance*. Wedgwood asserted that the existing distribution of wealth contravened common ideas about social justice:

> Current ideas of justice do not, it is true, indicate clearly whether the distribution of the product of industry should be according to the needs of the individual, or according to the amount of effort which he puts forth, or according to the value of its effects, under the circumstances of the time. But it is at least certain that they are *not* in harmony with inequalities of wealth which correspond *neither* to differences in need, *nor* to differences in effort, *nor* to differences in the amount and value of the personal economic services rendered to society by the individuals concerned.[106]

---

105 Cited in Rodney Harrison, 'Observing, Collecting and Governing "Ourselves" and "Others": Mass-Observation's Fieldwork Agencements', *History and Anthropology*, Vol. 25, No. 2 (2014), p. 235.
106 Wedgwood, *The Economics of Inheritance*, pp. 52–53.

In turn, Wedgwood suggested that the way wealth was allocated was not conducive to 'a high general level of ability'.[107]

It would be problematic to claim that this 'technocratic' social formation had become the bearer of a hegemonic social logic by the time the war was declared. But its values and beliefs did correspond with many of the political ideas that were being employed by politicians and intellectuals as they grappled with the economic and social problems that they observed.

Liberty, equality and 'planning for freedom'

We have used Penguin Books to trace the emergence of a regime of knowledge that helped to popularise a professional social ideal in the late inter-war period. In the remaining pages of the chapter, attention will be devoted to the ideological consequences of this regime of knowledge. One way of mapping these consequences is to consider the way in which key political concepts acquired and shed meanings as actors employed them to understand and describe the social and political crises that they encountered. Here, two such concepts – equality and freedom – will be explored in detail.

Much has been written about the influence that liberal ideas exerted upon the left intelligentsia in the inter-war period, with some accounts claiming that core liberal values, far from being the exclusive property of thinkers who identified as liberals, informed the way in which many socialists and social democrats defined their political objectives.[108] In various ways, Penguin's books expose this aspect of inter-war politics. Many of their authors, including those who identified as socialists, conceptualised fascism in terms inherited from the liberal tradition and reproduced the argument that the individual should be the basic unit of social

107 Wedgwood, *The Economics of Inheritance*, p. 56.
108 Peter Clarke, *Liberals and Social Democrats* (Cambridge: Cambridge University Press, 1978). Freeden, *Liberalism Divided*, pp. 295–330. Renwick, *Bread for All*, pp. 8–9.

analysis. But if liberal values were the focus around which different political groups converged, they were also modified in important ways in response to the problems of the late inter-war period. Ben Jackson, in a discussion of wartime policy-making, has drawn attention to the way in which socialistic ideas were incorporated into the thinking of liberal reformers like William Beveridge.[109] A similar argument can be made about the pre-war moment. As they confronted the crises of that moment, liberals drew upon social democratic ideas and theories and became much more willing to embrace egalitarian language.

Freedom was a concept that was frequently evoked to critique the fascist enemy. It is perhaps unsurprising, then, that Penguin published a number of books that sought to give it meaning. Among them was Harold Laski's *Liberty in the Modern State*, which was published as a Pelican in 1937. The first chapter of the text was concerned with establishing an appropriate definition of liberty. Laski's first task was to consider the nature of freedom. Rejecting the idealist approach to this matter, he opted for the following formulation: 'I mean by liberty the absence of restraint upon the existence of those social conditions which, in modern civilisation, are the necessary guarantes of individual happiness.'[110] In essence, this formulation traversed the distinction that Isaiah Berlin would later draw between 'positive' and 'negative' liberty.[111] On the one hand, it preserved the notion that the essential quality of freedom was the absence of constraint. But on the other, it acknowledged that individual freedom could not be achieved in an environment in which certain social conditions were not present. It was a way of thinking about liberty that, despite its logical tensions, was to become ascendant in the years preceding the Second World War.

---

109 Ben Jackson, 'Socialism and the New Liberalism' in Ben Jackson and Marc Stears (eds), *Essays in Honour of Michael Freeden* (Oxford: Oxford University Press, 2012), pp. 34–52.
110 Laski, *Liberty*, p. 49.
111 Freeden, *Liberalism Divided*, p. 304.

A similar conception of liberty is present in W. B. Curry's Special, in which Curry dedicated a chapter to an expansive restatement of liberal values. One of Curry's principal claims was that liberalism had been contaminated by its association with *laissez-faire* economics. *Laissez-faire* principles, he argued, were often incompatible with individual liberty because they failed to account for the way in which economic security interfered with the individual's capacity to realise their desires. Two conclusions followed: first, that the liberty of all, not of the 'rich and powerful', should be respected; second, that private property should be widely distributed. Curry would not, of course, have agreed with all of Laski's propositions regarding the appropriate function of the state. Laski was much more sceptical of the claim that private property was a conduit to freedom. On the question of the desirable relationship between equality and liberty, however, they occupied some common ground. Both believed that liberty could not be defined in strictly negative terms, and both were critical of the notion that the planned allocation of resources was inimical to individual liberty.

It cannot be claimed that Laski's social democratic conception of liberty was upheld by all major political factions prior to the Second World War.[112] Nonetheless, it was a definition that became acceptable to an increasingly wide range of actors. In defining liberty as something that was essentially negative but which could not be achieved unless certain basic social conditions were present, Laski offered a way of thinking about freedom that could be accommodated by thinkers in different ideological traditions. It may even be possible to argue that by 1939, the argument that individual liberty could only be achieved in a social order that secured economic freedom for all was hegemonic. We can trace, for instance, the way in which Conservative thinkers like Harold Macmillan came to regard the establishment of a 'social minimum'

---

112 It is also notable that Laski had, by the late 1930s, moved beyond many of the propositions that he had offered in *Liberty in the Modern State*.

as an urgent task. Reproducing the kind of organicist language that had been employed by Edmund Burke, Macmillan attempted to forge a 'middle way' between socialism and unbridled capitalism. He justified his variant of capitalist planning by appealing to the idea that an individual could not be free unless they possessed the means to utilise their talents and skills.[113] It is perhaps unsurprising that Macmillan's ideas brought him into collaborative discussions with some of Penguin's leading authors, most notably G. D. H. Cole and Norman Angell.[114]

The success of the social democratic definition of liberty can be partly attributed to the ascendency of the professional ideal. According to its logic, inequalities of reward could be tolerated if they benefited the most disadvantaged members of society. It was therefore possible to endorse it when making the case for awarding rewards according to merit. Moreover, it created space for the argument that professional experts could receive greater rewards if their labour helped to improve the conditions of the poorest.

These principles could be endorsed by a wide range of policymakers and intellectuals. Tawney and other socialists had, in their efforts to construct an alternative to capitalist enterprise, suggested that the criterion of social function could be employed to determine how rewards were allocated.[115] Liberals like J. M. Keynes and Beveridge often placed emphasis on the distinctive social function performed by the professional class to which they belonged.[116] And Burkean Conservatives, who tended to see society as an organic whole whose different components needed to work in harmony with one another, could accommodate the idea that individuals should have an equal opportunity to be

---

113 Macmillan, *The Middle Way*, pp. 19–30.

114 Ritschel, *The Politics of Planning*, pp. 292–300.

115 R. H. Tawney, *The Acquisitive Society* (First edition 1921. London: Fontana, 1961), pp. 80–86.

116 Perkin, *Professional Society*, p. 341.

unequal.[117] Important ideological divisions did, of course, survive. While socialists were anxious to ensure that the privileging of professional skills and talents did not erode communal bonds, many conservatives and liberals were suspicious of the rationalist impulses that the professional ethic appeared to sanction.[118] Nonetheless, the argument that a society that rewarded technical expertise would be more efficient and more harmonious than those which did not was hegemonic by the time war was declared.

Conclusion

Situating Penguin's pre-war books within the broader intellectual debates to which they contributed reveals a series of ideological settlements that would inform wartime discussions about the possibility of a new post-war social order. These settlements were uneasy and fraught with contradictions. But they managed, for a time at least, to impose some boundaries upon political contestation. They were informed by a set of broad assumptions that took root following the perceived crisis of the 1930s. Chief among them was the assumption that emotionalism and irrationality were the source of those human impulses that had brought about fascism and war. In some instances, this notion was anchored to a critique of capitalism and its alleged vagaries. It was not only those on the left, however, who came to advocate the conscious organisation of the social and economic order to impair the advance of undemocratic forces. Many Liberals and Conservatives, albeit for rather different reasons, were also willing to endorse a politics of expertise that would harness the achievements of science. The professional ideal can thus be located at the locus of a new ideological settlement that had implications for the way in which political

---

117 See Reginald Northam, *Conservatism: The Only Way* (London: Ebenezer Baylis, 1939), pp. 97–98.
118 Stapleton, 'Resisting the Centre at the Extremes', p. 286.

elites and commentators conceptualised the social order. In part, this was because its basic assumptions regarding merit and reward cut across the ideologies that were competing with one another. This is not to say that all of Britain's main ideological traditions were satisfied with these principles. But they were all rejecting the entrepreneurial ideas about distributive justice that had been dominant until at least 1914.

Although they may have continued to offer different visions of the future that were informed by their distinctive core beliefs, Britain's major ideological traditions shared some common enemies by the time war was declared: they were all committed to resolving the perceived inefficiencies and inequities of the inter-war social order; they were all convinced that equality of opportunity was desirable; and they all rejected *laissez-faire* economics. There were, of course, dissenting voices, and it would be difficult to describe the emergent consensus as anything other than putative. But by 1939, it was possible to identify areas of political agreement that had been forged by agents like Penguin.

2

WHERE DO WE GO FROM HERE?

In response to the outbreak of war in 1939, Allen Lane declared that the primary objective of Penguin's political publishing should be to contribute to debates about post-war reconstruction: 'more and more people', he wrote, 'are talking of the economic changes which are bound to ensue than they are of the question of winning or being defeated. As far as publishing is concerned, we are switching over very considerably from books on international politics to those discussing the possibility of a new world order when all this mess is over.'[1] Many of Lane's contemporaries shared his concern with post-war reconstruction. Ordinary citizens, they claimed, would be more willing to make sacrifices if they had a clear sense of why the war was being fought, so it was essential that they were given a clear sense of what the post-war world would look like. When they attempted to envisage this world, these individuals often arrived at different ideas about changes that should be made. What they all shared, however, was a commitment to reconstituting the prevailing political and social order. This chapter explores these competing visions of the future and offers an argument about the nature of the political settlement that followed from the attempts

1 Allen Lane to Charles Laughton, 1 February 1940. Cited in *Fifty Penguin Years*, p. 38. In a letter to Agatha Christie, Lane criticised the 'diplomatic bungling' of the Chamberlain government. Allen Lane to Agatha Christie, 28 September 1939. PA: DM1819/26/1.

made to realise them. In doing so, it contributes to some long-standing historiographical controversies. One such controversy concerns the political consequences of the war. Whereas some accounts, such as those of Paul Addison and Colin Hay, have argued that the wartime period witnessed the emergence of a more consensual political order in which Britain's main parties shared considerable common ground, other scholars have maintained that the 'post-war consensus' is an illusory construct. As well as citing the persistence of ideological conflict in the wartime period, these authors also suggest that in the decades that succeeded 1945, successive governments significantly modified the state regime.[2] This chapter sheds new light on this controversy by offering an alternative account of the intellectual politics of the wartime period.

Most narratives have suggested that if the wartime period did generate a political consensus, it was one that was social democratic. Drawing attention to the broadly egalitarian consequences of the reconstruction programme that the post-war Labour government inherited, many argue that the war created space for a set of collectivist beliefs and values that became hegemonic. These accounts possess some validity. The wartime period did generate widespread enthusiasm among elites for policies that were designed to redistribute wealth from the rich to the poor. Yet it is difficult to argue that this common enthusiasm fundamentally resolved the ideological conflicts of the inter-war period. The debates about wartime reconstruction reveal a remarkable range of ideological objectives that motivated individuals across the political spectrum. While Conservatives and centrist liberals were suspicious of the state and sought to protect the principle of private property, socialists and progressive liberals sought to erode the rights of property owners, envisioning wartime innovations as a starting point for a more

---

2   Paul Addison, *The Road to 1945* (London: Cape, 1975). Colin Hay, *Re-Stating Social and Political Change* (London: Open University Press, 1996). Harriet Jones and Michael Kandiah (eds), *The Myth of Consensus: New Views on British History, 1945–64* (Basingstoke: Palgrave, 1996).

egalitarian social order that would be administered by a centralised state. It is necessary, then, to look elsewhere for a concept that can best describe the ideological settlement that was forged in the 1940s. This chapter suggests that merit might be one such concept.

The beliefs and ideas that were articulated in Penguin's wartime publications offer an insight into a consensus that was, above all else, meritocratic. This consensus did not chiefly concern the visions of the future that political elites advanced, which continued to be informed by very different ways of thinking. Instead, it concerned their beliefs about the most efficient means of executing the war effort and the appropriate relationship between ability and reward. At its core was a range of assumptions regarding the relationship between reason and politics. By 1945, many political elites from Britain's main intellectual traditions had accepted that the preservation of democratic politics depended upon the political authority of scientific knowledge and the expansion of educational opportunity. In turn, they often endorsed reforms that were accordant with a certain kind of meritocratic logic. That is not to say that they wanted to realise a meritocracy. Yet they all became more sympathetic to the argument that strengthening the relationship between merit and reward would, in the short term at least, be conducive to social progress. In part, this was because this principle was the lowest common denominator of their respective belief systems.[3] Under the conditions of war, it became necessary for different political factions to identify principles and arguments that could foster co-operation across the political divide. Equal opportunity and reward according to ability were two such principles.

---

3   Jose Harris has hinted at this kind of argument. In a survey of wartime social change, she argued that while the political class might have rejected the notion of a hereditary class hierarchy during the war, it replaced it with the aspiration to create 'a meritocracy of measurable intellectual talent'. Jose Harris, 'War and Social History: Britain and the Home Front during the Second World War', *Contemporary European History*, Vol. 1, No. 1 (March 1992), pp. 17–35.

The tacit endorsement of meritocratic arrangements was also the result of electoral pressures. Meritocratic arguments seemed to reconcile the twin objectives of liberty and equality in a way that chimed with popular conceptions of social justice. And when they endorsed them, political elites could not be accused of privileging the interests of a particular social class. In the context of war, when national unity appeared to be a prerequisite of the social order's survival, appealing to the ideal of a classless social order was politically attractive. It was also accordant with the principle of equality of sacrifice, which, as Sonya Rose has demonstrated, framed popular understandings of the war effort.[4]

Alongside other agencies of ideas, Penguin helped to forge this consensus by popularising a set of ideas about the nature of the conflict that Britain had entered and the means of establishing a more harmonious post-war order. Its authors tended to agree that the war was a moment of opportunity that could only be won by constructing a more collectivist state regime that enshrined democratic principles. Many of the publisher's authors, in their efforts to justify their prescriptions for change, appealed to the virtues of equality of opportunity and anticipated the creation of a classless social order. In doing so, they often established arrangements that were fraught with logical contradictions. These contradictions would, in the post-war period, prompt the emergence of new ideological formations that actively resisted meritocratic reasoning. But for a time at least, meritocratic logic was the ideological adhesive that held together a putative and fragile political settlement.

An audit of the status quo

Once Britain declared war, many intellectuals and commentators began to undertake an audit of the state institutions that would be

---

4 Sonya Rose, *Which People's War? National Identity and Citizenship in Wartime Britain 1939–1945* (Oxford: Oxford University Press, 2004), pp. 8–14.

charged with the task of executing the war effort. Some of the forums in which this scrutiny took place were concealed from the popular gaze; however, the Penguin Specials, which continued to sell in remarkable quantities, ensured that the existing system of governance became a subject of public debate. Some of these books devoted attention to the democratic institutions that had been brought under scrutiny by the Popular Front campaign. Harold Laski's *Where Do We Go from Here?*, for instance, cast its gaze upon the nature of capitalist democracy and blamed the contradictions of capitalism for the coming of war.[5] Elsewhere, H. G. Wells, in a Penguin published in 1940, advocated a new world order in which nationalism would be displaced by a 'unification of the common interests of mankind'.[6] The upshot of capitalist productive relations, he argued, was conflict, for it was the waste and inefficiency of competitive capitalism that had created the antagonisms that fascism had channelled.[7]

Some Penguin authors identified the establishment of the Churchill-led coalition as an opportunity to break decisively with a moribund political order. The Political Secretary of the Transport and General Workers' Union, John Price, made this point with particular force. In *Labour in the War*, Price claimed that the Chamberlain government had represented a 'system that had failed' and urged readers to regard May 1940 as the starting point for a new form of democracy. 'Democracy,' he wrote, 'implies something more than the enjoyment of political right; there must be industrial and social democracy before a State can be truly democratic ... And liberty does not mean only physical liberty ... It presupposes equality of opportunity, without which true liberty is unattainable.'[8]

In their audit of the status quo, these authors often criticised the way in which the existing social order had suppressed the forces of

5   Harold Laski, *Where Do We Go from Here?* (Penguin, 1940), p. 39.
6   H. G. Wells, *The Common Sense of War and Peace* (Penguin, 1940), p. 62.
7   Wells, *The Common Sense of War and Peace*, p. 28.
8   John Price, *Labour in the War* (Penguin, 1940), p. 173.

reason. According to their analyses, the capitalist state was not only guilty of wasting the productive capacity of labour; it was also suppressing human talents and impairing the development of scientific and technical knowledge. In his wartime Special, John Gloag, a broadcaster and industrial design consultant, lamented the way in which the prevailing social system allowed inferior individuals to acquire positions of authority:

> People with less spectacular ability, and people who lack ability of any kind, are frequently furnished with opportunities because they have influential friends, inherited wealth or inherited social status.[9]

Other commentators did not only privilege the skills and ability of the talented; they also suggested that disproportionate status should be given to those individuals who were contributing to the acquisition of objective, scientific knowledge. The novelist Phyllis Bottome articulated such an argument in her contribution to *Our New Order or Hitler's?*:

> The field is open to all who are prepared to work in it with unswerving loyalty to truth, so far as can be ascertained by perspective observation, crucial experiment and unprejudiced interpretation … These are the only conditions of which all volunteers are welcome and high rank is given by general assent to those who have proved themselves worthy of it by their contributions to knowledge.[10]

A number of arguments followed from this way of understanding the war. First, it was often assumed that political regeneration would be made possible by extending access to, and enhancing the authority of, scientific knowledge. According to many progressives, the war was, above all else, a product of the moral decay that had followed from capitalist development and the pursuit of

---

9   John Gloag, *What about Business?* (Penguin, 1942), p. 8.
10 Cited in Phyllis Bottome (ed.), *Our New Order or Hitler's?* (Penguin, 1943), p. 50.

self-interest. They thus believed that the war effort had to be accompanied by a social revolution that could replace prejudice with rational logic. This reasoning informed Wells' insistence that the status quo was morally bankrupt:

> The main battle is an educational battle, a battle to make the knowledge that already exists accessible and assimilable and effective ... The new brains ... are being waylaid by the marshalled misconceptions of the past, and imprisoned in rigid historical and political falsifications.[11]

Striking a similar tone, Aleck Bourne, in his Special on healthcare, stated that 'the very foundations of our thoughts, ideas and way of life must be altered. So great a change seems impossible during the ordered run of modern life, but the upheaval of a major destruction, which is the present war, may provide the opportunity for a change of human values.'[12]

Second, it followed that a successful war effort would require the dismantling of certain social inequalities. If the fascist enemy was attempting to suppress freedom and defend greed, it was difficult to defeat it while denying freedom to a large proportion of the population. Bottome articulated this sentiment in clear terms when she stated that 'Men [sic] are judged by their deeds; and we cannot refuse our own share of responsibility for the Nazi logic until we shift all of our activities into the opposite direction.'[13] As Sonya Rose has noted, the notion of equality of sacrifice became central to much discussion of the war effort. This principle was more easily propagated by the forces of the left, but even the Conservative party sought to defend it in order to break with the perceived injustices and inequities of the inter-war period.[14] One way of reconciling this principle with the existence of substantial

---

11   Cited in Aleck Bourne, *Health of the Future* (Penguin, 1943), p. 186.
12   Bourne, *Health of the Future*, p. 15.
13   Bottome (ed.), *Our New Order*, p. 8.

inequalities of reward was to modify the justification for such disparities. Rather than justifying inequalities in defence of the entrepreneurial ideal, conservatives and liberals argued that they could be
justified on the basis of efficiency and effort. This logic had been present in the writings of progressive Conservatives like Harold Macmillan in the late inter-war period. But in the wartime period, it found
allies among an increasingly large section of conservative opinion.[15]

To some extent, the general shift towards this meritocratic justification of inequality had been in progress since the late nineteenth
century, when the rise of the Labour party and ascendency of a
more collectivist New Liberal tradition of thought brought the
aristocratic defence of privilege under threat. But the Second
World War helped to vanquish the residues of the class-based conception of society on which this defence had been premised. By
May 1940, the entrepreneurial ideal, which had been predicated
on the notion that the individual's entrepreneurial spirit was the
engine of progress, was in abeyance. Policy-makers from across
the political spectrum were searching for new ideological frame-
works that could be employed to map a new social order.

If the call for change was heard across the political spectrum,
there was significant disagreement about what form this change
should take. Conservatives and centrist liberals tended to be suspicious of the state and cautioned against policies that might impose
restrictions upon property owners and business leaders. Conversely, socialists and left-liberals proposed a significant extension
of state authority and the creation of a planned economy that
could distribute resources according to social needs.[16] These

---

14 Winston Churchill, 'Objectives after the War' in Bottome (ed.), *Our New
    Order*, p. 14.
15 Macmillan, *The Middle Way*, pp. 372–374. David Clarke, *The Conservative
    Faith in a Modern Age* (London: Conservative Political Centre, 1947), p. 14.
16 Jose Harris, 'Political Ideas and the Debate on State Welfare' in H. L.
    Smith (ed.), *War and Social Change: British Society in the Second World War*
    (Manchester: Manchester University Press, 1986), pp. 233–263.

differing approaches to post-war reconstruction could not be easily reconciled. There were, however, some ideas that were able to cut across the ideological divide and provide the basis for a new political settlement. Many of these ideas deferred, rather than resolved, the ideological questions that had been provoked by the outbreak of war. Yet they did provide the basis for political agreement in a period when co-operation between different political formations was both necessary and desirable.

Science in war

As Rodney Barker argued, the ascendency of collectivist policy solutions in the wartime period can, in part, be explained by tracing their sponsorship by experts.[17] Although collectivist ideas might have acquired consent on the basis of their logical force, they were also legitimated by their epistemological authority. By the time the war began, it had become common for policy-makers across the political spectrum to regard expert knowledge as both dispassionate and authoritative.[18] And matters that had once fallen within the realm of politics came to be regarded as technical problems whose resolution required objective expertise, not subjective moralising. Penguin's wartime texts expose the political consequences of this regime of knowledge. They reveal that arguments about the nature of scientific knowledge and its appropriate relationship with politics fostered enthusiasm for certain policy prescriptions and formed the basis of new social alliances.[19]

In many instances, Penguin's authors regarded the expert as the servant of objective reason who was unreceptive to the moralising of political debate. Such an idea was clearly evident in David Lilienthal's Special on the Tennessee Valley Authority (TVA), a

17 Barker, *Political Ideas in Modern Britain*, pp. 145–146.
18 Perkin, *Professional Society*, pp. 407–418.
19 David Edgerton, *Britain's War Machine: Weapons, Resources and Experts in the Second World War* (London: Allen Lane, 2011).

federally owned institution that had been established in the United States to modernise Tennessee's economy. Lilienthal celebrated the institution's system of democratic planning and rested his case on a particular understanding of the expert. The expert, it was assumed, was the handmaiden of reason and could, in turn, identify the 'facts' of a situation. Lilienthal regarded the expert as an antidote to prejudice and self-interest, and a bulwark against social conflict.[20] This description of the expert had important consequences. It not only protected expertise from the accusation that it was one kind of knowledge among others; it also invited policy-makers to regard the expert as an agent of democratic advance. Such an argument was advanced by the contributors to *Science and the Nation*, a Pelican that was produced at the end of the war. The last chapter offered an explicit argument about 'the politics of science', claiming that 'democracy needs a greater technical awareness, a rise in the standards of social and technical thinking'.[21] Similar ideas were advanced in other Penguin texts. In *Our New Order or Hitler's?*, the astronomer Richard Gregory claimed that the 'guiding principles of science are among the basic principles of democracy. They combine independence with co-operation; they recognise fundamental human rights; and they are essential factors in the establishment of a worthy and righteous form of society.'[22]

When they celebrated the virtues of scientific discovery, writers often constructed a declinist narrative about the inter-war period. The social and economic crises of this period, it was argued, had followed from ignorance of scientific knowledge among the political class. Perhaps the most widely read exposition of this narrative can be found in *Science in War*, one of the most successful Specials of the wartime period. The genesis of the book can be traced to a meeting of the Tots and Quots dining group. Comprised of some

20 David Lilienthal, *Tennessee Valley Authority: Democracy on the March* (Penguin, 1944), pp. 105–108.
21 *Science and the Nation* (Penguin, 1947), p. 246.
22 Bottome (ed.), *Our New Order*, p. 52.

of Britain's leading scientists, this group assembled in London to discuss how scientific knowledge could be applied to assist the war effort. Among the attendees was Allen Lane, who, after listening to the speakers, remarked that a transcript of the proceedings would have made an excellent Penguin Special. One of the group's founders, Solly Zuckerman, seized upon the comment and issued Lane with a challenge: if a manuscript was delivered within a fortnight, could Penguin publish it within a month? Lane accepted, and, remarkably, the book rolled off the printing presses only weeks later.[23] Throughout the book, it was argued that scientific knowledge had been marginalised within the state institutions that wielded power. Rather than embracing the scientific community, these institutions, it was argued, were wedded to the 'Victorian liberalism' that had done so much to impair social progress in the inter-war period.[24] Implicit here was a critique of the entrepreneurial spirit that liberals had often endorsed.

In policy terms, the chief beneficiary of these ways of thinking was the concept of planning. We have already discovered the centrality of this concept to pre-war discourses. But the war, by compelling the state to radically expand its sphere of influence, allowed advocates of these ideas to draw attention to the concrete benefits of its implementation. Much like the phrase 'equality of sacrifice', planning concealed a range of ideological positions. Nonetheless, it would be problematic to assume that its apparent ubiquity did not reflect a profound ideological shift. Embedded within its conceptual architecture was a set of epistemological assumptions, and these assumptions ran against the grain of the Victorian entrepreneurial ideal. Chief among them was a hostility to waste. In opposition to the conservative notion that such waste was the inexorable by-product of the natural scarcity of both resources and skill,

---

23 Brenda Swann and Francis Aprahamian (eds), *J. D. Bernal: A Life in Science and Politics* (London: Verso, 1999), p. 172.
24 *Science in War* (Penguin, 1940).

wartime planners sought to minimise waste by placing faith in the ability of experts to determine the most efficient distribution of resources and human capital.[25] More often than not, these experts were imagined as professionals who were motivated, above all else, by their sense of duty rather than their self-interest.

These ideas about expertise and reason were bound up with broader questions about the appropriate distribution of status and wealth. If Britain was to become populated by an increasing number of experts who could construct a more rational and efficient economic order, it was assumed that the state would need to remove barriers to educational attainment and reward relevant talents and attributes. These matters cut across a range of ideological debates, not all of which can be discussed here. But one concept that often drew them together was that of class. It is instructive, then, to consider the way in which actors understood this concept in the wartime period.

Class, citizenship and merit

There has been much disagreement about the impact that the wartime period had upon Britain's social order. Some accounts have suggested that the war blurred class boundaries and laid the basis for a more equitable social order.[26] Others, by contrast, have argued that the war exposed the severity of social inequality and did little to temper class antagonisms.[27] Our concern is not with the objective 'fact' of class in the wartime period. Rather, it is with the languages of class that were employed by political elites to conceptualise and understand it. These elites did not conceive of class

25 Perkin, *Professional Society*, p. 409.
26 Arthur Marwick, *Class: Image and Reality in Britain, France and the USA since 1930* (Basingstoke: Palgrave, 1990).
27 Penny Summerfield, 'The Levelling of Class' in H. L. Smith (ed.), *War and Social Change: Britain and Society in the Second World War* (Manchester: Manchester University Press, 1986), pp. 201–202.

in identical ways; however, there was a general enthusiasm for arrangements that could unite different social groups behind the war effort. It registered most commonly in support for 'equality of sacrifice', and it could be observed in the ideas about citizenship that proliferated in the period.[28]

As Jose Harris noted, while several conceptions of citizenship competed with one another in the 1940s, their exponents often shared a common aversion to class-based arguments.[29] Even members of the Labour party were reluctant to privilege the interests of the working class. While they acknowledged that the working class was disproportionately disenfranchised by capitalist relations of production, they believed that all workers deserved the full fruits of their labour.[30] On their part, Conservatives, despite maintaining that disparities of status and reward were immutable, were becoming hostile to the idea that an individual's class status should determine their opportunities. This was, in part, because they believed that class prejudices were threatening to dissolve the bonds between different social groups. This hostility to class-based conceptions of citizenship had significant consequences. First, in their efforts to reconcile the interests of different social groups, many intellectuals and policy-makers celebrated the principle of equal opportunity. Socialists and left-liberals had, of course, regarded this as an objective long before the war. But in wartime conditions, it was anchored to an increasingly wide range of arguments that could gain the approval of non-progressives. Among them was the notion that

---

28 Rose, *Which People's War?*, p. 68.
29 Harris, 'Contract and Citizenship' in Marquand and Seldon (eds), *The Ideas That Shaped Post-War Britain*, p. 132. Also see Jon Lawrence, 'Labour and the Politics of Class, 1900–1940' in David Feldman and Jon Lawrence (eds), *Structures and Transformations in Modern British History* (Cambridge: Cambridge University Press, 2011), pp. 237–260.
30 After the war, the Deputy Leader of the Labour Party, Herbert Morrison, remarked that technicians, managers and experts would come to be regarded as 'if not the salt of the earth, then at least as some of its salt'. 'What Future for the Middle Classes?', *Picture Post*, 6 March 1948.

equality of opportunity would foster a more harmonious social order. Envy was seen as a source of social antagonism that could be curtailed if inequalities were deemed to be fair and just. Previously, this argument had run up against some liberal and conservative traditions of thought.[31] But as it became acknowledged that certain inequities had contributed to both the rise of fascism and the social turbulence of the inter-war period, even those on the right of the political spectrum became more receptive to the idea that equality of opportunity was desirable.

Penguin's progressive authors were particularly enthusiastic about the idea of equal opportunity and the meritocratic argument that rewards should be earned rather than inherited. In *Why Not Prosperity?*, A. J. Evans, an educator and financier who was serving as an intelligence officer in the RAF, envisaged a state-owned system of production in which economic activity would be motivated by service rather than selfishness. Although Evans proposed this 'Economic Democracy' as a solution to the injustices fostered by capitalism, he was anxious to protect differential rewards for different kinds of work. When he came to identify a criterion for determining the value of work, he seized upon ability:

> E[conomic] D[emocracy] will arrange that men and women have an equal chance in life, and consequently those who rise to the top in each generation will be those who are best suited to their posts, and they will be selected out of the whole nation. Supporters of E[conomic] D[emocracy] contend that many able men do not rise to positions worthy of their ability, owing to lack of opportunity.[32]

Evans went on to sanction disparities of income that would follow from disparities of talent: 'To exceptionally able men, who under capitalism were managers and part owners of huge businesses,

---

31 D. J. Ford, 'W. H. Mallock and the Socialism in England, 1880–1918' in Kenneth D. Brown (ed.), *Essays in Anti-Labour History: Responses to the Rise of Labour in Britain* (London: Palgrave, 1994), pp. 336–338.

32 A. J. Evans, *Why Not Prosperity?* (Penguin, 1943), p. 36.

E.D. will offer ample rewards.'[33] Many of Evans' meritocratic assumptions were shared by other progressive writers. Phyllis Bottome, for instance, seized upon the principle of merit in her attempt to describe a new post-war order. After drawing attention to the way in which the Soviet state selected exceptional children for 'pioneer schools', which trained them in professions of their choice, she suggested that a similar arrangement could be introduced in Britain:

> It might be a good use of our Public Schools to turn them into state-endowed Pioneer Schools open only to these children of exceptional merit. To every ambitious child – and almost all normal children are ambitious – this incentive would more than take the place of our present individual competitive system.[34]

The notion that merit was an appropriate criterion for determining the distribution of wealth and status was implicit here, and it was one that informed many actors' thinking about Britain's productive capacity. Maximising the exploitation of Britain's natural resources, it was argued, was a task that required the elevation of ability and skill. This logic was particularly prominent in the Special authored by John Gloag, who endorsed meritocratic ideas in his attempt to reconcile the twin objectives of equality and efficiency. Gloag's central claim was that revolutionary and reactionary politics were the enemy of reasoned progress. He was particularly critical of those socialists who were pursuing equality of rewards, and he proposed an alternative system of distribution that could preserve liberty but promote social justice. This system was, in essence, meritocratic:

> No political party has yet had the courage and prescience to demand equality of opportunity and adequate reward for ability ... A state

---

33 Evans, *Why Not Prosperity?*, p. 39.
34 Bottome (ed.), *Our New Order*, p. 114.

where such conditions were established would allow enterprise to flourish, so that people could cultivate their creative gifts and make best use of their lives to advance and enrich civilisation.[35]

Significantly, Gloag believed that meritocratic arrangements would promote, rather than stifle, democratic co-operation. Whereas systems that were designed to bring about equality of outcome tended to generate resentment and envy, a system of equal opportunity, it was argued, would foster mutual respect and co-operation.[36]

It was not only policy-makers and intellectuals who made the case that the extension of educational opportunity could resolve social conflict. Theologians and Christian leaders also saw in this objective a potential source of spiritual and moral renewal. In his last major statement of political theology, the Archbishop of Canterbury, William Temple, suggested that the time was 'ripe for a development by which it should be possible for children from every kind of home to come into any kind of school provided that they are qualified by mental, physical and personal talents'. Significantly, he did not privilege 'intellectual' ability and favoured assessments that could measure a wide range of attributes and talents.[37] Under the influence of R. H. Tawney, he was concerned that the distribution of rewards according to intelligence would result in the creation of a more stratified society. Yet he, like many others, acknowledged that there would be a need for 'disciplined intelligence'.

---

35 Gloag, *What about Business?*, pp. 93–94. Hostility to abstract ideology can be found in other Penguin texts. Wickham Steed's pre-war Special on the press, for instance, suggested that 'the true choice of free communities does not lie between the "ideologies" of totalitarian Communism, on the "Left" and of Fascism and Nazism, on the Right, but must be fixed upon the ideology of ordered freedom'. Wickham Steed, *The Press* (Penguin, 1938), p. 61.

36 Gloag, *What about Business?*, pp. 14–15.

37 William Temple, *Christianity and the Social Order* (Penguin, 1942), p. 68. The book sold 140,000 copies. Also see John Kent, 'William Temple, the Church of England and British National Identity' in Richard Weight and Abigail Beach (eds), *The Right to Belong*, p. 25.

The authors discussed above did not share common visions of the future. Some Penguin authors, like Gloag, imagined a meritocratic order in which inequities were justified by a common respect for distinctions of ability. By contrast, others, like the Liberal MP Tom Horabin, saw equality of opportunity in functionalist terms. Here, equality of opportunity was tied to the idea of service and duty: 'The individual's position in society must depend on the function he performs and not upon his social status.'[38] For this reason, Horabin was unsatisfied with the provisions of the 1944 Education Bill, which was then passing through Parliament. But if the war did little to resolve the broader distributive questions that the problem of class raised, the very fact that class was understood as a problem to be solved was itself significant. If there was a hegemonic idea that informed debates about post-war reconstruction, it was the notion that a more classless order was desirable. Penguin's authors frequently alluded to this aspiration, and when they did so, they often constructed, whether implicitly or explicitly, a conception of the ideal citizen. This citizen was a civic-minded professional who had abandoned class-based prejudices by embracing the value of scientific knowledge. Evans described the way in which education could expand the productive capacity of an individual, noting that 'The happiest and most desirable "average man" [sic] is the cultivated artisan.'[39] Elsewhere, Richard Acland drew attention to the peculiar moral disposition of skilled workers. Identifying self-interest as inimical to the war effort, Acland referred to 'the men who would carry on British industry without a moment's pause even if every shareholder died intestate and without heirs to-morrow. I speak of the salaried technicians and mangers of industry.'[40]

From a different ideological perspective, Gloag's Special made reference to a 'new class of worker' and endorsed Sir William Bragg's suggestion that 'we should place a high value on their

38   Tom Horabin, *Politics Made Plain* (Penguin, 1944), p. 110.
39   Evans, *Why Not Prosperity?*, p. 68.
40   Cited in Bottome (ed.), *Our New Order*, p. 59.

services'.[41] This was, in part, because he believed that its expansion and elevation could smooth out the differences between capital and labour.[42] William Temple arrived at a similar reading of this class of worker:

> 'Management' is fast becoming a profession, with its own standards and objectives. Its primary interest is not dividends for the shareholders, but efficiency of service.[43]

These authors seemed to assume that skilled professionals were located outside of the traditional class struggle and were thus more likely to behave in ways that served the common good. As a corollary, they often regarded professionals as altruistic citizens who could be the vanguard of a new social settlement. The widespread enthusiasm for the extension of educational opportunity can, in part, be attributed to this understanding of professional expertise. By permitting a greater share of talented individuals to acquire professional skills, meritocratic arrangements could be the solvents of the envy and self-interest that had brought about the rise of fascism. That is not to say that all advocates of equal opportunity shared common ideological objectives. Yet they all could regard meritocratic arrangements as staging posts in the realisation of a more harmonious and productive social order.

Because they were predicated on the notion that the classless individual would pursue objectives that were altruistic, these meritocratic conceptions of citizenship were, in some respects, social democratic. Yet they did not necessarily violate the principle that inequalities of rewards could be justified if they resulted in greater efficiency. They only stipulated that those who received greater rewards and status should do so on the basis of their earned attributes. It was thus possible for many on the right to have at least some sympathy with the logic that informed them.

---

41 Bragg was one of Britain's leading physicists.
42 Gloag, *What about Business?*, p. 80.
43 Temple, *Christianity and the Social Order*, p. 70.

We can register these developments when we explore the way in which book readers were described by wartime commentators.[44] As the preceding chapter noted, several commentators had been drawing attention to a 'new reading public' since the early 1930s. But in the wartime period, this social category was awarded a more explicitly 'technical' identity. Writing in *The Bookseller*, Sydney Hyde claimed that 'the new reading public are not browsers … they have a striking facility for sizing up a book from the most rapid examination … Where a few years ago books played little or no part in the technical equipment of manual workers, now they are eagerly sought after.'[45] Comparable observations were made by Mass-Observation, who published a number of studies on reading habits in the wartime period. According to responses collected from booksellers, the largest decline in reading took place within the 'former leisured classes', but this had been offset by a 'new growth of reading in the working class'.[46] Respondents devoted particular attention to the way in which skilled workers had taken an interest in non-fiction:

> The most unlikely people buy books now … We've extended sales tremendously among the working-classes. Just to give you an example: there a parcel here, we're sending it off to a factory hand in the Midlands. He used to ask for a book occasionally. Now he sends us a pound a week, regularly, and we send him books. Most of them are technical books, but not all.[47]

These statements reveal some broader shifts in understandings of class. The author recognises class as a concrete feature of the social order. But when they refer to the factory hand as an 'unlikely' consumer of 'technical' books, they also imply that

44 Valerie Holman, *Print for Victory: Book Publishing in England, 1939–1945* (London: British Library, 2008), p. 51.
45 Sydney Hyde, 'The New Reading Public Are Not Browsers', *Bookseller*, 15 January 1942.
46 M-O File Report 2018, p. 58.
47 M-O File Report 2018, p. 71.

individuals can transcend their class identity by engaging with scientific knowledge.

As these ways of thinking about class proliferated, an imagined classless citizen began to cast a shadow over debates about post-war reconstruction.[48] This citizen was understood as an individual who had shed their class prejudices by engaging in some form of further education. They were imagined, that is, as the bearer of what Perkin termed the 'professional ideal'. This new citizen's ability to reconcile the interests of labour and capital was dependent on their commitment to public service and efficiency, while their status followed from their perceived merits rather than their inherited social status.

These ideas about class did not, of course, dissolve concrete social distinctions, which continued to punctuate the conditions of everyday life.[49] What they did do, however, was orientate policy-makers towards arrangements that could resolve such conflict.

In their efforts to apply the professional ideal, political elites began to think about policy problems in new ways. We can consider, for instance, the way in which policy-makers thought about land use. Under wartime conditions, this matter was of pressing concern, since it had implications for the efficiency of industrial and agricultural production. Yet it was also a contentious one, as any attempts to extend the state's control over land tended to provoke the hostility of land owners. It would be problematic to claim that a happy consensus on the question emerged during the war. But some ideas were able to garner the support of a sufficiently wide range of policy-makers to pass into the government's legislative agenda. Many of these ideas appeared in the 1942 publications of two parliamentary

---

48 Morgan and Evans gesture towards this notion in their study of the war-time period. David Morgan and Mary Evans, *The Battle for Britain: Citizenship and Ideology in the Second World War* (London: Routledge, 1994), pp. 106–107.

49 Rose, *Which People's War?*, p. 68.

committees: the Scott report on land utilisation and the Uthwatt report on compensation and determent. A summary of their provisions was published as a Penguin Special in 1943, and its author, the historian G. M. Young, drew attention to the way that they approached the issue of property rights. His central observation was that although both reports rejected widespread nationalisation of land, they enshrined the notion that landowners had corresponding 'obligations of neighbourliness or citizenship'. For this reason, he arrived at the conclusion that their provisions amounted to a substantive attack on the principle of ownership itself.[50]

As Perkin noted, the idea that the value of private ownership should be determined by the property's service to the community was one corollary of the professional ideal. This could not be reconciled with the class-based claims that were made in the name of both wholesale nationalisation and absolute property rights.[51] And because it awarded primacy to the function of producers and their ability to achieve efficient production on behalf of the community, it could be reconciled with the meritocratic notion that rewards should be determined by ability. Importantly, this principle cut across the political divide. An early advocate was the socialist R. H. Tawney, whose *The Acquisitive Society* (1920) had argued that 'propriety rights shall be maintained when they are accompanied by the performance of service and abolished when they are not'.[52] Yet those on the right could also find themselves in sympathy with its basic logic. Shortly after the war, David Clarke, who was then the director of the Conservative Political Centre, observed that property had become increasingly detached from obligation, writing

---

50 G. M. Young, *Country and Town: A Summary of the Scott and Uthwatt Reports* (Penguin, 1943), p. 104. Michael Ticheler, *The Failure of Land Reform in Twentieth-Century England: The Triumph of Private Property* (London: Routledge, 2018).

51 Perkin, *Professional Society*, p. 136.

52 Gary Armstrong and Tim Gray, *The Authentic Tawney: A New Interpretation of the Political Thought of R. H. Tawney* (Exeter: Imprint, 2010), pp. 67–88.

that 'Profits made by withholding from the community beneficial inventions are immoral.'[53] Progressives and conservatives continued to disagree on these matters. The former placed a greater burden of proof upon the private property owner, while the latter tended to define private property as a prerequisite for individual liberty. But the professional ideal cut across their different visions of the appropriate relationship between the individual and the community. When representatives of both ideological traditions came in search of practical starting points for a plan for a new political settlement, they often fell back upon its logic.

Finding a middle way

As the prospect of Allied victory appeared on the horizon, elites from across the political spectrum became increasingly anxious to establish concrete commitments to legislative reform. Within progressive circles, this anxiety frequently stemmed from a desire to seize the opportunity for egalitarian change that the war had offered. The war had placed the forces of privilege in a vulnerable position. But if some kind of reconstituted social order was to be established, the middle classes, it was argued, would need to be assured that a more equitable order would not endanger their social status. In many cases, this fed enthusiasm for gradualist reforms that would allow for power and wealth to be transferred peacefully. Even the more radical of Penguin's authors favoured reform rather than revolution. Wells, for instance, noted that:

> One necessity in the process is a clear statement, in the broadest and most acceptable terms, not of any remote Utopia ahead, nor of any acceptance of things as they are, but of the world as reasonable people want to have it now.[54]

---

53 Clarke, *The Conservative Faith in a Modern Age*, p. 24.
54 Wells, *The Common Sense of War and Peace*, p. 80.

In his Special, Harold Laski relinquished his pre-war radicalism and endorsed a moderate programme of wartime social and economic reform. The Labour party leadership, he wrote, 'need neither to demand, given efficiency and good will, proscription of persons or expropriation of property. They need only to insist, as the price of their support, upon the necessity, for this government, of using the procedures of democracy to inaugurate the process of adaptation its victory requires.'[55] Laski argued that such a strategy would permit, 'by the evolutionary basis on which it is built, the forces of privilege to prepare themselves for, and adapt themselves to, the idea of fundamental change'. In his review of the volume, Thomas Cook suggested that Laski recognised 'the need for hard-headedness if enlightenment is to result'.[56]

Mirroring Laski's intellectual transition, G. D. H. Cole began to modify his thought in the early wartime period. His editorial file in the Penguin archive contains a proposal for an unpublished book with the provisional title *Forward to Socialism*. Cole outlined 'a policy of liberal Socialism as the basis on which reconstruction ought to rest'. Rather than advocating a transformative programme of nationalisation, Cole proposed a moderate programme of reform that would only affect Britain's principal productive industries. In 1942, Gollancz published Cole's *Great Britain in the Post-War World*, a book which carried forward many of the ideas from the Penguin proposal. Departing from his pre-war beliefs, Cole argued for the advantages of a mixed economy.[57] The conventional argument that widespread nationalisation was necessary to put an end to the exploitative nature

---

55 Laski, *Where Do We Go from Here?*, p. 105.
56 Thomas I. Cook, 'Reviews', *Political Science Quarterly*, Vol. 56, No. 1 (1941), p. 139. Margaret Heston, writing in the Communist Party of Great Britain's monthly journal, suggested that Laski's strategy had parallels with the gradualism of Ramsay MacDonald. Margaret Heston, 'Following Ramsay MacDonald', *The Labour Monthly*, December 1940.
57 G. D. H. Cole, *Great Britain in the Post-War World* (London: Gollancz, 1942), pp. 75–76.

of capitalism had, he argued, lost some of its appeal, since 'trade unionism and social legislation have between them narrowed considerably the opportunities for the grosser forms of economic exploitation in Great Britain itself'.[58] According to his analysis, the principal malaise in the modern economy was monopolistic capitalism, something which was best defeated by bringing into state ownership 'only those parts of industry in which monopoly is already entrenched, or could throw up fresh entrenchments if it were driven from its present points of vantage'.[59] Anticipating the arguments that would be posed by moderate Labour thinkers in the 1950s, he stated that public ownership was 'a means, and not an end'.[60] This represented a departure from Cole's earlier belief that 'the essence of Socialism is not public interference but public ownership'.[61] Moreover, in response to the question 'are Socialists not out to abolish the profit system?', he replied, 'I, for one, am not.'[62] Cole's intellectual conversion was symptomatic of a broader enthusiasm for establishing a 'middle way' policy agenda that could be endorsed by a wide spectrum of opinion.

By 1942, Penguin was publishing books that were trying to reconcile egalitarian demands with capitalist enterprise. John Gloag's *What about Business?* is one example. Gloag prefaced his argument by questioning whether politicians were best equipped to solve economic problems:

> Political loyalties and political beliefs confuse the situation. It is difficult for their exponents to identify a revolution that is dissociated from social prejudices and economic conflict.[63]

William Temple struck a similar tone. When he came to defend his Penguin from the charge that he was advocating socialism, he referred

58 Cole, *Great Britain in the Post-War World*, pp. 75–76.
59 Cole, *Great Britain in the Post-War World*, pp. 76–77.
60 Cole, *Great Britain in the Post-War World*, p. 75.
61 Cole, *Socialism in Evolution*, p. 198.
62 Cole, *Great Britain in the Post-War World*, pp. 96–97.
63 Gloag, *What about Business?*, p. 79.

to Britain's 'peculiar genius for working out in practice the correlation of principles which seem to be logically opposed to each other'.[64]

When we consider the prominence of these ideas, it becomes possible to account for the popularity and influence of William Beveridge's report into social insurance. Published in December 1942, this document provided a central point of reference for public debate about post-war reconstruction.[65] A full description of its principles and propositions cannot be offered here. But it is instructive to note that the main thrust of its provisions was accordant with a certain kind of meritocratic logic. That is not say that Beveridge was seeking to construct a perfect meritocratic order in which the rewards of individuals were commensurable with their intelligence. Yet his proposed reforms could be reconciled with a professional ideal that celebrated equality of opportunity and social mobility. When he identified ignorance as one of the sources of deprivation, Beveridge conceptualised it in relation to two problems: the injustice of unequal opportunity and the inefficiency of wasting talent. As he put it in a discussion of child allowances: 'The people who are being employed below their capacity are the unhappy ones, and we want to abolish that cause of unhappiness as well as use their talents.'[66]

Although Beveridge did not write a Penguin in the wartime period, a summary of his report and some accompanying speeches appeared in Bottome's *Our New Order or Hitler's?* Bottome addressed these contributions to the volume in her preface:

> Sir William Beveridge has kindly allowed us to include his own summary of his Report. The Report is in the nature of an acid test

---

64 William Temple, *Some Lambeth Letters, 1942–44* (London: Oxford University Press, 1963), p. 92. Temple was writing to Guy Kindersley, who had been a Conservative MP in the 1920s.

65 Tony Cutler, John Williams and Karel Williams, *Keynes, Beveridge and Beyond* (London: Routledge, 1986).

66 William Beveridge, *The Pillars of Security* (London: Allen & Unwin, 1943), p. 84.

of our sincerity as a nation. It is the first concrete and feasible plan that has been produced at the request of a responsible government towards making better and freer conditions of life for every citizen.[67]

Not only were these remarks indicative of the central place that Beveridge's plan had acquired in debates about reconstruction; they also exposed the enthusiasm for 'concrete and feasible' proposals for a new policy consensus.

While many of Penguin's authors adopted ideological positions that were incompatible with the full range of principles that informed Beveridge's scheme, they often endorsed his arguments about educational inequality. This could be regarded as an unsurprising feature of wartime political debate. Yet we should resist the temptation to regard the widespread approval of equality of opportunity as being of little ideological significance. Here, two points can be made. First, it must be noted that the objective of equal opportunity had not been a common denominator of political thought in the inter-war period. Dominant educational ideas had been rooted in class-based assumptions about ability, and the notion that the state could take action to equalise opportunity was treated with suspicion by large sections of opinion. Second, attention can be drawn to the way in which ideas about the expansion of educational provision became the starting point for a broader reworking of ideas about democracy and citizenship. The argument that equality of opportunity was a prerequisite for social progress did not only follow from ideas about justice; it also emerged from more expansive conceptions of citizenship that had been fostered by the conditions of war. The intellectual trajectory of Liberal MP Tom Horabin, who, until the late 1930s, had been broadly sympathetic to the classical liberal tradition, demonstrates this shift. In response to the crises of that period, Horabin adopted

---

67   Bottome (ed.), *Our New Order*, p. 9.

more socialistic ideas. By the time he came to write a Penguin Special in 1944, he was convinced that widespread nationalisation and a redistribution of wealth were necessary. Much of Horabin's Special was preoccupied with exposing the evils of the inter-war order and the way in which power had been concentrated in private hands. He came to advocate a wider distribution of power, arriving at the argument that ability, not inheritance, should determine the distribution of rewards:

> Power must go to those who prove their ability to use it, not to those with the social status to monopolise it.[68]

He then extended this notion to make an argument about educational reform:

> It is in our power, however, to secure equal opportunities for all. The facilities for advanced education must be evened out and multiplied. Nobody who can take advantage of higher education should be denied this chance. You cannot conduct a modern community except with an adequate supply of persons upon whose education, whether humanitarian, technical or scientific, much time and money has been spent.[69]

Harold Laski, in *Where Do We Go from Here?*, also placed the principle of educational opportunity at the core of his proposed programme of social reform. Victory, he argued, could only be assured if the masses could be convinced that there was to be 'no vast denial of genuine equality of educational opportunity'.[70]

We might conclude that two principles provided the ideological adhesive for the construction of a putative wartime consensus. The first was that professional expertise and the concomitant expansion of scientific knowledge was an antidote to the forces

---

68 Horabin, *Politics Made Plain*, p. 109.
69 Cited in Bottome (ed.), *Our New Order*, p. 17.
70 Laski, *Where Do We Go from Here?*, p. 88.

that had brought the war into being. The second was that equal opportunity could provide the basis for a more harmonious social order in which older forms of class prejudice were rendered redundant. These principles did not exhaust all of the aspirations that were provoked by the debate and post-war reconstruction, but they did resonate with some objectives that were held across the political spectrum.

Conclusion

The political settlement that emerged from debates about post-war reconstruction has typically been understood a 'social democratic' entity that was designed to redistribute wealth and power.[71] While the wartime debates about reconstruction did result in the Attlee government inheriting a political order that was ripe for being reconstituted along social democratic lines, we might need to look elsewhere for a concept that can adequately describe the hegemonic aspirations and beliefs that informed wartime political thought. A study of Penguin's wartime books suggest that it might be appropriate to refer to the post-war settlement as a meritocratic entity. That is not because these books reveal a widespread desire to realise a perfect meritocracy. Rather, it is because the logic that informed meritocratic ideas was the ideological adhesive that bound together the different aspirations that these books articulated. Actors located in different ideological traditions may have endorsed this logic for different reasons, but they shared a common commitment to the twin principles of equality of opportunity and reward by ability. It was these principles that were the central pillars of what Ortolano has termed Britain's 'meritocratic moment'.[72]

---

71 Kavanagh and Morris, *Consensus Politics from Attlee to Major*, p. 6.
72 Ortolano, *Two Cultures*, p. 17.

To suggest that the wartime consensus was the result of meaningful agreement would be problematic. In many respects, the political settlement that was forged after 1940 concealed the persistence of substantial ideological disagreement. Nor should we regard 1945 as a moment of ideological resolution. In many respects its architects had deferred, rather than resolved, the central distributive questions posed by the crises of the preceding decades. As Morgan and Evans have suggested, the post-war settlement sought to reconcile two contradictory objectives: the pursuit of social equality and the maintenance of private property relations.[73] It was hoped, of course, that these objectives could be reconciled by the attainment of economic growth and the erosion of class conflict. Yet, as subsequent chapters demonstrate, this hope became increasingly difficult to realise.

---

73 Morgan and Evans, *Battle for Britain*, p. 2.

3

THE RISE OF THE MERITOCRACY

In 1960, Penguin published a collection of essays to commemorate its twenty-fifth anniversary. One of the most provocative contributions was by Richard Hoggart, who, in the preceding decade, had established himself as one of Britain's leading public intellectuals. Hoggart praised Allen Lane's achievement, noting that Penguin had fed the more 'responsible needs' of its vast and expanding audience, but in the closing paragraph of his essay, he suggested that the publisher's political zeal had waned in the preceding decade. Whereas Penguin had, in its early period of development, been a vibrant source of ideas, it had, he argued, struggled to maintain its relevance in the post-war world. Hoggart did not attribute this to any lack of ambition on behalf of the publisher but to the social and political climate of the period. 'Intellectually,' he wrote, 'the fifties have been a cloudy period.'[1] When we explore Penguin's engagement with the intellectual politics of the immediate post-war period, it is possible to discern some of the reasons why Hoggart might have arrived at such a reading of Penguin's post-war history. In a number of respects, the publisher retreated from the battle of political ideas in the decade that succeeded the Second World War. Between 1947 and 1955, only six titles appeared

---

1   Richard Hoggart, 'The Reader' in *Penguins Progress, 1935–60* (Penguin, 1960), p. 29.

in the Specials series, and although some current-affairs titles did appear in other lists, they often sold in modest quantities.[2] Some evidence suggests that Penguin's retreat from the political stage followed from commercial concerns. A letter sent by Richard Lane, co-director of Penguin, in August 1947 reveals that he advised his brother to 'put a ban on Current Affairs', citing production troubles and low unit sales.[3] Although Allen Lane frequently disagreed with his more financially prudent sibling, it appears that on this occasion he was willing to accede to his advice. In an interview with the *Daily Telegraph* that was conducted months later, he explained that 'the demand now is for cultural books' rather than those that are overtly political.[4] It is difficult to assess the accuracy of Lane's statement, but some evidence does suggest that the demand for political ideas declined in the immediate post-war period. Attention can be drawn, for instance, to the range of progressive journals, publishing imprints and organisations that exited the political arena. Gollancz's Left Book Club was dissolved in 1948; *Picture Post*, whose circulation was over half its wartime peak by 1949, published its final issue in 1957; and Mass-Observation became a commercial market-research organisation in 1949.

This decline in progressive publishing can be understood as one consequence of the relative political stability of the post-war period. As Mark Blyth has argued, political systems that are able to contain social conflict are likely to impair the advance of new ideas.[5] These systems not only generate positive feedback effects that can stave off uncertainty; they also encourage political actors

---

2   One of the most significant Specials of the period, Mark Abrams and Richard Rose's *Must Labour Lose?*, sold only 10,146 copies. PA: DM1107/S188.

3   Richard Lane to Allen Lane, 5 August 1947. PA: DM1294/3/2/94.

4   In 1949, Allen Lane's accountants insisted that 'ethical aims and financial prudence do not always run side by side' and suggested that the latter should take priority for the time being. PA: DM1294/4/2/5.

5   Mark Blyth, *Great Transformations: Economic Ideas and Institutional Change in the Twentieth Century* (Cambridge: Cambridge University Press, 2002).

to be more risk-averse. Such a state of affairs emerged in the aftermath of the Second World War, a consequence of which was a decline in the demand for new ideas and a corresponding fall in the number of readers who purchased the kinds of political texts that Penguin had sold in such vast quantities prior to 1945.

We need to be attentive to the way that ideas contributed to this political stability. When actors arrived at the conclusion that they were living through a period of consensus, they did so because they had adopted particular beliefs and assumptions about the conditions in which they were living. Some of these beliefs concerned the apparent 'affluence' that seemed to follow from the ending of wartime controls on consumption. Observers often claimed that older forms of political conflict were being rendered redundant by the rising living standards prompted by post-war growth.[6] They did so, in part, because they assumed that such growth would ease the conflict between different social classes. Since such conflict had followed from the scarcity of resources, the prospect of material abundance seemed to open up the prospect of a future in which class distinctions would wither away.

Many policy-makers were sympathetic to this reading of post-war change, and they responded by reconfiguring their priorities. Most importantly, they became increasingly preoccupied with facilitating social mobility. By creating a more fluid social order in which individuals could obtain opportunities commensurable with their talents and attributes, they hoped to reconcile the twin objectives of equality and efficiency.[7] It would be inappropriate to suggest that there was a bipartisan enthusiasm for creating a meritocracy. Each of Britain's major ideological traditions had

---

6   Ferdynand Zweig, *The Worker in an Affluent Society: Family Life and Industry* (London: Heinemann, 1962). Robert Millar, *The New Classes* (London: Longmans, 1966).

7   Perhaps the most notable advocate of this argument was C. P. Snow. See C. P. Snow, *The Two Cultures* (Cambridge: Cambridge University Press, 1959).

reason to believe that such a state of affairs would be undesirable. But they tended to see meritocratic policies as starting points for further political action, and the idea that rewards should be awarded according to merit did marginalise the more radical ideas about distributive justice that had often been upheld by the left and the right. In his perceptive study, Guy Ortolano gestures towards this kind of argument when he describes the three decades that followed the 1945 election as a 'meritocratic moment' in Britain's social and political development This period, he notes, was one in which ability and expertise were regarded as being of increasing importance and when alternative distributive logics were marginalised.[8] This chapter adds weight to Ortolano's claim by exposing some of the ways in which ideas about post-war social change fed the proliferation of a professional ethic and extended its range of meanings.

Penguin was implicated within the cultural politics of this meritocratic moment. In its first decade, it had done much to facilitate its emergence. As well as contributing to the democratisation of knowledge, it had also played a role in extending the role and authority of expertise. Yet in the post-war period, Penguin came to be suspicious of the social and cultural changes that meritocratic arrangements seemed to facilitate. Allen Lane and his fellow editors were not only concerned about the apparent decline of cultural standards that had followed from the arrival of mass consumption; they were also suspicious of the way in which social mobility could undermine communitarian social values. Indeed, like many cultural institutions with leftist sympathies, the publisher was destabilised by the politics of post-war affluence.[9] By observing Penguin's fraught engagement with the social and political change of the 1950s, we can better understand the tensions that

---

8   Ortolano, *Two Cultures*, pp. 16–18.
9   Lawrence Black, *The Political Culture of the Left in Affluent Britain, 1951–64* (Basingstoke: Palgrave, 2003).

were present in the fragile intellectual consensus that sustained the meritocratic moment.

The post-war settlement

In 1947, one of Penguin's advisory editors, H. L. Beales, wrote an essay on Britain's electoral politics.[10] His central claim was that the 1945 General Election had been a watershed in Britain's democratic history. Far from representing a regular swing of the electoral pendulum, Labour's victory had followed from a fundamental shift of social attitudes. In turn, Beales claimed that unless Labour departed from its programme of reform, the party would dominate parliamentary politics for a generation. 'Nationally and internationally,' he declared, 'the politics of Labour will be British politics and world politics.'[11] In one regard, Beales' forecast was falsified by subsequent events: in October 1951, the electorate awarded the Churchill-led Conservatives a small parliamentary majority, initiating thirteen years of uninterrupted Tory governance. It is more difficult, however, to dismiss Beales' argument that 1945 marked a critical moment in Britain's political development. After all, the Conservative governments of the 1950s did not dismantle the central pillars of the state regime that they inherited, and many of the ideas that were sanctioned by Labour's electoral victory were accommodated by their political opponents. Here we reach the long-standing debate about the existence of a post-war political 'consensus'. Though Penguin's post-war publishing cannot be a basis for a decisive intervention in this controversy, it offers an insight into how the wartime period had reshaped the boundaries of political contestation. Two

---

10 Beales was a historian as the London School of Economics. See Alexander Hutton, '"A Repository, a Switchboard, a Dynamo": H. L. Beales, a Historian in a Mass Media Age', *Contemporary British History*, Vol. 30, No. 3 (2016), pp. 407–426.

11 H. L. Beales, 'Has Labour Come to Stay?', *Political Quarterly*, Vol. 18, No. 1 (1947), p. 59.

of the publisher's post-war texts are particularly useful in this regard: John Parker's *Labour Marches On* and Quintin Hogg's *The Case for Conservatism*. Published simultaneously in a short-lived 'World Affairs' series, these books provided the opportunity for two leading thinkers within Britain's main parties to espouse their views, and they expose a number of ways in which the locus of British politics had shifted following the 1945 election.[12]

Parker and Hogg held different views on a range of matters. While the former was enthusiastic about extending the programme of social reform that was being initiated by Clement Attlee's Labour government, the latter was suspicious of the state's expanding authority and defended capitalist enterprise from its socialist critics. Yet their books do suggest that the parameters of ideological conflict had narrowed since 1939. In his book, Hogg, who had been a leading member of the Tory Reform Group during the wartime period, provided a comprehensive restatement of conservative values. One of his central objectives was to reimagine the organicist conception of the social order that conservatives had often espoused. Distancing himself from the *laissez-faire* doctrines that had been employed to defend free enterprise, Hogg placed emphasis on the 'unity of interests' between social classes, suggesting that the maintenance of social bonds required the intervention of the state. A key passage of the book attempted to align his conception of conservatism with what he called 'Social Democracy without socialism':

> By Social Democracy I mean so-called 'Equality of Opportunity' – and a basic minimum for all those who are handicapped in the battle of life … To each man and woman, rich and poor, must be offered an opportunity limited only by his capacity, skill and energy.

---

12   John Parker, *Labour Marches On* (Penguin, 1947). Quintin Hogg, *The Case for Conservatism* (Penguin, 1947).

Hogg detailed two criteria that could be used to determine the appropriate allocation of wages:

(a) That skill always receives its reward in comparison with want of skill;
(b) That effort always receives its reward in comparison with laziness.[13]

These criteria were compatible with a certain kind of meritocratic logic. They also contravened many of the older arguments conservatives had made about equality. Edmund Burke, Benjamin Disraeli, W. H. Mallock and other writers in the British conservative tradition had claimed that inequalities of opportunity were inexorable and desirable.[14] In 1898, Mallock, had written a comprehensive critique of the principle of educational opportunity, in which he advanced two key points. First, that the cultivation of talents would provoke social disharmony by encouraging individuals of 'average' abilities to develop aspirations that they could not realise. Second, Mallock claimed that the type of education which was appropriate to one social class could not be deemed appropriate for another: As he put it, 'the education proper for the rich is not a type but an exception'.[15] Hogg's arguments ran counter to this reasoning. He not only embraced the principle of equal opportunity; he also implied that the aristocratic justification of inequality could no longer hold. In a sense, he had embraced the key tenets of the professional ideal.

John Parker, who was then the Vice Chairman of the Fabian Society, departed from many of Hogg's views. His statements on

---

13 Hogg, *Conservatism*, p. 300. Also see Christopher Hollis, *The Rise and Fall of the Ex-Socialist Government* (London: Hollis & Carter, 1947), p. 113.
14 P. J. Marshall, Donald C. Bryant and William B. Todd (eds), *The Writings and Speeches of Edmund Burke, Vol. 4: Party, Parliament, and the Dividing of the Whigs: 1780–1794* (Oxford: Oxford University Press, 2015), p. 448. J. P. Parry, 'Disraeli and England', *The Historical Journal*, Vol. 43, No. 3 (2000), p. 708.
15 W. H. Mallock, *Aristocracy and Evolution: A Study of the Rights, the Origin, and the Social Functions of the Wealthier Classes* (London: Adam and Charles, 1898), pp. 334–349.

economic planning and private property were, for instance, at odds with those that Hogg had advanced. Yet he did arrive at some propositions about distributive justice that overlapped with Hogg's. When he attempted to describe his party's approach to equality, he constructed a formulation that placed considerable emphasis on the criterion of ability:

> [Socialists] believe in equality of opportunity. They wish to build up a society in which each boy or girl will have the education best suited to bring out his [*sic*] natural ability and to develop his various tastes. A community which had an effective system of education would have the whole people from which to choose the best individuals to occupy all the most important posts whether in industry, the universities, the arts or Government.[16]

Unsurprisingly, Hogg and Parker parted company on the question of how far an individual's ability was determined by extra-human forces. Whereas Hogg was more willing to regard inequalities at the product of biological factors, Parker suggested that much could be done to 'neutralise' what were often regarded as 'natural' inequalities.[17] Nonetheless, they both sought to expand the repository of expertise within the social order, believing that equality of opportunity was a desirable objective. Significantly, they also maintained that the nature of political contestation was being transformed by social change. Parker stated that:

> The break-up of the big capitalist vested interests and the growth of general interest in politics following an expansion of education are likely to make the distinction between Left and Right dependent more upon differences in mental outlook than at present.[18]

Hogg arrived at a similar view. But while Parker drew attention to the way in which education established common values that

16 Parker, *Labour*, p. 201.
17 Parker, *Labour*, p. 201.
18 Parker, *Labour*, p. 206.

militated against social conflict, Hogg was preoccupied with the emergence of a new consensus on the appropriate distribution of wealth and opportunity:

> The vast majority of our fellow countrymen ... wish to see equal opportunity and social security; they desire to see industrial policy subordinated to the national will and made the subject of a conscious plan. But they do not desire equality of income.[19]

In different ways, both Hogg and Parker argued that post-war social conditions would require a political settlement that could stave off the social antagonisms of the inter-war period. In their efforts to describe such a settlement, both seized upon the objective of equality of opportunity. The views of two politicians cannot, of course, be taken as evidence of a broad political consensus. But as the below discussion will argue, it is possible to locate this shared enthusiasm for educational opportunity at the nodal point of a broader intellectual settlement.

The politics of class in post-war Britain

In the post-war period, class remained central to political debate. But as new technologies were developed to empirically observe its character, and as post-war economic changes began to modify Britain's occupational structure, it began to be understood in new terms. The emergent discipline of sociology played an important role in bringing this about. From the mid-1950s, a number of influential studies were published that were informed by a particular set of methodological assumptions. Their authors not only aligned themselves with the positivist notion that social facts could be deduced through empirical observation; they also conceptualised society in broadly functionalist terms. They assumed that the structure of complex societies followed from their need to fulfil

---

19 Hogg, *Conservatism*, p. 306.

certain functional prerequisites, such as maintaining social integration and providing an adequate food supply. When they turned to the political consequences of the social changes that they observed, these authors tended to be preoccupied with the phenomenon of *embourgeoisement*: that is, the apparent adoption of 'bourgeois' values among those working-class communities that had traditionally voted for the Labour party but whose party allegiances seemed to be weakening. *Must Labour Lose?*, published as a Penguin Special in 1960, was one of the most important studies of this phenomenon.[20] Written in response to the Labour's party third consecutive election defeat, in 1959, the book was co-authored by two leading sociologists, Mark Abrams and Richard Rose. Using the findings of a survey into social attitudes and voting behaviour, Abrams and Rose traced an erosion of class consciousness and a declining relationship between class identity and voting behaviour.[21] They devoted particular attention to the way in which working-class electors were becoming less receptive to the class-based appeals of the Labour party. Two conclusions followed: that the Labour party could only reverse its electoral decline by changing its policy programme and image, and that the politics of consumption was replacing the politics of production. Regardless of their accuracy, these kinds of narratives exerted a considerable influence on the way in which many policy-makers and commentators understood post-war social change. Leading figures in the Labour party were particularly receptive. One of the party's leading intellectuals, Anthony Crosland, cited Abrams' survey in his own diagnosis of the Conservatives' election victory in 1959, while

---

20 As Jon Lawrence has demonstrated, other approaches to describing post-war social change were available, but the distinctive political conditions of the 1950s help to foster a preoccupation with social mobility and its electoral consequences. Jon Lawrence, 'Class, "Affluence" and the Study of Everyday Life in Britain, c. 1930–64', *Cultural and Social History*, Vol. 10, No. 2 (2013), pp. 273–299.

21 Mark Abrams and Richard Rose, *Must Labour Lose?* (Penguin, 1960).

the socialist thinker Rita Hinden, in her commentary on *Must Labour Lose?*, stated that 'the old working-class ethos is being eroded by prosperity and the increasing fluidity of our society'.[22] On the other side of the party divide, the Conservatives began to employ the 'affluent worker' as a trope within its campaign literature, and it became increasingly willing to associate the national interest with the interest of the expanding middle class.[23]

As they outlined their narratives of *embourgeoisement*, many writers referred to apparent changes in the nature of British capitalism. Attention was directed to the increasing complexity of the capitalist economies that were fuelling the post-war boom in consumption.[24] Production methods had become increasingly complex, and this shift had changed the relationship between labour and capital. In their efforts to describe this transformation, many accounts took their cue from James Burnham's *The Managerial Revolution*, published as a Pelican in April 1945. A former communist who had become disillusioned with Marxism prior to the war, Burnham had claimed that the inter-war war period had witnessed the ascendency of a new class of managers who were the new source of power in America's capitalist order. His conclusion was a pessimistic one. The 'managerial revolution', he argued, would result in the emergence of a more oligarchic world order in which a managerial elite would suspend basic individual freedoms. Yet when British intellectuals imported Burnham's thesis into British political debate, many, particularly those on the moderate wing of the Labour party, substituted his gloomy prophecies for a more optimistic vision. Instead of regarding the expansion of a managerial class as a threat to social democracy, they argued that it would be a conduit for its advance. This followed from an understanding

---

22   Anthony Crosland, *Can Labour Win?* (London: Fabian Society, 1960), p. 10. Abrams and Rose, *Must Labour Lose?*, p. 106.
23   Stuart Laing, *Representation of Working Class Life, 1957–1964* (London: Macmillan, 1986), p. 12.
24   Zweig, *The Worker in an Affluent Society*.

of the role of the managerial class in society. It was argued that because managers tended to be salaried professionals whose rewards were not directly linked to the profits of the companies for which they worked, they would be more likely to engage in altruistic activity.[25]

These ideas punctuated the writing of some Penguin authors. *Twentieth Century Socialism*, a Special written by leading members of Socialist Union, a Labour-affiliated group that published the influential journal *Socialist Commentary*, acknowledged that the social order from which the labour movement had emerged had been replaced with a very different one. Its principal authors, Rita Hinden and Allan Flanders, wrote:

> The twentieth century has witnessed how, step by step, the old unrestricted rights of ownership in regard to labour have been whittled away – through legislation, through trade union organisation, through full employment – with the result that the power relationship between capital and labour to-day stands transformed, even when ownership is still in private hands ... This, in essence, is the 'managerial revolution' which has gone so far to divorce the exercise of economic power form ownership.[26]

According to Hinden and Flanders, this shift in the nature of British capitalism was having a significant impact upon social attitudes. They drew attention to the change in aspirations of the salaried worker: 'His [*sic*] concern is, primarily, with his personal reputation; he wants to be esteemed for his success, to win recognition for his ability and his efforts and to be promoted to positions of higher esteem.'[27] This esteem, they argued, did not necessarily follow from material rewards. Rather, it was bound up with the social value of their work. It followed that the twin objectives of economic

---

25 Anthony Crosland, *The Future of Socialism* (London: Jonathan Cape, 1956), pp. 74–75. Also see Roy Jenkins, *The Labour Case* (Penguin, 1959), pp. 54–55.
26 *Twentieth Century Socialism* (Penguin, 1956), p. 126.
27 *Twentieth Century Socialism*, p. 99.

efficiency and social equality could be reconciled by securing a social order that was predicated upon a 'strong' conception of equality of opportunity. After rejecting the notion of an 'equal start with the race left to the swiftest', Hinden and Flanders noted that:

> The classless society, which has been the continuing inspiration of socialists, would give no one group ... superior opportunities. They would be open equally to all who could use them. The elimination of class distinctions is thus a measure of the achievement of equality.[28]

Provided that social status was determined by an individual's moral positions as well as their social function, opportunities for attainment could be satisfied without doing harm to the interests of the community. Hinden and Flanders' arguments accorded with those of leading figures within the parliamentary Labour party, particularly those, like Anthony Crosland and Hugh Gaitskell, who were coming to be identified with its 'revisionist' wing. As Ben Jackson has demonstrated, these figures did not wish to realise a perfect meritocracy.[29] Drawing upon arguments that had been made by R. H. Tawney and others, they were concerned that the elevation of merit as a criterion for distributing rewards would result in the legitimation of certain kinds of inequality.[30] Nonetheless, they believed that the advance of meritocratic practices was, in the short to medium term, desirable.[31] Not only did they argue that rewarding ability and effort was necessary to incentivise effort, but they also assumed that equal opportunity would ensure that talents were not wasted. Some of the arguments outlined in Roy Jenkins' *The Labour Case*, a Penguin Special that was published in advance of the 1959 election, are telling. At one juncture, Jenkins, who was affiliated with the moderate 'revisionist' wing of the

---

28 *Twentieth Century Socialism*, p. 26.
29 Ben Jackson, *Equality and the British Left* (Manchester: Manchester University Press, 2005), pp. 169–176.
30 Crosland, *The Future of Socialism*, pp. 237–237.

Labour party, intervened in the debate about educational reform, and he arrived at the following conclusion:

> So long as a tiny minority of schools, with pupils recruited almost exclusively from one class, command much of the entry to Oxford and a high proposition of the best jobs, so long will equality of opportunity remain unreal, and so long will it be impossible to make the best use of available talents … Equality of opportunity is not in itself enough either as a social or an educational aim. It needs to be supplemented by a respect for the unsuccessful and by a scepticism towards the values and rights of elites. But it is a great deal better than inequality of opportunity.[32]

Many conservatives had also arrived at the conclusion that the expansion of educational opportunity and the elevation of the criterion of merit could generate prosperity and social harmony. But there were some who railed against meritocratic logic. A number of Conservatives, for instance, were concerned that if intelligence became the supreme criterion for determining the distribution of status and wealth, those traditions and customs that could not be developed through formal education would become redundant. One of the clearest statements of this argument appeared in Roy Lewis and Angus Maude's *The English Middle Classes*, which was published as a Pelican in 1952. At the time of the book's publication, Maude was the director of the Conservative party's research department, while Lewis was an economic journalist, and they shared the belief that the English middle classes were inhabiting an increasingly hostile social and political climate. It was the middle classes, they argued, that were the repository of the virtuous customs and traditions that Britain's social and political health was predicated upon. Yet the expansion of the state, combined with

---

31 Crosland, *The Future of Socialism*, p. 229 and p. 231.
32 Jenkins, *The Labour Case*, p. 87. An extensive summary of the book was published in the *Daily Telegraph*. See 'Socialism Could Not Survive 3rd Defeat', *Daily Telegraph*, 15 September 1959.

the redistributive policies of the post-war Labour government, were eroding their relative status and wealth. In support of their argument, Lewis and Maude constructed a particular description of the middle class: opposing the idea that the function of middle-class expertise was to manage the increasingly complex productive system, they argued that the middle class was best understood as the fount of social and moral dispositions that were eternally virtuous:

> A great part of the strength, and the value, of the middle classes in English political life has been their ability to set off, within themselves, intellect against money, common sense against intellect, and a tradition of gentility against all three. Therein lies the great advantage of a social class over a body of experts, or an elite chosen by means of examinations or intelligence tests.[33]

But even Maude and Lewis acknowledged that in the conditions of the post-war world, technicians and organisers were becoming indispensable: 'the English middle classes', they wrote, 'are destined to become increasingly "managerial"'.[34]

As the 1950s wore on, the kinds of arguments that Maude and Lewis advanced became increasingly marginalised within Conservative discourses. Far from attempting to resurrect the notion of a middle class that was defined by its relationship with tradition, the party appealed to a more functionalist conception of its interests. By the end of the decade it was common for Conservatives to appeal to the idea of classlessness and to promote the fluid mobility of individuals across class boundaries. In his updated edition of *The Case for*

---

33 Roy Lewis and Angus Maude, *The English Middle Classes* (Penguin, 1949), p. 72. For a discussion of the way in which Conservatives attempted to reconstruct the political and cultural middle ground, see Clarisse Berthèzene, *Training Minds for the War of Ideas: Ashridge College, the Conservative Party and the Cultural Politics of Britain, 1929–54* (Manchester: Manchester University Press, 2015), pp. 160–165.

34 Lewis and Maude, *English Middle Classes*, p. 235.

Conservatism, Quintin Hogg was willing to privilege the social role of those individuals who had acquired measurable talents and attributes:

> We live in the age of the qualified man and woman, the man and woman who has earned a place of respect in society by some socially desirable skill or qualification.[35]

Nor did Maude and Lewis' anti-meritocratic conception of the social order resonate with broader social changes that were taking place in the early post-war period. As Savage has argued, many members of the lower middle classes came to deny 'culturist' arguments for their superior social status. Seizing upon the opportunities provided by the expansion of technical education, they derived their status from their possession of rational expertise and practical skills.[36] Their identities were bound up with the cultural politics of the post-war settlement, and the 'technically trained expert' came to be situated at the nodal point of a social consensus that reconciled traditional forms of political contestation.[37]

One facet of this consensus concerned the relationship between capital and labour. There has been a protracted debate about the existence or otherwise of a 'corporatist' model of economic management in post-war Britain.[38] But regardless of whether such a model was realised in practice, contemporaries certainly believed that the relationship between employees and employers was being transformed in the post-war period. In many instances, they identified rational experts as mediators who were resolving older forms

---

35 Quintin Hogg (Viscount Hailsham), *The Conservative Case* (Penguin, 1959), p. 166. Also see Iain Macleod, 'The Political Divide' in *The Future of the Welfare State* (London: CPC, 1958).

36 Savage, *Identities and Social Change*, pp. 80–84.

37 Becky Conekin, Frank Mort and Chris Waters (eds), *Moments of Modernity: Reconstructing Britain, 1945–1964* (London: Rivers Oram, 1999), pp. 14–16.

38 Alan Booth, 'Corporatism, Capitalism and Depression in Twentieth-Century Britain', *British Journal of Sociology*, Vol. 33, No. 2 (1982), pp. 200–223.

of class conflict. It is difficult to see these arguments in the few political texts that Penguin published in the post-war period, but some of its authors did draw attention to the way in which professionals, experts and technocrats were located outside of traditional interest groups and were, in a sense, 'classless'. Perhaps the most well known of these authors was J. K. Galbraith, an American economist and public intellectual. In 1958, Galbraith published one of the most important non-fiction books of the post-war period, *The Affluent Society*, which was published as a Pelican in 1962. The book's central argument was that private opulence was being achieved at the expense of public squalor. Rather than observing a universal increase in living standards, Galbraith traced the emergence of a society in which artificial needs were being generated in order to serve an economy that was excessively preoccupied with producing more and more private goods. But Galbraith did not deny that technological change was creating the opportunities for greater prosperity, and in his penultimate chapter, he outlined a solution to the malaise that he had described. This solution followed from a sociological observation about what he termed the 'New Class'. This class was distinguished by its relationship with work. Comprised of professionals, its members did not suffer pain and discomfort as a result of their labour. Instead, they drew satisfaction from their work and privileged enjoyment over material gain. Galbraith concluded that the 'rapid expansion of this class should be a major, and perhaps next to peaceful survival itself, the major social goal of the society'.[39] Since the qualification for membership was, above all else, educational attainment, he believed that investment in education should become the basic index of social progress.

If Galbraith seemed to frame the expanding class of professionals as a source of social progress on the basis of its relationship with labour, other commentators drew attention to their capacity

---

39 J. K. Galbraith, *The Affluent Society* (Penguin, 1958), p. 276.

to acquire and circulate knowledge. The expert was conceived as the bearer of objective, empirical knowledge, the dissemination of which benefited the community as a whole. This was not, of course, an entirely novel notion, and its origins can be traced to a much earlier period. What was distinctive about the post-war moment, however, was the extent to which politicians were willing to regard expert knowledge as the foundation for political thinking.

The architects of these ideas came from different intellectual traditions, but they shared a common hostility to the forms of reasoning that they believed had contributed to the totalitarian ideologies of the inter-war period. Few were more influential than Karl Popper. Together with other philosophers and intellectuals, Popper constructed a critique of the historicism that he detected in totalitarian ideologies.[40] In turn, he advocated a positivist epistemology and favoured gradual political change that could be easily reversed. Although it is difficult to find explicit statements of Popperite ideas in Penguin's post-war texts, it is possible to identify a growing hostility to historicism and the political logic that followed from it. Several Penguin authors developed critiques of what they regarded as the utopianism of the pre-war period. In his Special, Roy Jenkins cautioned against the notion that there were any universal solutions to political problems:

> [The Labour party is] a practical party. It is quite concerned with immediate reforms as with ultimate purposes ... It is always difficult to see how the course of politics will develop. The solution of one set of problems invariably uncovers new ones, the nature of which often cannot be seen in advance.[41]

For Jenkins, the task of the post-war socialist was not to identify universal political 'ends' but to engage in piecemeal social reform and to evaluate its consequences through empirical observation.

---

40 Karl Popper, *The Open Society and Its Enemies* (London: Routledge, 1945).
41 Jenkins, *The Labour Case*, p. 12.

Ideas about the appropriate relationship between merit and reward fed into these conceptions of politics. According to many commentators, utopian ideas were more attractive to those social groups that had been denied positions of authority. It followed that if a greater proportion of talented individuals were able to ascend the social ladder, it would be possible to produce a governing class that was unreceptive to utopian ideas. Accordingly, meritocracy was conceived as both a symptom and cause of the 'end of ideology'. This notion that ideological modes of thought were being made redundant influenced both sociologists and policy-makers from the late 1950s.

Meritocracy and the 'end of ideology'

As we have seen, meritocratic ideas were a feature of different traditions of political thinking long before 1945. But it was not until 1958 that a word was introduced into Britain's political vocabulary that could describe a society that was governed by their logic. In that year, Michael Young published his influential work of satirical sociology, *The Rise of the Meritocracy*, offering commentators and policy-makers a convenient point of reference in their debates about equality, education and economic change. By 1961, when Penguin published a paperback edition, the concept of a meritocracy had captured the attention of intellectuals and commentators across the political spectrum.[42] The book was both peculiar and provocative. Projecting himself into the year 2034, Young, who had co-authored Labour's 1945 election manifesto, offered a satirical account of the social and political changes that had taken place in Britain since the late nineteenth century. Central to his story was a particular phenomenon: the emergence of a 'meritocracy', an oligarchic group of individuals who, by virtue of their intelligence, had been selected to govern the community, and who

---

42 Michael Young, *The Rise of the Meritocracy* (Penguin, 1961).

received the greatest rewards for their work. Young traced the origins of this class to the 1950s, a period when political elites embraced the argument that rewards should be distributed on the basis of merit rather than inheritance. The result of this shift was the emergence of an unequal order that was not bound by ties of mutual responsibility. Elites did not feel compelled to express sympathy for those whom they governed, and the lower social classes, who could no longer blame their inferior status on the absence of opportunity, were unable to construct an effective moral argument for equality.[43] By telling a story about how meritocratic arrangements could perpetuate inequality, Young challenged the assumption that equality of opportunity was conducive to social justice, and, in turn, he invited his readers to contemplate a more expansive conception of equality. This way of thinking about equality placed emphasis on the principle of equal worth.[44] An equal society, Young seemed to argue, was one in which all individuals, regardless of their peculiar attributes, were able to make a full contribution to the common good.[45] From this proposition, Young developed an argument about the way rewards should be distributed: a society that was concerned, above all else, with the distribution of opportunity and reward according to intelligence would be unjust, since selfishness and competition would prevail over altruism and co-operation. A just order, it followed, was one in which rewards were distributed on the basis of the individual's contribution to the community. Finally, Young challenged the assumption that equality of opportunity aided productivity. Far from generating an 'Age of Plenty', the meritocratic society that he described created a scenario in which resources were directed not towards public provision but towards the purchase of mechanical equipment and the training of the social and political elite. As Young

43   Young, *The Rise of the Meritocracy*, pp. 106–109.
44   R. H. Tawney, *Equality* (London: Allen & Unwin, 1931).
45   Armstrong and Gray, *The Authentic Tawney*, pp. 133–137.

put it, 'We are all poor, and shall always remain so, because the demands of the scientific age are insatiable.'[46]

Young's book responded to broader tendencies in both intellectual politics and the field of social science that Young inhabited. From the early 1950s, the concept of social mobility became one of the central concerns of British social science. This development can, in part, be explained by the emergence of technologies and techniques that made the empirical study of the phenomenon possible. But as Chris Renwick has demonstrated, social scientists' concern with social mobility also reflected their enthusiasm for it.[47] Many of them regarded the creation of a more fluid social order as a solution to social problems. David Glass, a sociologist who published a major study into social mobility in 1953, noted that:

> There are two primary reasons for wishing to see the possibility of high social mobility in a community. First, in order to increase economic and social efficiency, since with a fluid social structure there is more likelihood that positions requiring high ability will in fact be held by individuals who possess high ability ... Secondly, from the point of the individual, social mobility should ensure that there are fewer square pegs in round holes, and the existence of opportunity to rise in status will in any case provide an incentive for the fuller utilization of a person's capacities. There may, as a consequence, be less feeling of personal frustration and a greater possibility of social harmony.[48]

Glass' comments reflected a broader movement of opinion. Prior to the war, progressive advocates of social mobility were preoccupied with the creation of a class of benign experts that could run the state efficiently. But now the phenomenon was anchored to a more functionalist conception of the social order. Societies were

---

46 Young, *The Rise of the Meritocracy*, p. 161.
47 Chris Renwick, 'Eugenics, Population Research, and Social Mobility Studies in Early and Mid-Twentieth Century Britain', *The Historical Journal*, Vol. 59, No. 3 (2015), pp. 845–867.
48 David Glass (ed.), *Social Mobility in Britain* (London: Routledge, 1953), pp. 24–25.

often conceived as self-perpetuating entities whose nature was determined by their ability to perform certain functions. In developed industrial societies, these functions were increasingly complex and required systems of selection that would allocate individuals to perform particular roles within the social order. Equal opportunity and the development of systems of educational selection were thus understood as the natural outcomes of post-industrial development. A number of arguments followed from this understanding of developed societies. First, it followed that certain kinds of political and social conflict were being rendered redundant. This notion was popularised by an influential body of sociological research, much of which drew upon a functionalist conception of the role of ideas. Notable sociologists like Karl Mannheim, Daniel Bell, S. M. Lipset and Raymond Aron were all convinced that the arrival of affluence was rendering ideology redundant.[49] Common to their accounts was a preoccupation with the role of the expanding class of scientists and technicians. These new occupational groups, it was argued, were less receptive to 'ideological' logic and were instead preoccupied with finding objective solutions to common social and political problems. Ideas had once performed the function of inspiring emotive beliefs and stirring political commitment. But the technocrat and the scientist were not motivated by emotion and passion but by rational logic.

As Peter Hennessy has noted, a certain kind of meritocratic reasoning complemented these narratives.[50] In a number of ways, meritocratic arrangements seemed to offer a means to resolve older forms of social and ideological conflict associated with the industrial order. In classical liberal and conservative traditions of thought, it had often been alleged that the twin objectives of equality and liberty existed in an inverse relationship, such that the

---

49 See Chaim I. Waxman (ed.), *The End of Ideology Debate* (New York: Clarion, 1969).
50 Peter Hennessy, *Establishment and Meritocracy* (London: Haus, 2013), p. 31.

attainment of one necessitated the absence of the other. But meritocratic arrangements could be conceived as a means of reconciling them.[51] On the one hand, they could replace older forms of inequality by ones that were determined by the socially agreeable criterion of merit. On the other, they could ensure than any individual, regardless of their social background, would have the freedom to develop their talents and climb the social ladder. It is unsurprising that some of the chief proponents of 'the end of ideology' drew attention to the way in which social mobility could temper political antagonisms. Although these writers admitted that social hierarchies would remain in a post-industrial order, they believed that such hierarchies would be less likely to provoke envy and anger. Daniel Bell's views were characteristic:

> One can acknowledge, as I would, the priority of the disadvantaged (with all its difficulty of definition) as an axiom of social policy, without diminishing the opportunity for the best to rise to the top through work and effort. The principles of merit, achievement, and universalism are, it seems to me, the necessary foundations for a productive – and cultivated – society. What is important is that the society, to the fullest extent possible, be a genuinely open one.[52]

How did these ideas about social mobility gain such resonance in the 1950s? In part, they did so because they were able to reconcile the egalitarian spirit of the wartime period with the functional needs of post-war capitalism.[53] At a time when the Cold War was exerting a significant influence upon the cultural and political climate of Britain, meritocracy could be conceived as an alternative to the excesses of unbridled individualism and statist collectivism.[54] It preserved the individual as the essential unit of the social

---

51 Ortolano, *Two Cultures*, pp. 24–25.
52 Daniel Bell, 'On Meritocracy', *Public Interest*, Vol. 29 (1972), p. 67.
53 Sinfield, *Literature, Politics and Culture*, p. 265.
54 Tony Shaw, 'Britain and the Cultural Cold War', *Contemporary British History*, Vol. 19, No. 2 (2005), pp. 109–115.

order and could be reconciled with the principle of private property. But because the professional classes that benefited from meritocratic practices claimed to serve the interests of the common good, they tended to be hostile to the waste of human capital and demanded that private property was functional. In a sense, then, meritocratic logic was so powerful not because it could be aligned with the objectives of Britain's major ideologies but because it provided a means of reconciling these ends with arrangements that were acceptable to a broad range of opinion.

As meritocratic ideas proliferated, alternative ideas about the appropriate distribution of wealth and rewards were increasingly marginalised. Penguin's engagement with ideas that ran counter to meritocratic logic reflect this development. When editors did commission texts that were informed by more radical conceptions of distributive justice, they often expressed anxieties. The editorial correspondence on William Gallacher's *The Case for Communism*, which was published in 1949, is revealing here. In response to the books by John Parker and Quintin Hogg that were discussed earlier, Gallacher, the Communist party's only MP, wrote a letter to Allen Lane. He argued that if, as the blurbs on the jackets of Parker and Hogg's books stated, Penguin had 'no politics', then they should be prepared to allow him to make the case for communism. The letter provoked a revealing dialogue between Penguin's senior editors. Initially, Lane acquiesced and believed that Penguin could not afford to ignore the ideas that Gallacher's advocated. In the following months, however, both Lane and Williams became increasingly concerned that the book would harm the firm's reputation. On his part, Williams wrote, 'there does linger in my mind the repercussions on the firm's prestige which publication might create. The public is a rather foolish animal, and might well jump to a wrong conclusion.'[55] To ensure that readers did not regard Penguin as a communist-affiliated publisher, he suggested that the

---

55   Bill Williams to Alan Glover, 9 October 1948. PA: DM1819/22/3.

cover of the book should include a note that declared the firm's political objectivity:

> We can, of course, make it abundantly plain in the blurb that we are only doing for Communism what we have already done for Socialism and Conservatism. But I think we also ought to consider some further announcement on the front cover itself.[56]

When the book was finally published, it included a publisher's note stating that the book 'must be read with the caution which all propaganda should arouse in the rational reader'.[57]

Penguin expressed similar anxieties after it launched *Russia Review*, a quarterly magazine that documented cultural life in the Soviet Union.[58] Only three issues were published before poor sales prompted Allen Lane to terminate the project. Writing to the magazine's editor, he stated: 'As I think you know, we went into this on a somewhat idealistic basis without thought of making enormous profits, but even bearing this in mind, the results are pretty catastrophic.'[59] Perhaps alluding to the onset of the Cold War, the firm's chief non-fiction editor, Alan Glover, suggested that the magazine's poor sale performance was 'mainly due to circumstances beyond the control of all of us'.[60] In the final issue of the publication, its editor, Edward Crankshaw, noted that 'the expected revulsion of feeling has already taken place, and on every side there is an increasing coldness towards Russia, which is in fact no better founded than the preceding warmth of admiration'.[61]

---

56 Bill Williams to Alan Glover, 9 October 1948. PA: DM1107/S156.

57 William Gallacher, *The Case for Communism* (Penguin, 1949), inside cover.

58 An internal memo introducing the magazine stated, 'the general reader in this country, in spite of an intense interest in Russia, has been impeded in his desire to understand her by the lack of suitable and adequate information'. PA: DM1879/11/7.

59 Allen Lane to Count Beckendorff, 24 January 1946. PA: DM1819/11/7.

60 Alan Glover to Edward Crankshaw, 8 August 1946. PA: DM1819/11/7.

61 Edward Crankshaw, 'Editorial Comment', *Russia Review*, Vol. 3 (1947), p. 1.

The cultural politics of affluence

Many members of Penguin's social milieu railed against merito-cratic logic. Of particular significance was Richard Hoggart, who, as we have seen, was wedded to many of the ideas that we might associate with Penguin's vision of cultural democracy. Hoggart challenged the conclusion that the move towards a 'classless' social order was a positive development. Writing in *The Uses of Literacy*, which was published as a Pelican in 1958, he admitted that the 1944 Education Act had made it possible for a larger proportion of working-class children to become socially mobile. Yet he was reluc-tant to regard this as either an egalitarian or a culturally beneficial development. His argument was rooted in an analysis of the his-torical role of the 'earnest minority' within the working class who were intellectually gifted. Previously, the individuals who com-prised this social group had employed their talents to advance the cause of the poorest sections of the community. But increased social mobility, Hoggart argued, was threatening to lift them from the classes into which they were born. The chief consequence was the decline of 'critically minded' individuals within the poorest sections of the community, and Hoggart concluded that if this process continued, 'we might find ourselves moving towards a kind of new caste system, one at least as firm as the old'.[62] Unsurpris-ingly, Allen Lane was sympathetic to many of the book's argu-ments, and he immediately suggested that Hoggart might be a suitable advisory editor. In a memorandum to a senior editor, he noted: 'I have a hunch he's the man we may be looking for on the editorial side ... [he] obviously has a feeling for popular edu-cation for the best reasons i.e. as a means of attaining an appreci-ation of the cultural life as opposed to mere job-getting.'[63] Hoggart would later remark that Lane had gravitated towards the book

---

62 Hoggart, *The Uses of Literacy*, pp. 337–338.
63 Allen Lane to Eunice Frost, 7 March 1957. PA: DM1843/8.

because it 'typified so much of what [he] had at the back of his head but hadn't himself made articulate'.[64]

Lane's chief editor, W. E. Williams, was also sympathetic to the kind of argument that Hoggart had advanced. Not only did he share Hoggart's cultural critique of post-war affluence, but he also expressed concerns about mass consumption. A letter that he wrote to the Director of Penguin USA, Victor Weybright, reveals his reasoning:

> I particularly liked your suggestion that periods of trial and depression promote a cultural view. If I believed that Britain was about to become luxuriously supplied with nylon legs and television sets, I should take a pessimistic view of the prospects of cultural activities. The fact is that poverty promotes reflection upon the less material values and therefore instigates an attention to serious books, music and the arts which is absent in more prosperous times. There are occasions when I hope Britain will not get the Loan and so be forced back into something of the spirit of 1940–41. For myself, if the cigarettes and the whisky hold out, I am willing enough to accept sweat, toil and tears.[65]

When the consumer boom of the 1950s arrived, it destabilised many of the assumptions that had informed Penguin's vision of cultural democracy. Lane and his editors had assumed that the wider distribution of good literature would foster co-operative values and erode social divisions. By the late 1950s, however, it was difficult to locate evidence of this democratisation. Revisiting John Lehmann, who had employed *Penguin New Writing* to facilitate the development of working-class literature, helps us to understand this shift. Despite the success of his project in the late 1930s and early wartime period, Lehmann's post-war editorial venture, *The London Magazine*, did little to privilege working-class authors. In 1955, when asked to explain the magazine's failure to adequately represent the writing of ordinary authors, Lehmann wrote a foreword to the magazine that reproduced two pillars

---

64 Taken from the transcript of an interview conducted in 1991. PA:DM1843/17.

65 W. E. Williams to Victor Weybright, 6 March 1946. PA: DM1294/3.

of the 'end of ideology' thesis. First, he suggested that because 'intelligent and ambitious' children were beginning to move up the social ladder, Britain was becoming more 'classless'. 'The social structure where good class was identical with good education,' he wrote, 'is crumbling away.' He concluded that the very notion of 'working-class literature' was being outmoded. Second, Lehmann argued that the injustice and adversity that had fuelled the boom in working-class literary culture in the 1930s had dissipated. Full employment and the welfare state, he argued, had both resolved older antagonisms and reduced the time available for writing.[66]

Hoggart, Williams and Lehmann shared a common hostility to the cultural consequences of affluence. But when they articulated their critiques of post-war cultural change, they all assumed that educational equality and relative prosperity were blurring class distinctions and impairing interest in 'serious' cultural activities. They adhered to the view that meritocracy was something of a sociological fact that could not be easily reversed.

Penguin was implicated within the contradictions of this meritocratic logic. On the one hand, it was a cultural institution that sought to remove the barriers to educational attainment and intellectual advance. On the other, it was hostile to the acquisitive impulses that seemed to follow from the wider distribution of opportunity. It was, at one and the same time, both a facilitator of social mobility and a cultural institution that challenged the social logic that legitimated a particular conception of it.

Conclusion

The dominant ideology that took root from the late 1940s cut across Britain's major ideological traditions. Neither progressives nor conservatives were entirely satisfied with the assumptions and beliefs that comprised it. Yet this explains, in part, its ability to form the basis of a fragile and contested political settlement. Far

---

66 John Lehmann, 'Foreword', *The London Magazine*, December 1955, pp. 11–12.

from being the product of a common enthusiasm for the realisation of a 'perfect' meritocracy, Britain's meritocratic moment followed from uneasy compromises between different ideological
formations. Social democrats regarded equality of opportunity as
an immediate objective in a long-term struggle for a more egalitarian social order; Conservatives regarded it as a buffer against a
more radical conception of equality; and liberals regarded it as a
means of resisting the twin evils of collectivism and conservatism.

In many instances, meritocratic arguments were accompanied by
a social logic that negated political conflict. Removing barriers to
educational attainment and distributing the material gains of affluence would, it was argued, militate against the kind of ideological
contests that had marked the inter-war period. The chief consequence was what Stuart Hall called an 'ideological closure'.[67] That
is not to say that all forms of political conflict dissipated. But oppositional formations that operated outside of the prevailing political
logic of 'affluence' were increasingly marginalised. For cultural institutions like Penguin Books, this posed a dilemma. Not only did this
development impair the demand for new ideas, but it also made it
more difficult for the publisher to align its cultural vision with conceptions of the future. In the 1930s and 1940s, the publisher had
constructed an imagined community of social democratic readers
whose aspirations could be reconciled with progressive political
ideas. This vision was difficult to reconcile with the 'Conservative
modernity' of the 1950s. As the consumer boom took root, the aus-
tere covers of Penguin's Specials seemed to become a relic of a wartime political culture that was being dismantled by technological
and social change. These changes did not generate their own meanings, but they did establish a fertile context for narratives and ideas
that marginalised the more utopian visions of the future that had
been propagated by Penguin in the early wartime period.

---

67 Stuart Hall, Chas Critcher, Tony Jefferson, John Clarke and Brian Rob-
erts, *Policing the Crisis* (London: Macmillan, 1978), p. 232.

4

THE STAGNANT
SOCIETY

In the early 1960s, the optimism that had punctuated the intellectual politics of the preceding decade began to dissipate. Rather than anticipating a future in which social harmony and economic efficiency would resolve political conflict, intellectuals and policymakers became increasingly preoccupied with explaining, and identifying solutions to, Britain's apparent social and economic decline. This decline, as Jim Tomlinson and others have demonstrated, was not an objective historical fact but a political construct that was, to a large extent, invented.[1] Yet regardless of its actuality, decline came to frame debates about all kinds of social, cultural and economic phenomena in the early 1960s. When we attempt to reconstruct these debates, Penguin's books are a particularly useful resource. The publisher was an active and significant agent in the 'state-of-the nation' debate that took place in response to decline, and the books that it published can be employed to map the cultural politics of declinist thinking.[2]

---

1   Jim Tomlinson, *The Politics of Decline* (London: Routledge, 2000).
2   Kenneth O. Morgan, *The People's Peace* (Oxford: Oxford University Press, 1999), p. 199. Jefferys, *Retreat from New Jerusalem*, p. 111. Matthew Grant, 'Historians, Penguin Specials and the "State-of-the-Nation" Literature, 1958–64', *Contemporary British History*, Vol. 17, No. 3 (2006), pp. 29–54. Also see Kenneth O. Morgan, *Ages of Reform* (London: I.B. Tauris, 2010), p. 228; Ian Budge, 'Relative Decline as a Political Issue', *Contemporary British*

These books invite us to regard the period as the zenith of Britain's meritocratic moment. Many give voice to a meritocratic vision of the future, demonstrating how social mobility came to be regarded as a solution to social and economic decay. Yet while this period witnessed the proliferation of meritocratic arguments, it was also one in which the fragility of the prevailing meritocratic settlement was exposed. The apparent ubiquity of meritocratic arguments concealed the tenuous ideological bonds that had held this consensus together. Increasingly, actors were employing the language of meritocracy to make arguments that broke decisively with the assumptions that had informed political thinking in the preceding decade, and by 1964, the concept of merit was bearing the burden of an increasingly wide range of ideological objectives.[3] If the post-war settlement had been built on meritocratic foundations, those foundations were beginning to fracture by the time Harold Wilson formed his first government. This settlement had been based on a putative bipartisan enthusiasm for meritocratic policies that would enhance social mobility. But as intellectuals and policy-makers grappled with the problem of decline, their deeper ideological commitments began to come to the fore; the apparent ubiquity of meritocratic ideas in this moment concealed some significant disputes. Rather than regarding Harold Wilson's victory in the 1964 election as the zenith of Britain's meritocratic moment, we can instead understand it as a moment when the idea of meritocracy began to be eclipsed.

History, Vol. 7, No. 1 (1993), pp. 1–23; Jim Tomlinson 'Thrice Denied: "Declinism" as a Recurrent Theme in British History in the Long Twentieth Century', *Twentieth Century British History*, Vol. 20, No. 2 (2009), pp. 227–251; Richard English and Michael Kenny (eds), *Rethinking British Decline* (Basingstoke: Palgrave, 1999).

3   Ortolano has drawn attention to the way in which the phenomenon of decline was seized upon by actors making very different political arguments. Guy Ortolano, 'Decline as a Weapon in Cultural Politics' in Wm. Roger Louis (ed.), *Penultimate Adventures with Britannia: Personalities, Politics and Culture in* Britain (London: I.B. Tauris, 2005), pp. 201–211.

Penguin's response to the commercial and cultural changes in this period offers a valuable insight into the social and political terrain on which debates about decline were fought.

Changing the guard

From the late 1950s, Penguin re-engaged with the political sphere. The Specials list, which had been dormant for much of the decade, was revived. Many of the titles that Penguin published generated significant debate, such that the publisher once again became an important agent of political opinion. This resurgence was, in part, the product of internal changes within Penguin. But it was also made possible by the emergence of a new political environment.[4]

In the decade that succeeded the 1945 election, Penguin Books was firmly integrated within Britain's cultural establishment. Its changing status can be traced in the trajectories of its senior staff: Allen Lane had been knighted in 1952, and his chief editor, W. E. Williams, became Secretary-General of the Arts Council a year earlier.[5] Inevitably, this eroded some of the firm's earlier dynamism. Even Richard Hoggart, one of Penguin's greatest admirers, noted this tendency. 'One is bound to wonder,' he wrote, 'whether Penguins have managed to give young people during the past ten years the kind of service they gave us.'[6] Lane reluctantly agreed with this sentiment. In 1957, he wrote that there was a need to '[re-introduce] the sort of spirit that we had in the old days'.[7] Towards this end, he initiated a significant change in the firm's editorial personnel. Editors that had shaped the character of the

---

4   For discussions of the economic ideas that emerged in this period, see Matthijs, *Ideas and Economic Crises*, pp. 85–86; G. C. Peden, *British Economic and Social Policy: From Lloyd George to Margaret Thatcher* (Oxford: Philip Allen, 1985), pp. 164–202.

5   Lewis, *Penguin Special*, p. 269. Hewison, *Culture and Consensus*, p. 79.

6   Hoggart, 'The Reader', p. 29.

7   Allen Lane to Richard Lane, 31 December 1957. PA: DM1819/2/0/2.

non-fiction list since the late 1930s, such as Alan Glover, Eunice Frost and indeed W. E. Williams, were replaced by a number of younger editors who were more familiar with the changing cultural landscape of late 1950s Britain.[8] Two appointments were of particular importance for our story: Tony Godwin, who assumed the role of chief editor in 1960, and Dieter Pevsner, who replaced Glover as the chief editor of the non-fiction list in the same year.

When he was appointed by Allen Lane in 1960, Godwin, a prominent London bookseller, had no prior editorial experience. Nor was he always sympathetic to the editorial policies that Penguin had pursued in the preceding decade. He was particularly critical of its preoccupation with its ever growing backlist of titles. In his view, paperback imprints needed to take greater responsibility for the cultivation of original books that could satisfy the demands of a changing audience. But on the central question of the book's cultural function, Godwin's views complemented Penguin's left-culturist agenda. He was suspicious of the notion that books were merely 'commodities', and he shared Lane's belief in the potential of ordinary readers.[9] Godwin was also concerned with cultivating the talents of his authors. The novelist Al Alvarez once remarked that he was 'most happy when dealing with the text and its creator'.[10]

But while Godwin shared Lane's instinctive egalitarianism, he departed from his narrow conception of 'good' culture. During his tenure as the owner and manager of Better Books, Godwin had become exposed to, and helped to support, various radical literary movements, many of which were emerging from the Bohemian sub-cultures of London and the United States. He greatly admired

---

8   Alan Glover's resignation letter, 30 March 1958. PA: DM1819/1/1. Lewis, *Penguin Special*, pp. 301–315. W. E. Williams became a director of the firm, but he exerted a less prominent influence over the firm's editorial direction.

9   Tony Godwin, 'Paperbacks', *New Statesman*, 14 July 1961. Also see Lewis, *Penguin Special*, pp. 343–348.

10   Al Alvarez, 'Author's Editor', *London Review of Books*, 24 January 1980.

Beat writers like Allen Ginsberg, and he had provided financial assistance to the feminist magazine *Spare Rib*.[11] Moreover, while he shared Lane's belief that a book's chief purpose was to educate and entertain, rather than return a profit, Godwin was much more comfortable with the competitive commercial environment that Penguin had come to inhabit. Under his direction, books were marketed much more aggressively than they had been hitherto. As well as introducing illustrated cover designs, he was also willing to spend large sums of capital on expensive advertising campaigns.[12] After he departed the firm in 1967, Godwin criticised Allen Lane's belief that quality paperbacks should not be sold by petrol stations and supermarkets. Such a view, Godwin argued, was sustained by a belief that culture was an 'attribute of middle-class values which must at all costs be protected from contamination by mass values … I believe in the widest sensible display and availability.'[13]

Godwin's political beliefs are difficult to classify. Although he frequently expressed sympathy with the politics of the New Left, he did not describe himself as a socialist.[14] And his entrepreneurialism and commercial acumen were not easily reconciled with the cultural values of Britain's Labourist tradition.[15] But if Godwin cannot be comfortably located within the confines of a clear ideological formation, it is clear that he was receptive to political ideas that were running counter to the parliamentary consensus of the 1950s.

Dieter Pevsner, who joined Penguin in 1959 and served a brief editorial apprenticeship under the guidance of Alan Glover, was sympathetic to Godwin's modernising vision. Although his egalitarian beliefs informed his editorial decisions, he maintained that

11   Rylance, 'Reading with a Mission'.
12   Lewis, *Penguin Special*, pp. 349–369.
13   Tony Godwin, 'Views', *Listener*, 15 May 1969.
14   In a letter that was written in December 1966, he expressed admiration for Robin Blackburn's contribution to the 1967 Special *The Incompatibles: Trade Union Militancy and the Consensus* (Penguin, 1967). PA: DM1107/S262.
15   Rylance, 'Reading with a Mission', p. 59.

the publisher's duty was to foster a dialogue between ideas from across the political spectrum. He also shared Godwin's suspicion of the rigid hierarchies of taste that informed some strands of left-culturist thought. He was particularly critical of the way in which some writers had refused to engage with new literary trends: 'If depth and permanence are to be provided in books, the audience, being only human, will demand books so presented that they can at least bear comparison with the vividness and painlessness of television communication.'[16]

From the late 1950s, Penguin's sales and profits expanded markedly. Between Godwin's arrival in 1960 and his departure seven years later, the firm's turnover more than doubled, and annual volume sales increased from seventeen to 28 million books.[17] As a result of this commercial success, Godwin and Pevsner were able to significantly increase the scale of Penguin's non-fiction output. The resurgence of the Specials list was particularly striking; whereas just twenty books had entered the list in the five years before their arrival, sixty-two new titles appeared between 1960 and 1965. To a large extent, this resurgence reflected a change in the intellectual climate of British politics. Pevsner and Godwin had to be confident that a sizable audience existed for new ideas, and this audience, it seemed, was expanding in the wake of a pervasive mood of disillusionment.

Britain after Suez

From 1956, a number of developments had eroded the optimism that marked the immediate post-war period. Not all of these changes were related, but they were often conjoined to construct a

16 Dieter Pevsner, 'The Demands of Another 30 Years', *Guardian*, 26 September 1968.
17 Eric de Bellaigue, 'The Extraordinary Flight of Book Publishing's Wingless Bird', *Logos*, Vol. 12, No. 3 (2001), p. 75.

sense of profound unease about Britain's future. The changing temper of the Cold War offers one context for the declinist mood of the period. This conflict had, of course, provoked considerable disquiet since the late 1940s, but as the threat of nuclear warfare became increasingly acute, anxieties took on a new form. This shift was articulated with clarity by Tony Godwin, who suggested that the debate over disarmament needed to be understood in metaphysical terms: 'In the welter of controversy over defence, we seem to have forgotten to ask not only whether there is anything to fight against but also what we are defending ourselves for.'[18]

The anxieties provoked by the Cold War were often channelled into extra-parliamentary forms of political activity. The rapid ascendency of the Campaign for Nuclear Disarmament was symptomatic. Some of its marches attracted as many as 150,000 attendees, and, as Kenny has noted, its expansion came alongside a decline of formal modes of political representation.[19] Godwin was sympathetic to its cause, and he invited one of its most prominent advocates, the philosopher Bertrand Russell, to write a Special on the issue.[20] Political antagonism was accompanied by a broader cultural unease. Stephen Spender, the editor of *Encounter*, noted in 1953 that a 'rebellion of the Lower Middlebrows' was beginning to gain momentum. Younger intellectuals, he argued, were beginning to quarrel with the cultural dominance of Britain's aristocratic and liberal elite.[21] The political and cultural democratisation that contributed to Penguin's rapid expansion had created a new generation of thinkers and writers who were dissatisfied with Britain's seemingly archaic and effete elite. By the end of the decade, these intellectuals began to reach a large audience.

---

18 Tony Godwin to Bertrand Russell, 7 March 1961. PA: DM1107/S206.
19 Michael Kenny, *The First New Left* (London: Lawrence & Wishart, 1995), p. 193.
20 Tony Godwin to Bertrand Russell, 7 March 1961. PA: DM1107/S206. Bertrand Russell, *Has Man a Future?* (Penguin, 1960).

Declaration, a collection of essays written by dissident authors such as John Osborne, Colin Wilson and Doris Lessing, sold 20,000 copies.[22] In his discussion of the literary formation that these authors had forged, David Marquand argued that the resilience of a hierarchical social structure had fostered a pervasive sense of disillusionment:

> the novels of Amis and Wain, and the play *Look Back in Anger* ... are characterised by bitterness: bitterness against the niceties and false-nesses of bourgeois life ... Greed and selfishness are still the motive force of the economy. Stupidity still reigns triumphant in the admin-istration. Democracy is still blanketed by the mass futilities of the popular press, the maiden aunt gentility of the BBC and emergent vulgarity of Independent Television.[23]

Concerns about Britain's changing world role also cultivated disil-lusionment.[24] An increasingly large number of commentators believed that imperial commitments were contributing to bal-ance-of-payments problems, and as the escalation of the Cold War increasingly constrained the Conservative government's diplo-matic independence, many began to argue that Britain needed to renegotiate its relationship with the outside world. The Suez inva-sion of 1956 marked something of a turning point.[25] Anthony Eden's apparent incompetence was widely perceived as evidence

---

21 Cited in Hewison, *Culture and Consensus*, pp. 89–91.
22 Tom Maschler (ed.), *Declaration* (London: Macgibbon & Key, 1957). Tom Maschler, *Publisher* (Oxford: Picador, 2005), pp. 44–45. One of the most popular 'Angry Young Men' texts, John Braine's *Room at the Top*, was pub-lished by Penguin in 1959.
23 David Marquand, 'Lucky Jim and the Labour Party', *Universities and Left Review*, Vol. 1, No. 1 (1957), p. 57.
24 Jeffrey Pickering, *Britain's Withdrawal from East of Suez* (London: Palgrave, 1998); L. J. Butler, *Britain and Empire: Adjusting to a Post-Imperial World* (Lon-don: I.B. Taurus, 2002); Jim Tomlinson, 'The Decline of the Empire and the Economic "Decline" of Britain', *Twentieth Century British History*, Vol. 14, No. 3 (2003), pp. 201–21; Michael Kandiah, Michael Hopkins and Gillian Staerck (eds), *Cold War Britain, 1951–64* (London: Palgrave, 2003).
25 Peter Calvocoressi and Guy Wint, *Middle East Crisis* (Penguin, 1956).

of Britain's imperial decline, and, as Andrew Shonfield's *British Economic Policy since the War* suggested, the crisis 'stimulate[d] a lot of fresh thinking on previously accepted assumptions about Britain's position in the world'.[26]

As anxiety about Britain's international status gathered momentum, many intellectuals and policy-makers became enthusiastic about establishing economic and political ties with the nation's continental neighbours. Following the Macmillan government's failed attempt to integrate Britain into the European Economic Community, Tony Godwin, who described himself as a 'pro-European', commissioned a number of tracts that discussed Britain's relationship with Europe.[27] Of these, John Mander's *Great Britain or Little England?*, published by Penguin in 1963, was perhaps the most influential. Mander's principal argument was that Britain's isolation from the European community was a symptom of its leaders' nostalgic yearning for an imperial past. To resolve its relative economic decline, he concluded, Britain would need to develop closer political ties with its European neighbours.[28]

These concerns about Britain's diplomatic status fed into wider anxieties about its economic productivity. Britain had, in the 1950s, achieved unprecedented rates of economic growth.[29] But by the end of the decade, as a number of international institutions published comparative data on the performance of Western economies, it became apparent that such rates of growth were, in a relative sense,

---

26 Andrew Shonfield, *British Economic Policy since the War* (Penguin, 1958).
27 Tony Godwin to Meaburn Staniland, 30 January 1967. PA: DM189/20/2.
    Nora Beloff, *The General Says No* (Penguin, 1963).
28 John Mander, *Great Britain or Little England?* (Penguin, 1963). Irving Kristol wrote that Mander's tract was 'the best work on any country's foreign policy that I have read in years'. Irving Kristol, 'The View from Miami', *Encounter*, November 1963, pp. 87–88.
29 Britain's GDP increased from £13,162m in 1950 to £25,681m in 1960. Cited in Hugh Pemberton, 'Affluence, Relative Decline and the Treasury' in Lawrence Black and Hugh Pemberton (eds), *An Affluent Society? Britain's Post-War 'Golden Age' Revisited* (Aldershot: Ashgate, 2004), p. 108.

poor.[30] Attention was devoted to Britain's rates of industrial productivity, which, it was feared, would lead to a declining share of world trade and, in turn, a fall in absolute living standards.[31] The emergence of this economic pessimism did not go unnoticed by Penguin. As early as 1955, W. E. Williams wrote that 'my economic relatives and friends are all muttering these days about clouds on the horizon'.[32] While this decline did have a 'real', material basis, it did not generate its own meanings. Indicators of economic performance did suggest that other national economies were outperforming Britain.[33] But these indicators, as Supple and Tomlinson have noted, did not have to be understood as symptoms of decline.[34] It is necessary, then, to draw a distinction between decline as a real, material phenomenon and what might be termed declinism.

As knowledge of relative decline permeated parliamentary and state arenas, politicians and intellectuals from both sides of the political spectrum became receptive to ideas that could explain, and indeed resolve, the phenomenon. Consequently, a new space was opened up in which hegemonic meanings could be contested, and Penguin, as several accounts have noted, published a series of texts that sought to colonise it.

Decline and the politics of planning

Andrew Shonfield's Special was one of the first books to draw attention to the phenomenon of decline. Its central argument was

30 Hugh Pemberton, *Policy Learning and British Governance in the 1960s* (Basingstoke: Palgrave, 2004), p. 47.
31 Tomlinson, *The Politics of Decline*.
32 W. E. Williams to Allen Lane, 24 March 1955. PA: DM1819/26/3.
33 Pemberton, *Policy Learning*, p. 49.
34 Barry Supple, 'Fear of Failing: Economic History and the Decline of Britain' in Peter Clarke and Clive Trebilock (eds), *Understanding Decline: Perceptions and Realities of British Economic Performance* (Cambridge: Cambridge University Press, 1997), pp. 9–31. Jim Tomlinson, 'Inventing "Decline": The Falling Behind of the British Economy in the Postwar Years', *Economic History Review*, Vol. 49, No. 4 (1996), pp. 731–757.

that successive post-war governments had failed to invest sufficient capital in Britain's manufacturing sector. Shonfield traced the source of this deficiency to Britain's excessive defence expenditure: 'in embarking on a defence programme which used up all the sources in sight and more', the Attlee government, he argued, had contributed to under-investment in several key industries.[35] Successive Conservative governments, he then suggested, had allowed destructive market forces to direct resources towards inefficient forms of activity. Shonfield offered a series of policy prescriptions that could remedy the problems he had described. Chief among them was what he termed a 'Five Year Plan'. Under its auspices he proposed a central authority that would set production targets for 'a few crucial sectors of the economy' and encourage private business to operate in a manner that was compatible with them. Such an agency could stimulate the sort of investment that would permit much higher levels of productivity. Recognising that such a programme of industrial expansion would exert pressure upon Britain's balance of payments, Shonfield outlined a series of measures to constrain domestic consumption, the most significant of which was a temporary but stringent incomes policy. Given that wage restraint was intended to promote a period of significant industrial expansion, most of Britain's major trade unions, he hoped, would be willing to endorse such a policy.[36]

Shonfield dismissed the suggestion that Britain's welfare system was an impediment to productivity, and in criticising the monopolistic practices that proliferated under unfettered capitalism, he rehearsed an argument that had been central to Britain's progressive critiques of the market since the late nineteenth century. It is possible to describe Shonfield's intervention as being 'centre-left' in character; however, several features of his analysis were at odds with the more expansive conceptions of equality articulated by

---

35 Shonfield, *British Economic Policy*, p. 57.
36 Shonfield, *British Economic Policy*, p. 277.

social democrats and others on the left. Shonfield articulated his general enthusiasm for private enterprise:

> To achieve the kind of commercial momentum necessary for success, the atmosphere created … should be something like that of a frontier boom town. The frontier would happen to be a technological one. But there should be the same feeling of big money waiting to be picked up by people ready to engage in certain activities, for which the demand is temporarily insatiable.[37]

Continuing this line of argument, he noted that 'no government will be able to set about the real business of the plan … if its main concern is with the minutiae of social justice in the process'.[38] It must also be noted that Shonfield's book was punctuated with a general antipathy to 'ideological' politics; his conception of planning was essentially technocratic and designed to achieve the sort of economic growth that would render traditional political conflict redundant.

Three years after the publication of *British Economic Policy*, Penguin published Michael Shanks' *The Stagnant Society*, a book which W. E. Williams described as 'a sequel to the highly successful Special by Andrew Shonfield'. Such a description was, in many respects, adequate. Shanks reproduced many of Shonfield's basic arguments, and when he was sent the original manuscript, Shonfield had '[thought] highly of the first two chapters'.[39] Yet some significant disparities can be identified. Unlike Shonfield, Shanks emphasised what he termed the 'social barrier' to economic growth. Features of Britain's social structure, he argued, were serving to restrict the productive capacity of its industrial base. Two phenomena – the insecurity of the working class and the absence of educational opportunity – were awarded particular significance. While the former discouraged workers from maximising their

---

37 Shonfield, *British Economic Policy*, p. 294.
38 Shonfield, *British Economic Policy*, p. 295.
39 W. E. Williams to Monty Woodhouse, 29 April 1960. PA: DM1852/A555.

productivity, the latter prevented the most intelligent individuals from exercising their talents.

In making these arguments, Shanks was offering a diagnosis of decline that was accordant with some features of the Labour party's ideological agenda. Both his critique of class divisions and his demand for equality of educational opportunity complemented the Labour's party long-standing commitments. But it must also be noted that Shanks' conception of equality was much less expansive than the one that had been articulated by many socialists. The following passage of *The Stagnant Society* is revealing:

> If we do these things, I believe Britain will become a more socially mobile, more genuinely classless society – a society which offers rich prizes but awards them solely on merit.[40]

For Shanks, then, a productive social order was one in which goods and wealth were distributed on the basis of merit. In *The Rise of the Meritocracy*, Michael Young had argued that the operation of this distributive logic could legitimate significant inequalities and harden, rather than erode, class distinctions. Shanks was not receptive to this kind of reasoning. Believing that the impulse to redistribute wealth was 'harmful and not constructive', he claimed that '[a] highly competitive society with great social mobility is by no means incompatible with considerable inequality in rewards'.[41] Significantly, Shanks admitted that his policy prescriptions were unlikely to offend large sections of Conservative opinion: 'I do not think I have advocated anything which should be anathema to the Conservative Party in its present markedly progressive mood.'[42]

The conception of planning advocated by Shanks and Shonfield differed markedly from the socialist variant that had been

40 Shanks, *The Stagnant Society*, p. 173.
41 Shanks, *The Stagnant Society*, p. 168.
42 Shanks, *The Stagnant Society*, p. 197.

advocated in many of Penguin's wartime publications. Traditional instruments of socialist planning, such as public ownership and physical production controls, were largely dismissed, with Shanks stating that, 'the scope for direct governmental controls in economic policy is in my view pretty limited'.[43] A system of indicative planning, in which the state would exert an indirect influence upon the private sector through the deployment of tax incentives and subsidies, was, they argued, the most effective means of securing higher growth. Moreover, their objective, in contrast to that of the socialist planners of the 1940s, was to correct instances of market disequilibrium rather than to dismantle the profit motive as the primary instrument of resource allocation. For his part, Shonfield suggested that 'the role of private enterprise is primary', and he warned against a scheme of planning that was driven by concern for social justice.[44]

Both Shanks and Shonfield were concerned, above all else, with identifying practices and reforms that could enhance Britain's rate of economic growth. In their efforts to do so, they acknowledged that some forms of egalitarian activity would be inimical to this objective, and they were more willing to sanction the idea that it was risk-takers who should reap its rewards. Although both authors celebrated the value of professional expertise, they did not express hostility to the idea that an individual's rewards should be determined by the market value of their labour.

Shanks and Shonfield's interventions are symptomatic of an important intellectual shift. Though the appeal of meritocracy stemmed from its perceived ability to reconcile the objectives of equality and liberty, by the early 1960s the assumptions that informed this notion were coming under strain. It was increasingly common for commentators to assert that these concepts existed in

43 Shanks, *The Stagnant Society*, p. 189.
44 Shonfield, *British Economic Policy*, p. 295.

an inverse relationship. And some of the more expansive conceptions of social citizenship that had been espoused in the wartime period were marginalised. Put simply, merit was increasingly being defined in entrepreneurial terms, and there was a greater tolerance for inequities of outcome that could enhance competition within the private sector.

Politicians and economists from both sides of the political spectrum came to endorse substantial elements of the diagnosis of decline offered by the likes of Shanks and Shonfield. Among Labour's intellectuals, Richard Crossman regarded *The Stagnant Society* as 'the most outspoken, sensible and sympathetic account of what has gone wrong in the unions that I have ever read', while Harold Wilson was prepared to offer Shanks a position at the newly established Department of Economic Affairs shortly after he assumed office in 1964.[45] Leading Conservatives also endorsed, albeit implicitly, the arguments that Shanks and Shonfield had deployed. Harold Macmillan, in a revised edition of *The Middle Way*, endorsed an interventionist policy that would achieve 'expansion in a balanced economy'.[46] Elsewhere, Viscount Hailsham, then Minister for Science, advocated the expansion of public investment in scientific research that could inform government policy.[47] This Conservative sympathy for what might be termed 'centre-left declinism' was reflected in the policy programmes of Macmillan's governments.[48] Two innovations – the introduction of a five-year

---

45 'Four Advisers Brought in from Industry', *Guardian*, 18 December 1964. Also see Michael Shanks, *Planning and Politics: The British Experience, 1960–76* (London: Allen & Unwin, 1977), pp. 17–30; Tomlinson, *The Politics of Decline*, p. 36.

46 Macmillan, *The Middle Way*, p. xxv.

47 Lord Hailsham, *Science and Politics* (London: Faber, 1963).

48 Jim Tomlinson, *The Labour Governments, 1964–70: Economic Policy* (Manchester: Manchester University Press, 2004), p. 8. Matthijs, *Ideas and Economic Crises*, p. 75. Stuart Mitchell, *The Brief and Turbulent Life of Modernising Conservatism* (Newcastle: Cambridge Scholars, 2006), pp. 77–90. Shanks, *The Stagnant Society*, p. 238. Pemberton, *Policy Learning*, pp. 77–79. *Growth in a Responsible Society* (Wider Share Ownership Committee, 1961).

plan of consumption and the creation of a National Economic Development Council – were key. In an article for the *Observer* in February 1960, Shonfield noted the Conservatives' abrupt accommodation with the concept of planning. 'Left Tories,' he wrote, 'are now more firmly in the ascendant than ever.' Macmillan's willingness to intervene in the operation of private enterprise was, in Shonfield's view, evidence that the party's *laissez-faire* traditions had been pushed firmly to the margins of its contemporary thinking.[49]

This bipartisan consensus reflected the hegemony of the centre-leftist narrative of decline. By 1964, many of its basic features were informing popular political debate, and some commentators drew attention to its apparent ubiquity. One reviewer of Penguin's 'What's Wrong with...?' series made the point in brisk terms. Far from offering original arguments, Penguin's authors were simply reiterating a conventional wisdom: 'Everybody knows that the unions are at loggerheads with management, and that for the most part British industry is up the spout ... You'd have to be very somnolent indeed if you were alarmed by the obvious.'[50]

By the time Harold Wilson led the Labour party to victory at the 1964 General Election, the Labour and Conservative parties had arrived at a common understanding of the nature of decline and had constructed similar policy programmes in an effort to resolve it.[51] This bipartisan convergence was reflected in a number of Penguin titles, including Rex Malik's *What's Wrong with British Industry?*, published as a Special in 1964. Despite being 'on the right of the political fence', Malik offered a reading of Britain's industrial decline that was compatible with the analysis of centre-left economists. Rational government intervention informed by scientific knowledge, he argued, was the most effective antidote to low productivity. And, like

49 Shonfield, 'Tories Steering with the Left Hand', *Observer*, 14 February 1960.
50 Gordon Thomas, 'I Mean to Say, It's So Obvious', *Brighton Evening Argus*, 5 March 1964.
51 Pemberton, *Policy Learning*, p. 190.

Shonfield, he regarded class divisions as being inimical to the social co-operation that was conducive to stable growth.[52]

According to centre-left declinists, political and social consensus was a prerequisite for a productive economic order. As a corollary, they tended to be hostile to 'ideological' modes of reasoning. Rex Malik, for instance, stated: 'what we must begin to realise – it has been obvious long enough – is that many problems now have not party solutions, but simply solutions, and it does not particularly matter what labels are put on them'.[53] Offering a similar view, Michael Shanks remarked: 'Ideally what this country wants is a party of the moderate Right confronted by a party of the moderate Left.' Challenging the 'traditional dogma' of the Labour left, he argued that the task of economic modernisation was a 'mission for moderates'.[54] According to centre-left planners, Britain's regeneration would require consensus and conciliation, not competition and conflict.

Britain and *The Affluent Society*

In the wake of concerns about Britain's cultural and economic decay, the idea that the post-war period had been marked by unprecedented affluence was brought under scrutiny. Penguin was a vehicle for this scrutiny, and, in turn, it helped to cast doubt on many of the assumptions that had informed political thinking in the 1950s. One of these assumptions concerned the social consequences of affluence. Class divisions, it had been assumed, would be rendered obsolete as Britain entered a new epoch of material abundance. Anthony Crosland, one of the leading intellectuals in

---

52 Malik, *British Industry*, p. 127. When he came to discuss solutions to Britain's decline, Malik wrote the following: 'Can one in fact establish a causal link between professionalism in its widest sense and success? I think one can.'

53 Shanks, *The Stagnant Society*, p. 175.

54 Malik, *What's Wrong with British Industry?*, pp. 10, 127. The book had sold 14,771 copies by the end of 1964. Lynne Wilson to Rex Malik, 1 February 1965. PA: DM1107/S221.

the Labour party, made this argument in *The Future of Socialism* (1956). He stated that:

> in contemporary British society the poor are no longer driven by want to invade the possessions of the rich; and I doubt whether at present levels of real wages they are individually much prompted by envy. Contrasts in wealth, taken in isolation, do not now seem to cause widespread resentment.[54]

Another assumption that informed the dominant narrative of affluence was related to the nature of post-war capitalism: that changes in the productive system had rendered the traditional conflict between labour and capital redundant. Such an assumption was articulated by T. H. Marshall in his post-war discussion of citizenship. Marshall suggested that the principle that the members of the community were the owners of social rights had become entrenched with the economic order, such that it had become possible to reconcile a degree of economic inequality with social equality.[56]

From the late 1950s, both assumptions were subjected to considerable scrutiny. Commentators not only exposed phenomena that failed to adhere to their logic, but the material conditions that permitted their hegemony were modified out of existence. One of the first mass-produced books to explore the social consequences of the post-war boom in consumption was J. K. Galbraith's *The Affluent Society*, which, as we have seen, argued that the rapid expansion of private consumption in the post-war period had starved the public sector of the resources that it needed to serve collective needs. While it had become possible for consumers to obtain a wider range of private goods, and while the productive capacity of the American economy had been vastly

---

55 Crosland, *The Future of Socialism*, p. 145.
56 T. H. Marshall and Tom Bottomore, *Citizenship and Social Class* (London: Pluto, 1992), p. 44.

enlarged, the public infrastructure, he argued, remained inadequate, and, as a result, deprivation and social unrest continued to blight many communities.

Galbraith also challenged the assumption that the increased availability of consumer goods had satisfied the material desires of consumers. Such a notion, he argued, failed to acknowledge that desires were relative rather than absolute. 'The more that is produced,' he wrote, 'the more that must be owned in order to maintain the appropriate prestige.'[57] In turn, Galbraith suggested that it was necessary to direct more resources to the production of goods and services that served fundamental needs.[58]

Despite being critical of the productive arrangements of America's economy, Galbraith's analysis did not amount to a critique of the profit motive. Instead of regarding private enterprise as being necessarily harmful to the social order, he believed that it could be reconciled with the interests of the community. And while he was critical of the free market, his prescriptions for economic intervention were broadly compatible with Keynesian orthodoxies. But despite Galbraith's distance from the conceptual terrain of socialism, British social democrats offered remarkably positive assessments of his thesis.[59] For his part, Anthony Crosland endorsed Galbraith's distinction between public and private consumption and employed it to critique the notion that social inequality had been eliminated.[60] Elsewhere, Richard Crossman referred to *The Affluent Society* as the 'most profound exposure of post-war Western society that has yet been published'.[61]

---

57 Galbraith, *The Affluent Society*, p. 150.
58 Galbraith, *The Affluent Society*, pp. 133–137.
59 'What Influences Labour MPs?', *New Society*, 11 December 1962. Noel Thompson, 'Socialist Political Economy in an Age of Affluence: The Reception of J. K. Galbraith by the British Social Democratic Left in the 1950s and 1960s', *Twentieth Century British History*, Vol. 21, No. 1 (2010), pp. 50–79.
60 Anthony Crosland, *The Conservative Enemy* (London: Cape, 1962), p. 103.
61 Galbraith, *The Affluent Society*, rear cover.

The works of another American, Vance Packard, were also imported into Britain by Penguin. Of these, *The Status Seekers* was particularly influential. In it, Packard challenged the assumption that the arrival of material abundance was eroding America's class system.[62] On the contrary, the post-war period, he argued, had hardened social hierarchies and had made it more difficult for individuals to move between different classes. Packard devoted attention to three tendencies: the emergence of large bureaucratic organisations that imposed rigid divisions of status; the expansion of specialised forms of schooling; and the appearance of large trade unions that discouraged initiative within the workplace. Together, these developments had created a more rigid social structure that was generating significant disillusionment.[63]

Packard did not suggest that class divisions were undesirable in themselves. Instead, he argued that some divisions of status were inevitable: 'Status distinctions would appear to be inevitable in a society as complicated as our own.' His dissatisfaction with the tendencies he observed did not emerge from a socialistic critique of class. Rather, it was rooted in a meritocratic argument about the desirability of equal opportunity. Identifying a solution to the social discontent that he observed, Packard suggested that the principal objective of policy interventions should be to 'make class distinctions less burdensome by making certain that people of real talent are discovered and encouraged to fulfil their potential regardless of their station in life'.[64]

Whyte's *The Organization Man* also suggested that new forms of social relations were generating undesirable consequences.[65] The principal subject of Whyte's Pelican was the 'Organization Men',

---

62 Vance Packard, *The Status Seekers* (Penguin, 1960). For a discussion of Packard's work, see Daniel Horowitz, *Vance Packard and American Social Criticism* (Chapel Hill: University of North Carolina, 1994).

63 Packard, *The Status Seekers*, pp. 257–268.

64 Packard, *The Status Seekers*, p. 289.

65 William Whyte, *The Organization Man* (Penguin, 1960).

whom Whyte described as the 'the ones of our middle class who have left home, spiritually as well as physically, to take the vows of organization life, and it is they who are the mind and soul of our great self-perpetuating institutions'.[66] These individuals, Whyte argued, were becoming servants of the collective will of the organisations they were employed within and were, in turn, being alienated from their authentic desires and impulses. Whyte's focus was a critique of what he identified as the 'Social Ethic', an ideology which claimed that the interests of the individual could be reconciled with those of the community. Such an ideology, he argued, not only eroded individual creativity but contributed to a complacent approach to social problems:

> In practice, those who most eagerly subscribe to the Social Ethic worry very little over the long-range problems of society. It is not that they don't care but rather that they tend to assume that the ends of organization and morality coincide, and on such matters as social welfare they give their proxy to the organization.[67]

Whyte did not seek to displace all forms of co-operation and organisation. He acknowledged that classical philosophies of individualism had venerated conflict, and he accepted that organisations would be a permanent feature of America's economic and social life. Instead, he suggested, somewhat ambiguously, that it was necessary to foster individualism within existing institutions and organisations. And in doing so, he arrived at a conception of desirable social relations that was meritocratic in nature. Thus, in his commentary on education, he stated that '[children] have to be taught to reach. All of them. Some will be outstanding, some not, but the few will never flourish where the values of the many are against them.'[68]

---

66 Whyte, *The Organization Man*, p. 8.
67 Whyte, *The Organization Man*, p. 12.
68 Whyte, *The Organization Man*, p. 372.

Identifying common threads of argument within this body of social commentary is difficult, but two shared assumptions present themselves. The first relates to the relationship between the individual and society. Galbraith, Whyte, Packard and other commentators may have offered different readings of post-war social change, but they agreed that affluence had failed to resolve conflicts between private and public needs. The expansion of private consumption and the emergence of large-scale institutions had, they argued, created new forms of social conflict. The second shared assumption relates to the cultural consequences of the variant of capitalism that had emerged in the post-war period. While *The Affluent Society* drew attention to the way in which 'Every corner of the public psyche is canvassed by some of the nation's most talented citizens to see if the desire for some merchantable product can be cultivated',[69] Packard lamented that the 'forces of the times seem to be conspiring to squeeze individuality and spontaneity from us. We compete for the same symbols of bigness and success.'[70]

Many of the themes that punctuated American social commentary permeated Penguin's Specials. Galbraith's suggestion that mass consumerism was fostering private opulence at the expense of public squalor was reproduced frequently. Reflecting upon the housing shortages of the late 1950s, Stanley Alderson, writing in his Special, wrote that 'the typical British worker can get champagne if he wants it, but he cannot get decent housing'.[71] In *The Other England*, Geoffrey Moorhouse, a journalist for the *Guardian*, argued that the benefits of Britain's economic growth had been distributed unevenly. Beyond the 'Golden Circle' of the South East, a great deal of absolute poverty could still be identified.[72] Writing in *The Long Revolution*, Raymond Williams, one of the architects of the

---

69 Galbraith, *The Affluent Society*, p. 214.
70 Packard, *The Status Seekers*, pp. 311–312.
71 Stanley Alderson, *Britain in the Sixties: Housing* (Penguin, 1962), p. 10.
72 Geoffrey Moorhouse, *Britain in the Sixties: The Other England* (Penguin, 1964), pp. 26–28.

nascent New Left, echoed this assessment of affluence: 'It is easy to get a sense of plenty from the shop windows of contemporary Britain, but if we look at the schools, the hospitals, the roads, the libraries, we find chronic shortages far too often.'[73] This triumph of private and individual wants was, he argued, the product of a moral deficiency: 'It is a poor way of life in which we cannot think of social use as one criterion of our economic activity.' Williams' Special – a study of the forms of communication generated by affluence – extended this analysis. Commercial television, the popular press and private radio broadcasting were, the book argued, corrupting the cultural lives of their viewers, readers and listeners.[74]

Some of Penguin's titles identified inequality as a source of economic and moral decline. Far from abandoning the archaic class distinctions that had impaired its social and economic progress in the inter-war period, Britain, they argued, continued to possess a highly stratified social order. Authors suggested that this inequality was a principal cause of Britain's poor economic performance. Stanley Alderson, for instance, noted that inadequate housing, 'bears down on mental and physical health, moral standards and even education', while John Vaizey, a social democratic economist who authored a Special on education policy, argued that Britain possessed an 'inefficient, class-ridden, out of-date society'.[75] Tony Godwin echoed this sentiment: 'can you produce a nation of scientists and technicians', he asked, 'where families still live in two rooms, with or without Granny?'[76]

Many of these arguments echoed Harold Wilson's reading of decline, which Penguin helped to popularise in *The New Britain*, a

---

73 Williams, *The Long Revolution*, p. 324.
74 Raymond Williams, *Communications* (Penguin Books, 1962).
75 John Vaizey, *Britain in the Sixties: Education for Tomorrow* (Penguin, 1962), p. 114. The book sold 28, 628 copies in the six years following its original publication. Lynne Wilson to John Vaizey, 23 July 1968. PA: DM1107/A832. The main arguments of the book were also advanced in a Fabian pamphlet. John Vaizey, *Education in a Class Society* (London: Fabian Society, 1962).
76 Tony Godwin to Dieter Pevsner, 22 August 1962. PA: DM1107/16/3.

Special that contained transcripts of a number of speeches delivered by Wilson in the twelve months prior to the General Election.[77] In these speeches, Wilson appealed to the rationality of
scientific enquiry and emphasised the uneven, partial and contested
nature of post-war affluence: 'We welcome the rise in living standards of so many of our people: this is what the Labour Party and
the trade-union movement were formed to achieve … But what the
Labour Party resents and condemns is the fact that in this so-called
affluent society there is still so much avoidable poverty…'[78] Endorsing Galbraith's argument that the public provision of resources was
a necessary corrective to the irrational practices of private business,
Wilson advocated a significant expansion of the state's sphere of
influence.[79] As an ideological formation, Wilsonism was a vehicle
for the ideas and programmatic proposals that had been propagated within the centre-left declinist discourse.[80]

Penguin helped to change dominant understandings of post-war
affluence. As well as exposing the deprivation that continued to blight
many sections of the population, it popularised the notion that private
opulence had fostered cultural decline. These shifts were noted by a
number of commentators and politicians. On the eve of the 1964
General Election, Richard Crossman, who praised many of Penguin's
titles in this period, suggested that the preceding five years had witnessed
a marked change in Britain's intellectual and electoral climate:

> suddenly the affluent society was out of fashion; *The Times* began to
> thunder against its immorality, and economic pundits started arguing
> that stagnancy could only be ended by economic planning and an
> incomes policy. Even the poor derided nationalised industries began to

---

77 Harold Wilson, *The New Britain: Labour's Plan* (Penguin, 1964).
78 Wilson, *The New Britain*, p. 127.
79 Glen O'Hara, *Dreams to Disillusionment: Economic and Social Planning in 1960s
    Britain* (London: Macmillan, 2007), pp. 28–29.
80 Michael Shanks praised *Labour in the Sixties*, a policy document that had
    been authored by Morgan Philips. Michael Shanks, 'Labour in the Six-
    ties', *Listener*, 18 August 1960.

creep back into favour. As so often before in British history, heresy had become orthodoxy almost overnight.[81]

Mirroring this sentiment, Giorgio Fanti, an Italian socialist, wrote in *New Left Review* that 'the "affluent society" is now an outworn myth … thanks to the pressure from the masses, the country has undergone a phase of self-examination of left-wing intellectuals and to considerable examination and is now convinced of the need for big changes'.[82]

To explain the persistence of the social stratification that they observed, Penguin's authors often drew attention to the character of British Conservatism.[83] With its reverence for tradition and hierarchical structures of deference, this ideology, it was argued, was ill suited to the demands of modernity. Following the revelation that John Profumo, the Secretary of State for War, had been involved in an affair with a young prostitute, these sentiments gained prominence.[84] In his account of the affair, which was published by Penguin in 1963, Wayland Young contributed to the argument that Conservatism was no longer equipped to serve the nation. Profumo's actions, he noted, '[were] the natural fruit of a period of government when convenience was set above justice, loyalty above truth and appearance above reality'.[85] As these kinds of arguments proliferated, some younger Conservatives attempted to embrace a 'modern' identity by allying themselves with the interests of 'meritocrats'. One such figure was the MP Eldon Griffiths. Speaking in the House of Commons, Griffiths remarked:

It is of one group in particular that I want to say a few words tonight, namely, the people who have been variously described as

81 R. H. S. Crossman, 'Scientists in Whitehall', *Encounter*, July 1964, p. 4.
82 Giorgio Fanti, 'The Resurgence of the Labour Party', *New Left Review*, March 1965.
83 Jefferys, *Retreat from New Jerusalem*, pp. 85–109.
84 Kevin Jefferys, *Politics & the People* (London: Atlantic, 2007), pp. 172–173.
85 Wayland Young, *The Profumo Affair: Aspects of Conservatism* (Penguin, 1963), p. 112.

the technocrats, the *meritocracy* or the salariat … It is they who form the centre. Those people are of immense importance to all of us in this House, because they are the fulcrum of British politics. They are neither to the Left nor to the Right; and as they go, so goes the nation … As I see it, however, the future of the country and of this House will rest upon which of the two great parties is most effectively able to persuade these people at the centre that it represents a modern, progressive, efficient and compassionate Britain. We are competing for the people at the centre. Let that be where the competition should lie. I do not think that there will be disagreement on either side about that.[86]

We could read Griffiths' remarks as evidence of a bipartisan consensus.[87] Yet the above passage demonstrates the fragility of the intellectual foundation that underwrote the technocratic settlement of the early 1960s. The meritocratic language that legitimated it was bearing the burden of an increasingly disparate range of ideological objectives.

Equality, meritocracy and decline

The early 1960s witnessed a significant shift in Britain's intellectual politics. Affluence, which, in the preceding decade, had been wedded to notions of classlessness and prosperity, came to denote a set of undesirable social, cultural and political phenomena. Penguin played an important role in this shift. But if its publications helped to displace optimistic readings of post-war prosperity, they also reveal a hollowing out of the meritocratic ideas that had accompanied these readings.

As we have seen, Michael Young's *The Rise of the Meritocracy* had challenged the idea that a meritocracy would reduce inequality. Awarding status and wealth on the basis of merit would allow those

---

86 HC Debates, Vol. 720, Cols 274–275.
87 Rodney Lowe, 'The Replanning of the Welfare State, 1957–1964' in M. Francis and I. Zweiniger-Bargielowska (eds), *The Conservatives and British Society 1880–1990* (Cardiff: University of Wales Press, 1996), p. 270. Also see Vic George and Paul Wilding, *Welfare and Ideology* (Hemel Hempstead: Harvester, 1994), pp. 51–58.

with certain attributes to justify their disproportionate rewards and, Young claimed, create a new oligarchy that was more resilient than the aristocracy that preceded it. Young's book was not prescriptive; however, the logical implication of its story was that a genuine egalitarian society would be one in which members of the community, regardless of their attributes, would possess equal worth within the social order. Such a notion had been present in the writings of R. H. Tawney and a central feature of Labourist discourses in the 1930s and 1940s. It had also, albeit in a diluted form, informed the New Liberal tradition of thought that exerted such a considerable influence upon the design of the post-war settlement.

Young's ideas about fellowship and equal worth were difficult to reconcile with the views of centre-left declinists like Michael Shanks. These writers were preoccupied with creating an efficient economic order in which 'people's work and responsibilities are adjusted to their talents'.[88] Unsurprisingly, many centre-left declinists criticised the arguments that followed from Young's intervention. For his part, Shanks suggested that differentiation was a necessary feature of a complex and dynamic society:

> If we are to have an elite – and really it is hard to see how society can operate without one – then let us at least see that we get the best elite we can, one based on merit and not on wealth or breeding.[89]

John Vaizey's Special offered a similar argument. It was desirable, he argued, for more intelligent individuals to acquire jobs that placed demands on intelligence: 'the clever *are* better at doing things. I would rather be operated on by a clever surgeon than a nice one.' Vaizey then went on to offer a broader challenge to the argument that a meritocracy was morally undesirable: 'Would a meritocracy, in any case, be such a disaster? It seems to me that it

---

88 Shanks, *The Stagnant Society*, p. 166. Martin Daunton, 'Michael Young and Meritocracy', *Contemporary British History*, Vol. 19, No. 3 (2005), pp. 285–291.
89 Shanks, *The Stagnant Society*, p. 166.

would at least have the value of being built on the assumption that knowledge and skill are important.'[90] Vaizey, like Shanks, was critical of Britain's class system. But because he believed that a large proportion of the population were capable of 'radical improvement', he maintained that awarding rewards on the basis of merit would erode, rather than strengthen, class distinctions.

At a more general level, centre-left declinists distanced themselves from the ethos of 'fair shares' that had informed the dominant egalitarian discourses of the wartime period. Any system whose principal objective was to distributive goods and wealth on a fair basis would, its advocates argued, erode the entrepreneurial impulses that were essential to economic dynamism. Reflecting on the Resale Price Maintenance system, Shanks noted:

> It is exactly the sort of system which a society that believes in stability and 'fair shares' tends to support. It is also, quite obviously, a major obstacle to dynamism and efficiency, because it limits competition and keeps prices up. It is hardly, therefore, a system which should commend itself to a society which wants to grow.

He applied a similar reasoning to the question of income distribution:

> We grumble over unofficial strikes and restrictive practices, but what we really get excited about is whether nurses are being paid a fair wage. This is in many ways an admirable trait, but it is a sure recipe for national decay.[91]

In part, the willingness of centre-left declinists to accommodate a meritocratic conception of equality was rooted in their reading of social change. Following the logic that had informed the analysis of Mark Abrams and other sociologists, they believed that the working class was becoming more acquisitive and, in turn, less receptive to communitarian appeals.[92] Thus Stanley Alderson, in

---

90 Vaizey, *Education for Tomorrow*, p. 18.
91 Michael Shanks, 'The Comforts of Stagnation', *Encounter*, June 1963.
92 Mark Abrams, 'The Future of the Left', *Encounter*, May 1960.

his Special, noted that the typical member of the working class 'has discovered that he never believed in egalitarianism proper ... He does not question the differentials between skilled workers and managing directors.' Continuing his description, Alderson suggested that a commitment to redistributive equality had been replaced by a commitment to equity. He did not elaborate on this claim, but he seemed to imply that members of the working class were more concerned with receiving equitable treatment than they were with dissolving material differentials.[93] Alderson then challenged Labour's traditional conception of equality:

> Worst of all, the Labour Party still presents itself as striving to achieve, in Douglas Jay's phrase, the minimum practicable equality. Could anything be more depressing, more insulting, more patronizing?'[94]

Vaizey offered a similar assessment of the social changes that had taken place in the post-war period, noting that young people had become self-reliant and that for many older children, 'the years of Conservative freedom presumably represent the ultimate in social values'.[95] These sociological assumptions were symptomatic of a broader characteristic of centre-left declinism, namely its belief that competition between individuals was conducive to economic and social progress. This was frequently echoed in the critique of the paternalistic impulses that informed some kinds of social democratic, and indeed Conservative, modes of thought. Alderson wrote:

> Under the Labour government [the working-class] experiences a namby-pamby mood, a readiness to rely for the future on working-class solidarity and the soaking of the rich. That mood is spent.

Shonfield echoed this argument. Commenting on the National Plan that he had proposed, he noted that 'the slogan for the

93 Alderson, *Housing*, pp. 172–173.
94 Alderson, *Housing*, p. 174.
95 Vaizey, *Education for Tomorrow*, p. 28.

businessmen who do the things required by the Plan should be: "Enrich yourselves!" The whole scheme depends in the long run on the initiative of entrepreneurs.'[96] According to the professional ideal of the post-war meritocratic settlement, disproportionate rewards and status were to be awarded to those individuals and groups whose expertise was of functional value. But in his efforts to reconcile the twin objectives of equality and efficiency, Shonfield allowed himself to gesture towards a more entrepreneurial social ideal. Risk-takers, as well as experts, were accommodated in his vision of a prosperous future.

Centre-left declinists' reservations about Young's dystopian narrative were reproduced by many on the right of the political spectrum. In a review of Young's book, *The Times* noted that 'there is no getting away from the rise of the meritocracy in a scientific world'.[97] *The Economist* offered a more expansive version of this argument: Young, it argued, had correctly identified a problem, but his book had failed to confront the 'real opposition between the claims of maximum economic progress (for which the masses are certainly no less eager than the elite) and those of a resolutely non-economic, equalitarian attitude to people'.[98] Economic progress, it was argued, was no less important to human flourishing than the latter.

These ideas threatened to punch a hole in the fragile consensus that had taken root in the post-war period. If individual enterprise remained the main source of economic growth, it followed that there was a trade-off between equality and efficiency. Centre-left declinists were, in many respects, trying to negotiate such a trade-off. But they also opened up space for those who believed that a clearer choice had to be made. Socialists could respond to their claims by looking to the principle of equal worth. Those on the right, by

---

96 Shonfield, *British Economic Policy*, p. 295.
97 'IQ + EFFORT = MERIT?', *The Times*, 30 October 1958.
98 'The New Caste System', *The Economist*, 1 November 1958.

contrast, could respond by returning to the idea that the free operation of the market was the best way of promoting enterprise.

Rationalism, science and the social order

Centre-left declinists tended to be technocrats who celebrated scientific knowledge and professional expertise.[99] David Marsh wrote that 'scientific attitudes and methods are just as practicable and essential in trying to understand the problems of government, industry, and human relations as they are in discovering the secrets of nature'.[100] Adhering to the logic of Marsh's proposition, Ronald Fletcher, in a Special on the role of the family, noted that 'we are greatly in need of more research on the family to clarify further the historical changes to which it has been subjected'.[101] And for his part, Malik identified rational thought as the 'miracle ingredient' that could resolve the deficiencies of Britain's industrial base.[102]

In offering statements of this kind, centre-left declinists suggested that scientific knowledge could offer objective solutions to social and economic problems. In part, this feature of centre-left declinism can explain its adherents' broader antipathy towards adversarial politics: if rational forms of thought were capable of identifying objective solutions to social problems, it followed that 'ideological' or 'doctrinal' modes of thought were an impediment to social and economic progress. Marsh articulated this notion in his Special:

> Policies should wherever possible and practicable be based on facts
> and not on assumptions and hunches. Politicians, administrators,
> and even hard-headed businessmen have a strange faith in the
> power of their own intuition.[103]

---

99 Ortolano, *Two Cultures*, p. 166
100 Marsh, *The Welfare State*, p. 133.
101 Ronald Fletcher, *Britain in the Sixties: The Family and Marriage* (Penguin, 1962), p. 205.
102 Malik, *British Industry*, p. 128.
103 Marsh, *The Welfare State*, p. 136.

Striking a similar note, Shanks, in an essay that he wrote for *Encounter*, brought under scrutiny both the 'niceness' of the British character and the idea that tradition was a useful repository of knowledge:

> Each section of the community stakes out its appeal, before the court of public opinion, by reference to what it has traditionally expected and enjoyed. The very niceness of the British, the national desire to 'do the decent thing', uninformed by any rational calculus of what constitutes the common interest, has become an enormous force for *immobilisrae*.[104]

Such arguments were not novel. In the late nineteenth century, similar reasoning had been advanced by a number of progressive intellectuals and politicians when they responded to concerns about 'national efficiency'.[105] But in the conditions of the 1960s, they took a particular form. Partly, this was because these arguments were anchored to a pervasive belief in the capacity of scientific enquiry to resolve the moral questions that had been the concern of traditional forms of political activity.[106] This feature of centre-left declinism had important consequences for how its advocates understood social conflict. Conflict, they claimed, was, more often than not, a consequence of irrational prejudice. It followed that education, not political activity, was the principal instrument of social consensus, and it is thus unsurprising that Penguin's centre-left authors tended to prioritise educational reform and the expansion of formal training.[107]

Centre-left declinists appealed to the notion of a national community to resolve social conflict.[108] Michael Shanks offered one of the

---

104 Shanks, 'The Comforts of Stagnation'.
105 G. R. Searle, *The Quest for National Efficiency: A Study in British Politics and Political Thought, 1899–1914* (London: Blackwell, 1971).
106 C. P. Snow, *Corridors of Power* (London: Macmillan, 1964).
107 Vaizey, *Education*, pp. 7–12. Malik, *British Industry*, pp. 90–116. Shanks, *The Stagnant Society*, p. 173.
108 Alan Warde, *Consensus and Beyond: The Development of Labour Party Strategy since the Second World War* (Manchester: Manchester University Press, 1982), p. 101.

most emotive examples of this sentiment: 'If we are to succeed, it will be because we are determined as a nation to succeed, and because we are prepared to subordinate all other considerations ... to this national aim'.[109] Similar views were expressed by Marsh, who, in his efforts to determine an adequate set of principles on which to base social policy, posed the following question: 'what are the best interests for society as a whole?'[110] The nation was conceptualised as a synonym for the general good, and it was deployed to negate the claims that sectional interest groups could make to specific rights.

These two features of centre-left declinism – its appeal to rationality and its elevation of the national interest – resolved a number of tensions that had been exposed by decline. First, they collapsed the traditional distinction between the public and the private. Even in the early 1950s, when high levels of growth had permitted the expansion of the welfare state, commentators had continued to remark upon the conflict between public and private interests. But centre-left declinists sought to reconcile this division by subordinating individuals' private claims to the logic of the general good. Second, centre-left declinists were able to claim that the conflict between capital and labour could be resolved through rational negotiation. Antagonism between trade unions and the representatives of business, it was assumed, was a product of irrational social prejudices and the hostility to the supreme authority of scientific enquiry. The speeches in *The New Britain*, in which industrial conflict was frequently described by Wilson as a chimera, offer a key example of this logic.[111]

For centre-left declinists, social consensus remained an objective. In their minds, however, the nature of this desirable agreement was reconceptualised. Whereas Tawney, Hobson and other progressive thinkers had appealed to a 'fair shares' ideology that was to be realised by generating ties of mutual responsibility, centre-left declinists sought to realise consensus by generating a meritocratic order that

---

109 Shanks, *The Stagnant Society*, p. 232.
110 Also see Wilson, *The New Britain*, pp. 42–56, 125–134.
111 Wilson, *The New Britain*, pp. 14–15.

could legitimate individual acquisitiveness and reconcile its presence with the needs of the community.[112] This reconfiguration introduced a number of conceptual elements into the discourse of the centre-left that could be awarded non-progressive meanings.

Contemporaries often noted these features of centre-left declinism. In their assessment of the intellectual climate of this period, David Butler and Anthony King, for instance, noted that while some declinist writers offered ethical arguments, most 'disdained to a remarkable degree to use moral concepts ... For them, the values Britain lacked were efficiency, enterprise, dynamism and tough-mindedness.'[113] For her part, one of Labour's leading ethical socialists, Rita Hinden, lamented the dominant response to decline. The expansion of 'technical' debate, she argued, had served to obscure the ideological objectives that the left sought to realise.[114]

The 1964 'election specials'

Prior to the 1964 General Election, Penguin, as it had done in 1947 and 1959, invited members of the Labour, Liberal and Conservative parties to 'acquaint the electorate ... with the attitudes of the principal political parties on the major issues of the day'. When read together, these texts reveal the common assumptions and beliefs that mediated the parliamentary contestation of the period. Labour's volume was authored by Jim Northcott, who was then a member of the party's research department. He reproduced a Galbraithian assessment of Britain's malaise, noting that the market-driven 'free-for-all' of the 1950s had generated strong pressure to 'spend more on the things which can be sold privately at a profit

---

112 J. A. Hobson, *Wealth and Life: A Study in Values* (London: Macmillan, 1929). Tawney, *Equality*.
113 David Butler and Anthony King, *The British General Election of 1964* (London: Macmillan, 1965), p. 35.
114 Cited in Nicholas Ellison, *Egalitarian Thought and Labour Politics* (London: Routledge, 1994), p. 124.

and to spend less on the things that are supplied publicly out of tax revenue'.[115] To repair this imbalance, Northcott proposed a 'national plan' that would allow the state to set production targets, break up monopolies and allocate resources. This programme was accompanied by a commitment to social equality, but this commitment was liberal in character. After expressing a concern for the 'personal fulfilment of each individual', Northcott stated that because such fulfilment depended on the equal availability and adequacy of public services, it was necessary to devote more resources to social uses. He did not, however, wish to eradicate all forms of private provision, and he suggested that Labour would not remove the 'scope for private initiative'.[116]

In his companion volume, Timothy Raison, a leading member of the Bow Group and the editor of *New Society*, largely adhered to the description of Britain's social problems that Northcott had offered: 'The essential task now, here as elsewhere, is to remove distortions of the natural working of the market.'[117] Achieving this objective, he argued, would require the state to intervene more directly in the operation of the economy. Although he was much more willing to praise the virtues of private enterprise than his Labour counterpart, Raison did not dispute the argument that the state had a responsibility to maintain full employment and to provide a sufficient standard of living to the poorest members of society.[118]

Raison's also shared Northcott's belief that class distinctions were an undesirable feature of Britain's social order:

> Class distinctions can be the most pernicious and wasteful means of disrupting society which can be imagined. It is not simply that class leads to the politics of envy which has marked the century; not even that it is the greatest obstacle to the concept of One Nation. The

---

115 Jim Northcott, *Why Labour?* (Penguin, 1964), p. 154.
116 Northcott, *Why Labour?*, p. 46.
117 Timothy Raison, *Why Conservative?* (Penguin, 1964), p. 50.
118 Raison, *Why Conservative?*, pp. 63–64.

fundamental injustice of class comes when it deprives any man [*sic*] of the right to make the most of the talents which he may possess.[119]

But if Raison believed that social conflict was undesirable, he did not suggest that the profit motive or the existence of competitive forces were incompatible with its resolution. He questioned the 'tender-mindedness' that informed socialistic approaches to social policy, and he asserted that a 'dynamic private enterprise system' was the most adequate means of securing growth.[120]

Reviewers of Raison and Northcott's texts identified them as evidence of a new parliamentary consensus. One journalist noted that Raison devoted 'little space to praising the Tory record and even less to condemning the Socialists'.[121] Striking a similar tone, the *Sunday Times* celebrated the apparent convergence of Raison and Northcott's views: 'there cannot be very much wrong with two parties or a country that produces political writing of this sort'.[122]

At one level, Raison and Northcott's Specials suggest that in the early 1960s, a set of assumptions and ideas that had been popularised by centre-left declinists came to exert a significant influence upon the thought of both main parties. Both authors shared a belief in the desirability of indicative planning as a means of achieving higher economic growth, and both believed that the principal objective of social policy was to reconcile individual liberty with social stability. And in their efforts to achieve this

---

119 Raison, *Why Conservative?*, p. 24.

120 Raison, *Why Conservative?*, pp. 46, 62, 139. Raison stated: 'If you encourage the individual to become rich by creating work and trade, the community will become richer with him.' Raison, *Why Conservative?*, p. 62.

121 'Homework Texts for the Coming Election', *Southern Echo*, 18 April 1964. Writing in his later life, Timothy Raison suggested that his party's welfare policies of the early 1960s did not, in reality, represent a shift towards greater selectivity. 'The health service, family allowances and education remained effectively free for all, and the selectivity in the national insurance scheme was still very limited.' Timothy Raison, *Tories and the Welfare State* (London: Macmillan, 1990), p. 48.

122 Drew Middleton, 'Blueprints for Autumn', *Sunday Times*, 12 April 1964.

reconciliation, they emphasised the virtues of equality of opportunity. Yet the books also expose some tensions that were emerging within the edifice of the post-war settlement, not least. Raison's discussion of education policy. Making reference to the recently published Robbins Report, which had advocated a significant expansion of educational provision, he posed the following question: 'do we see [expansion] as a mean of securing what may be termed an ever expanding elite, or are we are equality pure and simple?' In his efforts to provide an answer, Raison sought to reconcile these two objectives, and he made explicit reference to the concept of a meritocracy:

> while we need to make the best use of our ablest people we also need to make the best use of everyone else – otherwise we shall succumb to the dangers of the meritocracy. People are suited to all sorts of different things: all sorts of different things need to be done and are worth doing. Education can act as a broker between the two.[123]

In a sense, Raison was attempting to resolve the contradictions of the meritocratic settlement of the 1950s.[124] But actors who were operating outside of the parameters of this settlement were beginning to seize upon these contradictions in their efforts to undermine its authority.

---

123 Raison, *Why Conservative?*, p. 107.

124 Similar ideas can be found in some of the popular sociology of the period. Robert Millar's study of Britain's class system is notable. Millar traced the ascendency of meritocratic selection and suggested that 'There will be more social mobility, greater scope for ambitious and talented people ... If properly encouraged, it could do much to eliminate traditional class antagonisms which have retarded Britain's industrial and economic progress. The recognition that such a new class system is evolving should be the first step towards the creation of a new spirit of co-operation.' Robert Millar, *The New Classes* (London: Longmans, 1966), p. 294.

Beyond meritocracy: The New Left and the New Right

The New Left was not a homogenous formation. Its leading figures often disagreed about the nature of British capitalism and
offered different prescriptions for its dissolution, and throughout
its early history it hosted a number of different factions that
were rooted in different traditions of thought. Nonetheless, its
leading members were critical of the way in which Britain's relative decline had been understood by the Labour and Conservative parties. One of the most notable of these writers was
Raymond Williams, who, in the final chapter of *The Long Revolution*, offered a series of reflections on the nature of contemporary Britain. Challenging many of the assumptions made by
centre-left writers, he suggested that the dislocation of the early
1960s could only be understood by examining the basic principles of capitalist production. In a capitalist society, he argued,
the market necessarily generated forms of activity that were
inimical to a 'general conception of social use'.[125] Nor was Williams sympathetic to the meritocratic impulses that were present
in much literature on Britain's economic and social problems.
Reflecting on the social changes of the 1950s, he asserted that
'the operation of differential respect is evident enough to tempt
some people into accepting the scale so long as they can improve
their own position on it'.[126] This observation was accompanied
by a broader commentary on British society, in which Williams
challenged the assumption that class was a product of feelings
of inferiority and insecurity that were 'psychological' in nature.
In place of this assumption, present in the analyses of Penguin's
'centre-left' authors, Williams drew attention to the way in
which income differentials were a barrier to social cohesion:
'The differential is merely an operative function of a particular
kind of society, and to promote an even more tense competition

---

125 Williams, *The Long Revolution*, p. 327.
126 Williams, *The Long Revolution*, p. 349.

within it, setting one kind of worker against another, has the effect of directing social consciousness into forms that simply perpetuate the overall system.'[127]

Present in Williams' analysis were two formulations that were inimical to centre-left declinist writings. The first was concerned with the notion of production. In centre-left writing, it was assumed that the production of an economic surplus was compatible with the attainment of equality of status. By demonstrating the competitive attitudes that were fostered by disparities of reward, Williams challenged this notion. Williams also deviated from the conception of the individual that informed much of the centre-left writing on decline. Shanks, Shonfield, Vaizey and other centre-left declinists tended to regard the individual as a relatively autonomous actor whose function and worth could be determined. Williams, by contrast, placed emphasis on the idea of social use. It was not possible, he argued, to determine the value of an individual's labour, since that labour was intimately bound up with that of others.

Similar themes can be identified in Ioan Davis' review of Anthony Sampson's *Anatomy of Britain*. After locating Sampson's work within a broader formation of 'new radicalism', Davies, a sociologist who was affiliated with the New Left, drew attention to the deficiencies of its architects' egalitarianism. Within their writings, he noted, there was:

> [an] absence of any real concern for democratic institutions, for public participation in governmental processes, and even, simply, for political theory. Instead we have crude technological objectives coated with a humanistic candy-floss: unless we become more efficient the Afro-Asians will starve (Shonfield), a meritocracy means greater equality (Crosland), putting the managers in charge will give us a new, purposeful society (Sampson). The concern is not for quality of the society but for its efficiency.[128]

---

127 Williams, *The Long Revolution*, p. 376.
128 Ioan Davies, 'Phrenology of Britain', *New Left Review*, August 1962, pp. 124–128.

Like Williams, Davis attempted to collapse the conceptual framework in which centre-left declinism operated. In his view, centre-left narratives of decline had failed to offer an adequate conceptualisation of the social problems that had been generated by affluence and had, in turn, arrived at formulations that were fraught with contradictions.

It was not only the extra-parliamentary left that was seeking to challenge the authority of centre-left declinism; those on the right of the political spectrum were also forging critiques of its logic. One of the most notable initiatives operated under the auspices of the Institute of Economic Affairs, a think-tank established by Arthur Seldon in 1957. Its principal output was *The Rebirth of Britain*, a multi-author book that challenged the description of decline offered by centre-left writers. Strongly influenced by Hayekian ideas, its contributors attributed Britain's slow economic growth to the suppression of private enterprise by the restrictive practices of both the state and the trade unions. Only by reducing the state's responsibilities and imposing deflationary measures, they argued, could economic dynamism be restored.[129]

The nascent New Right also challenged the professional ideals that coloured the writings of centre-left declinists, including that rational enquiry was a solvent to social and economic problems. Thus John Brunner, a former member of the Economic Section of the Treasury, lamented the ascendency of 'professionalism': 'We seem to be excessively prone to believe in objective solutions to problems which, particularly in public policy, are not capable of solution.'[130] Brunner drew upon traditional conservative propositions to sustain his critique. He argued, for instance, that the capacity of human reason was limited, rehearsing Burke's suggestion that patterns of social organisation were determined by extra-human forces.

---

129 Arthur Seldon (ed.), *The Rebirth of Britain* (London: Pan, 1964).
130 John Brunner, 'The New Idolatry' in *The Rebirth of Britain*, p. 36.

The New Left and New Right shared some common enemies. Both denied the argument that meritocratic arrangements could foster social unity, and both railed against the descriptions of post-war social change that had propped up the fragile consensus of the preceding decade. In the early 1960s, they were unable to decon-struct the dominant meanings and assumptions that centre-left declinists had helped to popularise. Indeed, their preoccupation with the 'orthodoxy' of the centre-left's narrative serves to illus-trate the hegemony of the ideas and prescriptions that Penguin had articulated. Nonetheless, the very emergence of the New Left and New Right suggested that the prevailing consensus was begin-ning to fracture. Here, we can return to the analysis of Brunner, who concluded his assessment of the 'present consensus' by offer-ing a prophetic assessment of its prospects:

> I would not expect this phase of the cycle to outlive another Labour government … When the pendulum swings back, it may be an exaggeration to talk about the rebirth of Britain, but only because it will then become clear that we never committed suicide.[131]

Conclusion

Penguin was an important contributor to the 'state-of-the-nation' debate that began in the wake of the Suez crisis. Its books helped to reconfigure dominant narratives of Britain's economic and social order, and they fed an increasingly vibrant marketplace of ideas. Perhaps its principal achievement was to popularise a partic-ular kind of response to the problems that threatened Britain's social and economic security. This 'centre-left declinism' challenged the more paternalistic ideas that had informed the fragile political consensus of the 1950s. No longer was the public-spirited expert conceived as the ideal citizen; it was now the 'tough-minded' entrepreneur who could make maximum use of their capital who

---

131 Brunner, 'The New Idolatry', p. 43.

was imagined as the agent of progress. And although centre-left declinists were concerned with improving the living standards of the poorest, they were relaxed about overall disparities of wealth.

The success of centre-left declinism reflected a movement away from the ideas that had held the post-war political settlement together. Many of the architects of this settlement had assumed that capitalist efficiency and social equality could be reconciled by creating a fluid social order in which ability was rewarded and the beneficiaries of social mobility would be altruistic and civic-minded. Centre-left declinists arrived at a different view. They sanctioned the inequalities that would follow from entrepreneurial activity, and they accepted that there was often a trade-off between efficiency and equality. In some ways, they provided an alternative argument for social consensus that was rooted in utilitarian ideas about the common good. But in doing so, they also opened up space for more radical arguments about distributive justice that broke decisively with meritocratic arguments. Once the economic growth that declinists yearned for could not be realised, these arguments began to gain much more traction.

5

MATTERS OF PRINCIPLE

By the time voters went to the polls in 1964, both of Britain's main parties were committed to ambitious programmes of state reform, and while their respective policy programmes were informed by different ideological objectives, they shared some common themes. They both identified a system of indicative planning as the principal means of resolving Britain's relative economic decline, and they both advocated expansive programmes of welfare reform.[1] This bipartisan policy convergence reflected a set of common assumptions about the means by which social antagonism could be contained. Put simply, both social democrats and moderate Conservatives believed that the acquisition of a high rate of economic growth, combined with the creation of a more meritocratic social order, could reconcile the objectives of economic efficiency and social equality. The following decade witnessed the collapse of this fragile consensus. Policy-makers across the political spectrum come to reject many of the assumptions that had been hegemonic in the preceding decade, and new social and political movements emerged that were the vehicles for new ideas.

Most accounts argue that the late 1970s amounted to a critical juncture in Britain's political development that shifted the locus of

---

1   Hugh Pemberton and Michael J. Oliver, 'Learning and Policy Change in Twentieth-Century British Economic Policy', *Governance*, Vol. 17, No. 3 (2003), p. 427. Tomlinson, *The Politics of Decline*, pp. 88–89.

British politics to the right. The crises of the period, they suggest, exposed the frailties of the post-war social democratic consensus and allowed Margaret Thatcher and her colleagues to impose a new ideology upon Britain's state regime.[2] But if there is relative agreement about the significance of the political changes that took place from the late 1970s, there is much less agreement about their causes. Some accounts regard the ascendency of Thatcherism as the outcome of structural social and economic changes that modified popular attitudes; others draw attention to the contradictions of the Keynesian economic policies that were pursued by successive governments in the 1960s and early 1970s.[3] By exploring the intellectual politics of the period, this chapter contributes to these debates by making two main arguments. First, it argues that the political turbulence of the 1970s stemmed from a crisis of the meritocratic settlement that was described in the preceding chapters.[4] This consensus, which Penguin had helped to forge, had sought to reconcile the objectives of capitalist growth and social unity by enhancing social mobility and strengthening the relationship between merit and reward. But when the perceived crises of the 1970s appeared to render these objectives unattainable, intellectuals and policy-makers began to construct new political visions. When they did so, they often awarded new meanings to the values and aspirations that had proliferated during Britain's meritocratic moment. In the case of Thatcher and the New Right formation that she led, the entrepreneurial spirit of the early 1960s was anchored to a monetarist economic vision and a desire to liberate individuals from the state. It may be necessary, then, to regard the

---

2   Dennis Kavanagh, *Thatcherism and British Politics: The End of Consensus* (Oxford: Oxford University Press, 1987). Colin Leys, *Politics in Britain: From Labourism to Thatcherism* (London: Verso, 1983), p. 101. David Marquand, *The Unprincipled Society* (London: Cape, 1988), pp. 40–62.

3   Eric Hobsbawm, *The Forward March of Labour Halted* (London: Verso, 1981).

4   In his seminal account, Stuart Hall noted that Thatcherism emerged from the hegemonic ideology that preceded it. Stuart Hall, 'The Great Moving Right Show', *Marxism Today*, January 1979, p. 16.

late 1970s as a 'tipping point' that exposed earlier ideological fissures in the meritocratic consensus. Rather than being a counter-revolutionary formation, Thatcherism was a project that gave new meanings to the values and aspirations that meritocratic arrangements had sought to advance.

The chapter's second argument concerns the political crisis that brought the post-war consensus to an end. This crisis stemmed from concrete social and economic problems that affected the lived reality of ordinary people. But as Colin Hay and others have noted, these problems did not generate their own meanings. It is therefore necessary to award causal significance to the discursive activities of political elites.[5] Actors engaged in a battle of ideas to determine popular understandings of the context that they operated within, and Penguin's books, as well as other vehicles for ideas, were active agents in this contestation. Once we acknowledge this understanding of crisis, we must avoid thinking about ideas as by-products or symptoms of societal change. We should instead place emphasis on the way they constituted the world in which political elites and intellectuals lived.

The politics of Harold Wilson

As the preceding chapter demonstrated, the early 1960s witnessed the emergence of a planning agenda that was sponsored by wide sections of Britain's political elite. This agenda exposed some of the tensions that had been built into the post-war political settlement, for it was designed to achieve two objectives that were seemingly contradictory: the rapid expansion of capitalist production and the eradication of social conflict. It was the figure of Harold Wilson, who seemed to embody a certain kind of meritocratic impulse, who came to embody the ideology of this planning agenda and who, as the leader of the Labour party following its

---

5   Hay, 'Crisis and the Structural Transformation of the State', pp. 317–344.

victory in the 1964 General Election, bore the burden of imposing it upon the institutions of the British state. This is not the appropriate place to offer a full account of Wilson's subsequent record in office.[6] It is instructive, however, to consider the way in which contemporaries understood this record, since it was a particular understanding of the Labour governments of 1964–1970 that informed much of Penguin's political publishing.

The 1966 General Election was a pivotal moment. Prior to polling day, many on the left had been willing to attribute Wilson's apparent failure to realise his modernising agenda to his small parliamentary majority. Once Labour increased this majority to ninety-eight seats, socialists became increasingly disillusioned.[7] Far from embarking upon a programme of legislative reform that could undermine the power of private capital, the government, they argued, was chiefly concerned with resolving Britain's balance of payments crisis and, in turn, introduced measures that ran counter to socialist principles. Penguin helped to popularise these critiques, publishing no less than four books that sought to explain the perceived failings of Wilson's project. The first of these was *May Day Manifesto 1968*, authored by leading figures of the New Left, including Stuart Hall, E. P. Thompson and Raymond Williams.[8] These writers claimed that British capitalism had entered into a new phase of development. Multinational corporations were acquiring a significant role in the British economy, and capitalists

---

6   Peter Dorey (ed.), *The Labour Governments, 1964–70* (Abingdon: Routledge, 2006). Glen O'Hara and Helen Parr (eds), *The Wilson Governments 1964–70 Reconsidered* (Abingdon: Routledge, 2006).

7   David Howell, 'Wilson and History: "1966 and All That"', *Twentieth Century British History*, Vol. 4, No. 2 (1993), p. 176.

8   *May Day Manifesto 1968* (Penguin, 1968). The book was an expanded version of a pamphlet that had been produced by the May Day Manifesto group. For a discussion of the group, see Nick Tiratsoo, 'Labour and Its Critics: The Case of the May Day Manifesto Group' in Richard Coopey, Steven Fielding and Nick Tiratsoo (eds), *The Wilson Governments, 1964–70* (Manchester: Manchester University Press, 1995), pp. 163–183.

were finding new ways to protect their profits. The net conse-quence was the repression of wages and a corresponding contrac-tion of workers' rights. The Labour party could not mount an effective challenge to this new form of capitalism. Because its lead-ers remained committed to protecting the fragile settlement between labour and capital, it was argued, they were unwilling to propose any measures that would protect workers.[9] Similar argu-ments were made by the journalist Paul Foot in *The Politics of Har-old Wilson*. Foot claimed that because he was, above all else, a meritocrat who had no clear socialist principles, Wilson was unequipped to bring about the change that was needed to protect the working class.[10]

In making this case, Foot and the authors of *May Day Manifesto* were not forging a novel assessment of post-war politics. Similar arguments had been advanced by figures across the parliamentary left since at least the late 1950s.[11] But in the context of 1968, when the fragility of Britain's post-war affluence was becoming more visible, they were able to achieve a new resonance and reach a wider audience. This shift can be demonstrated by drawing atten-tion to another Special that was published in the same year. *Matters of Principle: Labour's Last Chance* was co-authored by social demo-cratic economists and sociologists, and although these writers did not endorse the New Left's notion that welfare capitalism was fraught with contradictions, they did share its advocates' belief that Wilson, by virtue of his pragmatism, had failed to confront the barriers to socialist progress or expand Labour's electoral base.[12] In his contribution, Dudley Seers wrote that 'To continue drifting along without principles (trying to win the floating voter) is – as

9   *May Day Manifesto*, pp. 143–145.
10 Paul Foot, *The Politics of Harold Wilson* (Penguin, 1968), p. 347.
11 Stuart Hall, 'Crosland Territory', *New Left Review*, March 1960. Ralph Miliband, *Parliamentary Socialism: A Study in the Politics of Labour* (London: Allen & Unwin, 1961).
12 Tyrell Burgess (ed.), *Matters of Principle: Labour's Last Chance* (Penguin, 1968).

previous Labour governments have discovered – a sure recipe for electoral disaster.'[13] Similarly, John Grieve Smith, an economist who contributed to Fabian Society research groups in advance of the 1964 election, lamented the Wilson governments' willingness to tolerate rising inequality in pursuit of an incomes policy, and he suggested that the party required a 'new working ideology'.[14]

In an essay on Labour's 1968 party conference, the editor of the *Daily Telegraph*, Maurice Green, made reference to both *The Politics of Harold Wilson* and *Matters of Principle*. Both of these books, he argued, exposed a dilemma at the core of Labour's ideology. Green, who would come to be a staunch advocate of Margaret Thatcher's political project as it emerged in the mid-1970s, described this dilemma in terms of an ultimatum: 'Are [Labour] to be meritocrats or levellers?' Drawing upon Alexis de Tocqueville's thought, he suggested that equality and equality of opportunity were incompatible objectives.[15] The former, he seemed to argue, require the curtailing of opportunities for the more fortunate. The editor of *Matters of Principle*, Tyrell Burgess, responded to Green's argument by challenging this logic. 'Equality,' he wrote, 'is a prerequisite of equality of opportunity, not the other way around.' Burgess claimed that unless social policy in the fields of health and housing discriminated in favour of the 'otherwise underprivileged', a 'neutral meritocracy' could not be realised.[16] Burgess' comments are revealing. They demonstrate that although meritocratic aspirations continued to inform political thinking, these aspirations were being anchored to new arguments. Social democrats like Burgess were no longer willing to regard equality of opportunity as a starting point for the pursuit of social equality.

---

13 Burgess (ed.), *Matters of Principle*, p. 128.
14 Burgess (ed.), *Matters of Principle*, p. 114–115.
15 Maurice Green, 'Yet Another Impatient Conference', *Daily Telegraph*, 27 September 1968.
16 Tyrell Burgess, 'Labour Tradition of Levelling Up', *Daily Telegraph*, 4 October 1968.

Instead, they were more sensitive to the way in which environmental inequities could determine the opportunities available to individuals.

The politics of crisis

This renewed enthusiasm for 'ideological' modes of reasoning among social democrats was one symptom of a broader sense of crisis that took root in the late 1960s. Indeed, by the time Wilson's government began to retreat from the planning agenda it had outlined in 1964, many commentators had come to believe that Britain's economic and social problems were becoming increasingly pronounced. In a revised edition of *The Stagnant Society*, Michael Shanks declared that the crisis he had anticipated in the early 1960s had now become a reality: '[this] book originally carried as its subtitle the words: A Warning. That is now otiose. The warning has now come true.'[17] Elsewhere, Stephen Haseler, who had stood as a Labour candidate in the 1966 General Election, suggested that Britain's democratic system was on the brink of collapse, while the historian Isaac Kramnick edited a volume of essays titled *Is Britain Dying?*[18] As Tomlinson and others have demonstrated, these apocalyptic narratives exaggerated the depth of Britain's economic and social problems. Although the period did witness a sharp rise in inflation and a decline of growth, there was never a risk of hyper-inflation, and other European economies followed similar trajectories.[19] But following the relative prosperity of the 1950s and 1960s, many contemporaries came to believe that Britain was experiencing an unprecedented crisis whose resolution required

---

17 Michael Shanks, *The Stagnant Society* (Penguin, 1972), preface.
18 Stephen Haseler, *The Death of British Democracy* (London: Prometheus, 1976). Isaac Kramnick (ed.), *Is Britain Dying? Perspectives on the Current Crisis* (Cornell: Cornell University Press, 1979). Also see Robert Moss, *The Collapse of Democracy* (London: Sphere, 1977).
19 Tomlinson, *The Politics of Decline*, pp. 91–92.

urgent and radical action. In their search for ideas that could inform such action, some became receptive to ideas that were incompatible with the meritocratic consensus of the preceding decade.

Some writers regarded the crisis as one consequence of the failure to realise a genuine meritocracy. The most striking example is perhaps David Tribe's *The Rise of the Mediocracy*. The cover design of the book took its cue from that which adorned the Pelican edition of Michael Young's book, and Tribe began by engaging with the dystopian narrative that Young had offered. Far from resulting in the elevation of ability as Young had anticipated, the post-war period, he argued, had witnessed the rise of a mediocracy:

> when today we survey the whole landscape of human endeavour, where are the pinnacles of efficiency, craftsmanship, scholarship, creativity, culture and contentment that the forces of human potential might have thrown up?[20]

Tribe offered a gloomy response to this question. In the twentieth century, there had been an 'exploitation of the industrious by the lazy, the provident by the feckless ... and the able by the mediocre.'[21] When he searched for the causes of this social and moral decay, Tribe apportioned considerable blame to the eclipse of liberalism and the corresponding ascendency of sociology and other intellectual disciplines that were the 'ideological wing of the mediocracy'.[22] As he made his case, Tribe challenged many of the assumptions and tropes that had informed the meritocratic moment. The skilled bureaucrat, who had been lauded by writers like C. P. Snow as the arch-meritocrat, was reimagined as the beneficiary and architect of a social order that rewarded caution and hampered enterprise.[23] Comprehensive education was conceived

---

20 David Tribe, *The Rise of the Mediocracy* (London: Allen & Unwin, 1975), p. 21.
21 Tribe, *Mediocracy*, p. 10.
22 Tribe, *Mediocracy*, p. 111.
23 Ortolano, *Two Cultures*, pp. 48–52. Tribe, *Mediocracy*, pp. 145–154.

as a barrier, not facilitator, of human progress, and the Victorian aristocracy was described as a source of creativity and political stability.

Many of the themes that informed Tribe's libertarian critique of the status quo were taken up by the forces of the right.[24] But the left was constructing its own critique of the social and political arrangements that had been established in the post-war period. For their part, Penguin's editors began to commission texts whose arguments jarred with the fragile meritocratic consensus that had been forged at the start of post-war period. As we have seen, these editors had, in the early 1960s, been willing to propagate the centre-left ideas that had been articulated by Michael Shanks, Andrew Shonfield and other moderate commentators. But following the Wilson governments' failure to modify Britain's state regime, some editors became receptive to a different reading of Britain's social and economic problems. Its clearest articulation can be found in a letter that Robert Hutchison, the editor of the Specials series in the late 1960s, wrote to the Labour MP Trevor Park. Hutchison suggested that the Wilson governments had exposed the conservatism of many state institutions, the marginal power of Parliament and the media-constructed myth of the 'affluent worker'. Continuing his analysis, he then proposed a 'Britain in the Seventies' series that would perform the same function as the 'Britain in the Sixties' series, noted in the previous chapter. The books, he wrote, would

> start from the recognition that it is one of the tasks of the left to battle against the mass media's bewitchment of our intelligences, and that battle initially involves a restatement of the sought after ends of political action and social change – a radical re-examination of assumptions, those prevailing in society and those prevailing in the minds of socialists ... each volume in the series [should show] a concern with the interlocking structure of our society, and the

---

24 Keith Joseph and John Sumption, *Equality* (London: John Murray, 1979).

nature and necessity of structural change and how this can be effected.[25]

In the event, Hutchison's departure from Penguin prevented the series from being realised. But his successor, Neil Middleton, would commission and edit a number of books that served Hutchison's vision. One of the most notable was Andrew Glyn and Bob Sutcliffe's *British Capitalism*.[26] Reflecting on the industrial disputes of 1972, the book suggested that capitalist businesses, in their attempts to revive falling profits, were suppressing wages. The escalation of this process, they predicted, would engender a period of open class conflict that could only be resolved by 'a successful revolutionary struggle'.[27]

Peter Ambrose and Bob Colenutt's *The Property Machine* put forward a similar argument. By exploring the dynamics of urban development in major cities, Ambrose and Colenutt drew attention to the way in which Britain's property system benefited the wealthiest sections of society and deprived ordinary workers of access to adequate housing. Their analysis was informed by a Marxist understanding of property relations. 'The conflict,' they wrote, was 'between the property owners and the property users; between the gainers and the losers ... between finance capital and the people.'[28] Both *British Capitalism* and *The Property Machine* made arguments that ran counter to the prevailing consensus. Most

---

25 Robert Hutchison to Trevor Park, 3 March 1969. PA: DM DM1952/557. Park had been one of the most vocal critics of Wilson's government. See HC Deb., 23 April 1968, Vol. 763, cc. 27. Hutchison's list of proposed authors contained several members of the non-social democratic left, including Dorothy Wedderburn, Paul Foot, Ken Coates, Michael Barratt Brown and Trevor Park.

26 Andrew Glyn and Bob Sutcliffe, *British Capitalism: Workers and the Profits Squeeze* (Penguin, 1972), p. 212. The book originated as an article in *New Left Review*. Also see Andrew Glyn and Bob Sutcliffe, *Capitalism in Crisis* (New York: Pantheon, 1972).

27 Glyn and Sutcliffe, *British Capitalism*, p. 212.

28 Peter Ambrose and Bob Colenutt, *The Property Machine* (Penguin, 1975), p. 159.

notably, they rejected the assumption that the interests of labour and capital could be reconciled by a meritocratic system of selection that rewarded the talented.

As well as commissioning works that were challenging the prevailing consensus, Neil Middleton also contributed to a broader resurgence of Marxist thought.[29] His most notable achievement was the Pelican Marx Library. Published in association with the *New Left Review*, this series contained most of Marx's major works, including the first English translation of the *Grundrisse*.[30] This volume was particularly significant, since it contributed to the emergence of a 'Western Marxist' tradition within Britain that would exert a considerable influence upon the intellectual politics of the 1970s and 1980s.[31]

As Penguin began to expose a fracturing of the meritocratic consensus, the ideas that had informed this consensus came under scrutiny. We can register this shift when we look at the way that concepts like class were reimagined. As Jon Lawrence and Florence Sutcliffe-Braithwaite have demonstrated, languages of class were revived in the 1970s. Not only did many sociologists discover that class remained a pervasive feature of the social order, but the industrial conflict of the period also led to languages of class being employed as political resources. This development had significant consequences.[32]

The fall of the meritocracy

The meritocratic arguments that had been deployed in the 1950s were often based on a particular understanding of social class.

---

29 BBC interview with Neil Middleton, 1984. PA:DM1294/6/2/27.
30 The series was published from 1973 until 1978.
31 Stuart Hall, 'A "Reading" of Marx's 1857 Introduction to the *Grundrisse*' (CCCS Occasional Paper, 1973).
32 Jon Lawrence and Florence Sutcliffe-Braithwaite, 'Margaret Thatcher and the Decline of Class Politics' in Ben Jackson and Robert Saunders (eds), *Making Thatcher's Britain* (Cambridge: Cambridge University Press, 2012), pp. 132–147.

Social distinctions, it was argued, no longer emerged from disparities of material wealth. Rather, they were the product of feelings
of envy that emerged from disparities of opportunity. Centrist
meritocrats also believed that class was becoming a less pervasive
feature of British society. In *The Stagnant Society*, Michael Shanks
had traced the slow dissolution of older forms of working-class
identity, while John Vaizey had argued that the 'rise of the service
trades will be accompanied by a movement ... towards the sort of
middle-class life that has become characteristic of the more prosperous suburbs'.[33] From this reading of class, meritocrats identified
two means of resolving social conflict. First, they advocated an
education system that would expand educational opportunity. Second, they sought to dismantle those aristocratic institutions that
reproduced outmoded social prejudices.

In the late 1960s, these understandings of social change were
brought under scrutiny.[34] The work of sociologists was significant.
Challenging many of the approaches that had underwritten the
social surveys conducted in the immediate post-war period, scholars produced studies that seemed to reveal the resilience, rather
than the decline, of poverty. One of the most influential was Ken
Coates and Richard Silburn's *Poverty: The Forgotten Englishman*, published as a Penguin Special in 1970. Basing their analysis on an
extensive study of Nottingham's poorest communities, Coates and
Silburn claimed that severe poverty remained a significant feature
of Britain's social landscape. Overcrowding was contributing to
significant social dislocation, and malnutrition and underemploy-
ment continued to act as barriers to material improvement. To
account for the persistence of class inequality, Coates and Silburn
cast their gaze upon a familiar adversary: the market. In a society
in which goods and services were being allocated to serve the

---

33 Shanks, *The Stagnant Society*, p. 67. Vaizey, *Education*, p. 25.
34 Lawrence and Sutcliffe-Braithwaite, 'Margaret Thatcher and the Decline
of Class Politics'.

interests of private capital, inequalities and deprivation, they argued, were immutable. In many respects, this argument was comparable with that which Galbraith and others had offered in the preceding decade. But whereas Galbraith had believed that the imbalance he described could be repaired through quasi-Keynesian activity on behalf of the state, Coates and Silburn believed that the resolution of public squalor required a fundamental reassessment of the objectives of economic activity. Only the social control of production, it was argued, could dissolve the inequalities that were the inexorable outcome of market relations.[35] Coates and Silburn extended their argument to challenge the assumptions that informed the Beveridgean welfare state. In particular, they rejected the idea that the market could be reconciled with the interests of welfare. They also made explicit reference to T. H. Marshall's conception of social citizenship. Marshall, they argued, had failed to acknowledge that the extension of social rights had permitted, rather than eroded, the strength of market forces; for while the legislative reforms that had extended entitlement to social provision had placed some resources outside the price mechanism, they had also compelled poorer members of the community to enter into the market mechanism as a condition of their citizenship. This argument was anchored to a broader critique of the reformist 'consensus politics' of the preceding decades, which, they argued, had sought to demonstrate the redundancy of 'any politics that acknowledged continued opposition and conflict within the social system'.[36]

Similar arguments were articulated by Jack Shaw, who authored a Special that explored the living conditions of Britain's elderly population. Ameliorative reforms, Shaw noted, had failed to provide social justice for the elderly because they operated within a

---

35 Ken Coates and Richard Silburn, *Poverty: The Forgotten Englishmen* (Penguin, 1970), pp. 164–166.
36 Coates and Silburn, *Poverty*, pp. 183–184.

system which allowed individuals to profit from the 'labours of our fellow men'.[37] In turn, he argued that poverty could only be resolved if the allocation of resources was determined by public, rather than private, interests.

As well as challenging the 'myth of affluence', sociologists also defended traditional working-class values from those who had sought to displace class identities under its auspices. Brian Jackson's *Working Class Communities*, which was published by Penguin in 1972, did so with particular force. Jackson's analysis was punctuated by two arguments. First, he questioned the value of earlier sociological research into working-class communities. These studies had tended to regard working-class communities as the sites of social problems that required an administrative response on behalf of the middle class. In doing so, they had disguised the valuable features of working-class life that could not be found in middle-class environments.[38] Second, Jackson challenged the argument that the distinctive tastes and attitudes of the working class were being diluted by mass culture. Following Raymond Williams and other socialist commentators, he argued that this notion was predicated on a misunderstanding of the working classes' engagement with 'alien' cultural forms. Far from being the passive recipients of commercial cultural products, working-class consumers were able to reject those meanings and values that were incompatible with their lived experiences. What emerged was a more sympathetic reading of the working class that celebrated its communal values.

In another Penguin, co-authored with Dennis Marsden, Jackson directly challenged the meritocratic reading of class. Meritocrats had alleged that the creation of a society that distributed reward on the basis of merit would dissolve class antagonisms by

---

37 Jack Shaw, *On Our Conscience: The Plight of the Elderly* (Penguin, 1971), pp. 158–159.

38 Brian Jackson, *Working Class Communities* (Penguin, 1972), p. 176.

ensuring that there was considerable social mobility.[39] Yet Jackson and Marsden's study suggested that meritocratic policies had hardened, rather than eroded, class barriers. It not only demonstrated that many intelligence tests were unable to evaluate the full range of an individual's talents and attributes, but it also argued that middle-class children, by virtue of their social habits, were able to circumvent attempts that had been made to equalise opportunity. Jackson and Marsden also challenged the educational objectives that had informed the declinist writing of Shanks and other meritocrats. In an epilogue to the book, they wrote that 'it is now clearer to see that the old purpose of education – the training of a ruling elite – has not collapsed under the new purpose – the training of enough people to man our technological society'.[40] In many respects, the texts described above reopened debates that had been marginalised in the preceding two decades. As Chapter 3 demonstrated, the relative prosperity of this period had led many intellectuals and policy-makers to anticipate a social order in which distributive questions would be displaced and politics would be concerned, above all else, with post-material issues. But when the epoch of material abundance failed to become a reality, the concerns that had preoccupied writers in the 1930s and 1940s reasserted themselves. Not only did the question of how resources should be allocated acquire a new significance, but policy-makers were once again confronted with the prospect of significant class conflict.

It be wrong, however, to suggest that the political contestation of the 1970s was only conducted around distributive questions, for it was in the 1970s that new kinds of antagonisms came to the fore of political debate. These antagonisms also undermined the authority of the assumptions and beliefs that informed the

---

39 Shanks, *The Stagnant Society*, p. 168.
40 Brian Jackson and Dennis Marsden, *Education and the Working Class* (Penguin, 1966), p. 250.

technocratic consensus, albeit in rather different ways. In many instances, they exposed the parochialism of the technocratic consensus and its failure to reconcile its vision with the social and cultural changes that were reshaping the political landscape. The Specials of the early 1970s did not only reveal a growing disillusionment with the assumptions and beliefs that informed meritocratic ideas; they also articulated new antagonisms that could not be accommodated within their logic.

New antagonisms

Meritocratic prescriptions, as we have seen, were premised on a particular understanding of the social order. Their advocates often assumed that within a developed society, it was necessary for individuals to perform functions that matched their talents and intelligence. They also posited that some attributes would be more valuable than others. From this idea followed some other arguments. First, that social conflict emerged when an individual was denied access to the social role that was commensurable with the skills that they possessed.[41] And, second, that this conflict could be resolved by creating a social order in which merit determined an individual's occupation. Many of the antagonisms and discontents that emerged in the late 1960s and early 1970s could not be accommodated within the logic of these propositions, and Penguin, alongside other organs of opinion, helped to cultivate them.

Of the many extra-parliamentary formations that emerged in the late 1960s, few were more visible than the student movement. Recent studies have cautioned against the view that this movement possessed a coherent ideology that can be described in general terms.[42] Contemporary accounts, however, were often more

---

41 Shanks, *The Stagnant Society*, p. 166.
42 Caroline Hoefferle, *British Student Activism in the Long Sixties* (London: Routledge, 2013).

willing to identify it as a symptom of general forces that were condensing different antagonisms into a novel political agenda. One of the most notable was published by Penguin in 1969. Produced in association with *New Left Review*, *Student Power* contained a series of essays by activists, intellectuals and journalists who were seeking to understand the origins and significance of student protest. In his contribution, Perry Anderson identified student protest as a symptom of intellectual failure. Because Britain's dominant traditions of thought had ceased to provide an adequate explanation of the social totality, students, he argued, had begun to develop a 'revolutionary practice within culture'.[43] Elsewhere in the book, Gareth Stedman Jones suggested that student revolt was a response to a crisis of capitalist education. Having acknowledged that the principal function of universities was to produce an 'intelligentsia without ideas', many students, he argued, were beginning to articulate an alternative conception of education that could not be accommodated within a capitalist society. Stedman Jones traced the origins of student discontent to a contradiction in the meritocratic understanding of higher education. Meritocrats had sought to develop a class of specialised technicians who possessed the creative and critical intelligence required to manage new forms of capitalist production, but they also expected this class to be unaware of the social and economic uses to which their intellectual labour contributed: 'they must not apply the intelligence they are being urged to develop, either to the institutions where they are studying or to the society which produces them'.[44]

Similar arguments were popularised by Penguin Education, an educational imprint that Penguin established in 1967. The imprint's principal function was to provide textbooks for schools and

---

43 Perry Anderson, 'Components of the National Culture' in Alexander Cockburn and Robin Blackburn (eds), *Student Power: Problems, Diagnosis, Action* (Penguin, 1969).
44 Gareth Stedman Jones, 'The Meaning of the Student Revolt' in Cockburn and Blackburn (eds), *Student Power*, pp. 32–33.

universities, but it also published a series of Education Specials that contributed to political debates about educational issues.[45] *Education for Democracy*, a collection of essays that advocated progressive pedagogical ideas, was particularly influential. Its contributors were concerned, above all else, with creating an education system that could be conducive to a 'more democratic society', and in their efforts to imagine such a system, they challenged the meritocratic arguments that had been deployed in the early 1960s. In his contribution, Anthony Arblaster lamented the 'crudely utilitarian' doctrine that had been articulated by the Wilson government. This doctrine had not only anchored education to the demands of the capitalist economy, but it also impaired the development of a more 'sceptical and inquisitive' society.[46] Education, it was argued, should be for 'democracy, not for aristocracy, meritocracy, plutocracy, or any other kind of elitist system'.[47] In another Education Special, David Head, a teacher who had established a number of adult education schemes, lamented the educational initiatives that had been pursued by the Heath government: 'these programmes are based more on a demand for social mobility and a nearer-meritocracy-to-thee-devotion than an egalitarian society'.[48]

It was not only progressive educationalists who were challenging meritocratic principles. Socialist feminists, who were attempting to dispel the functionalist assumptions that had informed much

---

45 In 1976, the imprint's editor, Martin Lightfoot, acknowledged its egalitarian ethos: 'That Penguin Education attempted to redress some balances, and that it published books which put cases for the uncertain, the unprivileged, the inarticulate and the unnoticed is of course true, and perhaps no very bad thing.' Martin Lightfoot, 'Penguin Education', *Bookseller*, 14 August 1976.

46 Anthony Arblaster, 'Education and Ideology' in David Runciman and Colin Stoneman (eds), *Education for Democracy* (Penguin, 1970), p. 50.

47 Runciman and Stoneman (eds), *Education for Democracy*, p. 9.

48 David Head, 'Letter to an Educational Quisling' in David Head (ed.), *Free Way to Learning: Educational Alternatives in Action* (London: Penguin Education, 1974), p. 14.

post-war sociological writing, also rejected meritocratic reasoning. According to functionalist logic, the different roles assigned to family members reflected the broader prerequisites that societies needed to serve in order to reproduce themselves. Feminists, by contrast, suggested that the sexual division of labour was an exploitative arrangement that was designed to protect capitalist interests. Such an argument was clearly evident in Juliet Mitchell's *Women's Estate*, published as a Pelican in 1971. Patriarchal arrangements, Mitchell asserted, were socially constructed rather than fixed and immutable products of society's functional development.[49] Accordingly, Mitchell suggested that genuine equality could not be achieved within the current economic order. Other leading feminists, including Ann Oakley and Sheila Rowbotham, also published original Penguins that anchored feminist arguments to critiques of capitalism.[50]

As the preceding chapter demonstrated, the appeal of meritocratic values stemmed, in part at least, from the assumption that they were conducive to economic growth. A society with high levels of mobility, it was assumed, would also be efficient and would, in turn, achieve higher productivity. By the end of the end of the decade, a number of social movements and pressure groups were exposing the environmental costs associated with such productivity. One of the most important interventions was *A Blueprint for Survival*, which Penguin published as a Special in 1972. Originally printed as a special issue of *The Ecologist*, the book warned that the existing industrial order was unsustainable and advocated the creation of decentralised, deindustrialised communities that would be more likely to employ sustainable agricultural practices.[51] The central threads of the book's argument were reproduced in a number of Penguin texts. Robert Arvill's *Man and Environment* advocated an

49 Juliet Mitchell, *Woman's Estate* (Penguin, 1971), p. 95.
50 Ann Oakley, *Housewife* (Penguin, 1976). Sheila Rowbotham, *Women's Consciousness, Man's World* (Penguin, 1973).
51 *A Blueprint for Survival* (Penguin Books, 1972), pp. 50–58.

expansive planning system that would encourage sustainable activities and educate the public about the consequences of their consumption;[52] E. J. Mishan's Pelican drew attention to the environmental costs associated with high levels of productivity; and Theo Crosby, an architect and designer, authored a Special that exposed the negative consequences of the post-war zeal for urban expansion.[53] These books could not be easily located within Britain's major ideological traditions. On the one hand, their anti-materialist ethos was compatible with the moral arguments that had been advanced by ethical socialists. But on the other, the emphasis that their authors placed on the need for human communities to submit to the extra-human forces of the environment was compatible with traditional conservative beliefs.[54] What did bind them together, however, was a critique of the ideas and aspirations that had legitimated Britain's meritocratic moment. When they attempted to justify the cultural authority of merit, intellectuals and policy-makers had often celebrated the achievements of the scientific community and had assumed that the expansion of scientific knowledge was conducive to social progress. By contrast, the above texts tended to draw attention to both the fallible and politicised nature of scientific practice. They not only situated the scientific community as one interest group among others, but they also questioned whether the knowledge that they generated was socially valuable. Mishan's aforementioned Pelican, for instance, argued that the accumulation and application of scientific knowledge had done little to advance well-being:

> The innocent layman surrounded by a growing array of specialists of all kinds – in the social sciences by economists, sociologists,

---

52 Robert Arvill, *Man and Environment: Crisis and the Strategy of Choice* (Penguin, 1970).
53 Theo Crosby, *How to Play the Environment Game* (Penguin, 1973).
54 Stephen Driver, *Understanding British Party Politics* (Cambridge: Polity, 2011), p. 163.

anthropologists, psychologists and others – is deluded into believing that his welfare is in good hands.[55]

Mishan underwrote this claim by challenging the long-established idea that scientists were, by virtue of their rationality, committed to ends that were socially responsible. This idea, as we have seen, could be found in many of the declinist texts of the 1960s, and it was predicated on the assumption that the scientific community was autonomous and benevolent. Mishan's view, by contrast, was that scientific progress had always been subservient to technological changes. In turn, he concluded that the expansion of scientific knowledge could do little to resolve the most pressing social and environmental problems facing industrialised societies.

Polarisation

As preceding chapters have demonstrated, meritocratic ideas were hegemonic in the two decades that succeeded the Second World War. This hegemony did not eliminate political contestation, and nor did it eliminate the presence of counter-hegemonic ideas that could not be accommodated within it. But for at least two decades, most policy-makers believed that the expansion of equal opportunity could resolve social conflict and promote economic growth. The crises of the 1970s challenged these assumptions. The simultaneous presence of rising inflation and falling employment, combined with the industrial dislocation of 1972–1974, led many to hold the promise of meritocracy to account.

One consequence of these shifts was the 'hollowing out' of the political centre ground. For much of the post-war period, it had been assumed that centrist 'middle way' strategies could reconcile the interests of labour and capital and that the rival ideologies of socialism and capitalism had become redundant. But in the conditions of the mid-1970s, these strategies, which were broadly

---

55 E. J. Mishan, *The Costs of Economic Growth* (Penguin, 1971), p. 185.

compatible with egalitarian principles, came to be challenged by new political ideologies. Of particular significance was a new variant of conservatism. Its origins can be traced to the late 1960s, when many Conservatives, in response to the economic troubles of the period, became disillusioned with the 'middle way' ideas that had been espoused by Macmillan, Hogg and other moderate Conservatives.[56] But it was not until 1975, when Margaret Thatcher became leader of the Conservative party, that this ideology began to reshape Britain's political landscape. A full description of its character cannot be offered here, but it is instructive to sketch some of its basic beliefs and commitments. First, its advocates questioned the collectivist principles that had informed the postwar policy settlement. The Keynesian welfare state, it was argued, had discouraged individual enterprise and interfered with the operation of the market. And in doing so, it had contributed to the relative decline of the British economy. The New Right also railed against the 'permissive' attitudes that they believed had proliferated in the 1960s. In an effort to reassert values of self-reliance and enterprise, they argued that the erosion of deference and authority had contributed to a moral, as well as an economic, crisis.[57] Not only had British society become more undisciplined, but individuals had also forgotten the duties that were concomitant with citizenship. In her efforts to trace the origins of this permissiveness, Thatcher devoted particular attention to the kinds of sociological analysis that Penguin had popularised in the preceding decade:

> Twenty years of social analysis and woolly political theory have been aimed at trying to 'prove' that crime and law-breaking are not

---

56 David Howell, 'The British Right', *Listener*, 25 July 1968. Also see E. H. H. Green, *Ideologies of Conservatism* (Oxford: Oxford University Press, 2002), p. 215.

57 Notes for a conference speech: Churchill Archive Centre: THCR 5/1/4/24/24. Also see Matthew Grimley, 'Thatcherism, Morality and Religion' in Jackson and Saunders (eds), *Making Thatcher's Britain*, p. 83.

the responsibility of the individual, but are the fault of social conditions and society. The older language of morality and legality, of right and wrong, is conveniently forgotten. While we must do everything we can to improve social conditions where they are bad, the truth is that crime grows where the pressure of established values and conventions is removed.[58]

To restore social order and encourage self-discipline and respect for the rule of law, Thatcher and her colleagues advocated the creation of a more stringent legal system that would reassert traditional moral values.[59]

Significantly, Thatcher broke decisively with the meritocratic reasoning that had been deployed to sanction the post-war consensus. Under the influence of Hayekian economic thought, she believed that the market was the most effective instrument of resource allocation, and in a number of respects the market principle was inimical to meritocratic logic. Within a meritocracy, an external authority must intervene to ensure that rewards are distributed on the basis of merit. In a free market, by contrast, rewards are determined by the value that the price mechanism accords to an individual's labour or goods.[60] The concept of merit is not entirely incompatible with market values. After all, the market may reward particular kinds of measurable attributes. But in the last instance, a vision of society that is informed by the principle of the market cannot award supreme authority to the concept of merit.[61]

Thatcher's project offered a different ideological framework for reconciling the objectives of economic growth and social stability. In doing so, it often awarded new meanings to the concepts and arguments that had been deployed by the declinist writers of the

---

58 Speech to the Scottish Conservative Conference, Perth, 13 May 1978. Margaret Thatcher Foundation (subsequently MTF): Document 103684.
59 Raphael Samuel, 'Mrs Thatcher's Return to Victorian Values', *Proceedings of the British Academy*, Vol. 78 (1992), p. 15.
60 Friedrich Hayek, *The Constitution of Liberty* (London: Routledge, 1960), p. 99.
61 Ortolano, *Two Cultures*, p. 252.

early 1960s. They echoed, for instance, the claim that Britain's malaise was, above all else, a symptom of class conflict. But while the technocrats of the 1960s had sought to resolve social antagonisms by improving the material conditions of the working class and removing the barriers to educational attainment, the New Right interpreted industrial disputes as a by-product of collectivist politics. Undisciplined trade unions, it was argued, were pursuing their sectional interests as the expense of the national interest.

When they made these kinds of arguments, Thatcherites often contravened the ideas that had informed the post-war political settlement. As we saw in Chapter 3, Conservatives like Angus Maude had, in the immediate post-war period, challenged the argument that the middle class was a repository of technocratic skill that should serve the interests of the state.[62] Instead, they argued that the middle class was distinguished by its respect for tradition and its defence of liberty. These arguments had been marginalised during Britain's meritocratic moment, when the notion of a classless society was wedded to a politics of professional expertise and public service. But in the conditions of the 1970s they witnessed a marked resurgence. Angus Maude and other Thatcherites revived the notion that the middle classes were the guardians of the individualist and entrepreneurial values that had shaped the national character.[63] In doing so, they constructed an alternative conception of social mobility from that which had been hegemonic in the preceding decades. Their understanding of society fed the notion that risk-taking, effort and self-reliance were the human qualities worthy of reward.[64] In place of the declinists'

---

62 Lewis and Maude, *English Middle Classes*, pp. 235–237.
63 Margaret Thatcher, 'My Kind of Tory Party', *Daily Telegraph*, 30 January 1975.
64 In *The Stagnant Society*, Shanks had written the following: 'only when we feel ourselves to be genuinely one nation and one people will we be able to tap to the full the wonderful vein of courage, enterprise, and initiative which lies hidden in the British personality'. Shanks, *The Stagnant Society*, p. 174.

belief that 'highly competitive society' could be created by allow-
ing merit to determine the distribution of rewards, they instead
regarded the market as the instrument that could restore entrepreneurship.[65] Indeed Thatcher substituted the logic of the market for
the logic of merit in her efforts to diagnose decline. The New
Right thus operated upon the contradictions of the meritocratic
consensus, and by awarding new meanings to the values that it had
sought to harness, it helped to reconfigure the discursive terrain on
which politics was conducted.

As the New Right's ideas gained resonance, Penguin's progressive publishing became a source of political consternation. Those
on the left defended its egalitarian agenda, while many Conservatives came to regard the publisher as a sponsor of leftist propaganda. For his part, the conservative novelist Ferdinand Mount
lamented its willingness to publish Marxist works of theory:
'there is no Marxist from Europe, Africa or Asia too shrill and
shallow to be eagerly acclaimed by Penguin Books as the greatest
thinker of the age and the necessary scourge of our decadent
society'.[66] Other Conservatives devoted attention to the activities
of Penguin Education, which they identified as one of the principal vehicles for progressive educational ideas.[67] A particularly
fervent critique was authored by Maude. In his review of *Letter to
a Teacher*, Maude suggested that the text was a 'propaganda vehicle for the partisan views not of its authors but of its editors'.
These editors, he continued, 'do not believe that there can be any
respectable alternative viewpoint to the one – "progressive",
egalitarian, permissive and occasionally straight Marxist – which
they themselves so glibly and consistently propound'. Maude
even criticised his Conservative colleague Edward Boyle, a

---

65 Shanks, *The Stagnant Society*, p. 168.
66 Ferdinand Mount, 'Middle Classes of the World Unite, You've Got Noth-
    ing to Lose but your Guilt!', *Daily Mail*, 19 May 1977.
67 C. B. Cox and A. E. Dyson (eds), *Black Paper Two* (London: The Critical
    Quarterly Society, 1969).

supporter of comprehensive education who had written an after-
word for the book:

> *Letter to a Teacher* is a vintage specimen of the cult. It is guaranteed to
> bring a sentimental tear to the eye of every progressive egalitarian
> and to make almost everybody else feel faintly sick. It has been
> highly praised by progressive critics, and includes an enthusiastic
> afterword by Lord Boyle, one of the rulers of the Penguin Empire.[68]

Edward Boyle had embodied the post-war consensus. Throughout
the 1960s, he had encouraged a constructive dialogue between the
forces of the left and the right on a range of policy questions, and
during his tenure as Minister for Education he had introduced a
series of policies that were broadly compatible with Labour's educational agenda. But by the 1970s, his instinctive centrism led him
to be marginalised within his own party. A number of New Right
intellectuals went as far as to identify him as a fellow traveller who
had contributed to the advance of egalitarian ideas. One of them
was Rhodes Boyson, who, in October 1975, wrote a letter to Penguin that criticised the publisher's editorial policies. Commenting
on Penguin's failure to publish Caroline Cox's *The Rape of Reason*,
a book that documented alleged attempts by left-wing groups to
infiltrate a polytechnic institution, he argued that 'Penguin's educational reputation for a narrow propagandist purpose does no
credit to Penguins and has become a grave menace to the wider
community'.[69] Boyle disagreed and cited numerous Penguin texts
that were not authored by leftist writers.[70] Yet Boyle had his
own disagreements with Penguin's non-fiction publishing. In 1977,
he opposed the publication of *The Technology of Political Control*, a

---

68 Angus Maude, 'Biased Penguins', *Spectator*, 14 November 1970. Also see
Paul Johnson, 'Penguin Path', *Evening Standard*, 3 October 1978. Boyle was
then overseeing Penguin's takeover following Allen Lane's death.
69 Rhodes Boyson to Hans Schmoller, 13 October 1975. PA: DM1294/17/8.
70 Neil Middleton to Peter Wright, Anthony Mott and Jim Rose, 8 September 1978. PA: DM1952/383.

Marxist-inspired attack on the counter-insurgency techniques being deployed by the British state against the IRA and other extremists.[71] Writing to its editors, he remarked, 'I think Penguin has, with *The Technology of Political Control* reached the end of the path that one can fairly label as "international Marxist". And we shall be liable to really serious and merited criticism if we're not seen to explore other paths as well.' To repair the balance he suggested that Penguin should present the other half of the dialogue by offering the case of 'those "social-democrats" who are trying to make sense of the mixed economy'.[72] Boyle was no longer comfortable with the political orientation of either Penguin or the Conservative party.[73]

While Boyle continued to express enthusiasm for 'middle way' politics, other centrists became disillusioned with the social democratic ideas that had held the political centre together. John Vaizey's trajectory was characteristic. As Chapter 4 noted, Vaizey had been a prominent social democratic commentator on educational questions throughout the 1950s and 1960s. But in response to the economic and social problems of the 1970s, he came to abandon his commitment to the egalitarian cause. This commitment, as his 1963 Special had demonstrated, was broadly meritocratic in character. He had identified inequality of opportunity as unjust and wasteful, and he wanted to remove the barriers that prevented the talented from acquiring jobs that were commensurate with their skills. In the mid-1970s, Vaizey remained committed to improving social mobility. But in his efforts to identify practical means of realising a dynamic and meritocratic society, he came to reject the redistributive policies that social democrats had traditionally

---

71 Carol Ackroyd, Karen Margolis, Jonathan Rosenhead and Tim Shallice, *The Technology of Political Control* (Penguin, 1977). See Richard Moss, 'Left Wing of the Penguin', *Daily Telegraph*, 12 April 1977.
72 Edward Boyle to Jim Rose, 26 June 1977. PA: DM1952/Box 613.
73 R. E. Tyrell (ed.) *The Future That Doesn't Work: Social Democracy's Failures in Britain* (Doubleday: New York, 1977).

endorsed.[74] In part, his conversion stemmed from concerns about the rationalist ideas that informed social democratic thought. The failures of the post-war settlement, he argued, had demonstrated that human behaviour was neither rational nor predictable, such that any political philosophy that was informed by 'scientific' modes of reasoning was redundant: 'the only working set of political principles in free Europe', he wrote, 'is Tory pragmatism'.[75] Vaizey's move to the right was also informed by an economic argument. In his view, the industrial disputes of the period were symptomatic of the failure of Keynesian policies to control inflation.[76] His conclusion was that monetarism was 'as correct as any policy in this imperfect world'.[77]

It is problematic to regard Vaizey's move to the right as a symptom of a shift in his conceptual thinking. For while he did come to challenge many of the policies associated with the post-war settlement, his basic concerns, namely those of containing social antagonisms within an efficient economic order, remained consistent. What he did modify, however, was his understanding of how these objectives could be realised.

Another defector to the right, Hugh Thomas, deployed similar reasoning. Like Vaizey, Thomas had been one the leading contributors to the anti-establishment declinism of the early 1960s. But by the 1970s, he had become critical of many of the policies that had

---

74 In a conversation with Isaiah Berlin that took place in 1974, Vaizey argued that 'if there is any human organisation, it is quite clear that different people will perform different tasks and some of them will be obliged to give orders to others ... in normal human society some kind of hierarchy, in some degree, is bound to exist'. John Vaizey (ed.), *Whatever Happened to Equality?* (London: BBC, 1975), pp. 117–118.

75 John Vaizey, 'Lord Vaizey's Change of Party', *The Times*, 3 December 1980.

76 John Vaizey, *In Breach of Promise* (London: Weidenfeld & Nicolson, 1983), p. 96.

77 John Vaizey, 'Monetarism's Share of the Blame for Unemployment', *The Times*, 20 July 1981.

been pursued by the Wilson governments, and he was suspicious of trade unions. His principal concern was that Labour, in its efforts to redistribute power, had obscured the value of enterprise and had revived outmoded notions of class conflict.[78] In a sense, then, Thomas' defection did not follow from a disillusionment with his earlier values. Rather, it stemmed from a reconsideration of how those values could be realised.

Attention can also be devoted to another architect of the 'middle way' politics of the post-war period, Lord Hailsham (Quintin Hogg). As Chapter 3 noted, Hailsham's *The Case for Conservatism*, which Penguin had published in 1947, had reconciled a Burkean conception of the social order with the Beveridgean welfare state. Unless the gross inequalities of the inter-war period were resolved, it had argued, the organic social order would decay.[79] In the 1970s, Hailsham expressed the same Burkean concern for preserving the organic community, but this concern led him to repudiate, rather than defend, the post-war settlement. Reviewing the political crises of the period, he concluded that the threat to social stability was no longer inequality but uniformity. In turn, he suggested that the Conservative party needed to adopt a programme that could challenge the 'social engineering' and collectivism that was being advocated by the radical left.[80]

The trajectories of Vaizey, Thomas and Hailsham reveal much about the intellectual politics of the late 1970s. Not only do they expose the fragility of the meritocratic consensus that was established in the 1960s, but they also demonstrate that the aspirations that this consensus had sought to contain were easily appropriated by other ideological formations.

---

78 Hugh Thomas, 'A Letter to a Social Democrat' in Patrick Cormack (ed.), *Right Turn* (London: Leo Cooper, 1978), pp. 89–104.
79 Hogg, *The Case for Conservatism*, pp. 250–260.
80 Lord Hailsham, 'Foreword' in Lord Blake and John Patten (eds), *The Conservative Opportunity* (London: Macmillan, 1976), pp. vii–viii.

Not all of Penguin's publications sought to dismantle the post-war settlement, and the publisher commissioned books that sought to revitalise centrist arguments. Aubrey Jones' *The New Inflation* was one example. Jones, a Conservative who had been the Chairman of the National Board for Prices and Incomes during the tenure of the first Wilson government, used the book to outline a 'non-partisan' incomes policy. Such a policy, he argued, would restore political consensus:

> The only way of coping with the problem of wage and price leadership is to introduce or re-introduce ... the idea of a compact which both Right and Left accept as applicable to ordinary social behaviour.[81]

Elsewhere, Trevor Russel, a former Labour MP who had joined the Conservative party in the late 1960s, authored a Penguin Special that challenged the thought of the Tory right. With her free market philosophy and divisive social policy, Thatcher, Russel argued, had deviated from the core tenets of conservative belief. And the resolution of Britain's social and economic problems, he argued, could be achieved by forging an 'alliance of the centre' that comprised of those on the Tory left and Labour's social democrats.[82] But while Russel's book demonstrates that Thatcher's authority within the Conservative party was fragile, its reception also reveals that centrists were operating in a political landscape whose locus was moving rightwards. One reviewer wrote that '[Russel's] middle way has become a left lane; no place for a Tory, only Penguin's idea of one', while another described Russel as a 'Blue Leftie'.[83] Implicit in both reviews was the idea that moderate

---

81 Aubrey Jones, *The New Inflation: The Politics of Prices and Incomes* (Penguin, 1973), p. 184.
82 Trevor Russel, *The Tory Party: Its Policies, Divisions and Future* (Penguin, 1978), pp. 152–154.
83 'Turn Left for Middle Way', *Daily Telegraph*, 22 October 1978. *New Manchester Review*, 20 October 1978. Despite the considerable attention it received from the press, the book sold only 8,000 copies. Neil Middleton to Trevor Russel, 29 January 1979. PA: DM1952/329.

Conservatives were leftist fellow travellers who had abandoned Conservatism.

There was also something of a backlash against the progressive ideas about education that Penguin had done much to popularise.[84] When the *Bookseller* reviewed Anthony Flew's *Sociology, Equality and Education*, a book which attacked these ideas, it claimed that

> many people, positioned in the middle of the political road and with attitudes less vigorous than his, may well be influenced by his collection of essays in the philosophy of education to feel that grief at the demise of Penguin Education may now be decently contained.[85]

Even some progressive intellectuals were disillusioned with some of the sociological texts that Penguin had published since the late 1960s. Among them was Bernard Crick, a social democratic intellectual who had been an editorial advisor to Penguin in the 1960s. In a private memo to Penguin's editors, he wrote that the '"old Penguin ideal" of the general educated reader, not the socialist' should have been the publisher's target audience. Many of the Penguin Specials, he suggested, 'seem like a Left Wing dream of what the *Sunday Times* insight team should be doing', and the politics list was too full of books from the 'Western Marxist socialist camp', which were 'unlikely to be what most of your readers and a wider potential readership want'.[86] According to Crick, Penguin

---

84 For a discussion of the New Right critique of progressive education, see Martyn Hammersley, 'An Ideological Dispute: Accusations of Marxist Bias in the Sociology of Education during the 1970s', *Contemporary British History*, Vol. 30, No. 2 (2015), pp. 242–259.

85 *Bookseller*, 31 July 1976. *The Times* pursued a similar argument in an article that cited Penguin as an agency of Marxist ideas: 'the intellectual initiative which the left has enjoyed for years has to some extent passed to the right'. 'The Enemies of Liberty', *The Times*, 21 September 1977. Anthony Flew, *Sociology, Equality and Education* (Basingstoke: Macmillan, 1976). Also see Anthony Flew, 'Penguin Pedagogy', *Spectator*, 30 September 1972.

86 Crick, 'Political Penguins'. PA: DM1952/613. Also see Bernard Crick, *Essays on Citizenship* (London: Continuum, 2004), pp. 35–58.

was failing to accommodate the preferences of readers who were not ideologically committed to the left: 'the centre has been neglected, both in a political and an intellectual sense'. [87] Crick also noted that the political list of the 1970s, despite exhibiting a strong left-wing slant, was, 'extraordinarily heterogeneous'.[88]

The diversity of Penguin's non-fiction list reflected the proliferation of new identities and concerns that could not be contained within a clear ideological agenda. As Dennis Dworkin has observed, these new identities eroded the effectiveness of the categories that the left had traditionally employed, and as a result, the forces of the left were increasingly fragmented.[89] One of Penguin's most influential authors, Raymond Williams, noted these problems. Reflecting on *May Day Manifesto*, he acknowledged that in the 1960s and 1970s, Marxism had failed to acquire an 'operative' character:

> [*May Day Manifesto*] started out with a group of mainly Marxist socialists thinking they could put together their various analyses – economic, political, international, cultural and so on – and present, however briefly, a general position. What we found, and would still find, is that they simply do not add up; in the politics, most obviously.

Continuing his analysis, Williams drew a distinction between the 'productive popular formations of the Left of the thirties' and the 'largely critical milieu of one kind of later Marxism'. While the former had been able to operate upon the concrete experiences of ordinary people, the latter had tended to assume that 'the whole people, including the whole working class, [were] mere carriers of the structures of a corrupt ideology'.[90]

---

87 Crick, 'Political Penguins'. PA: DM1952/613.
88 Crick, 'Political Penguins'. PA: DM1952/613.
89 Dennis Dworkin, *Class Struggles* (Harlow: Longman, 2007), p. 215.
90 Raymond Williams, 'Notes on Marxism in Britain since 1945', *New Left Review*, December 1976, p. 89.

Conclusion

The 1970s witnessed the eclipse of Britain's meritocratic moment.[91] As the Wilson governments struggled to satisfy the aspirations that elites and voters had invested in the promise of meritocratic logic, new ideas emerged that could not be reconciled with the prevailing political settlement. Feminists, students, Marxists and progressive educationalists all railed against the notion that inequalities could be justified if they were the product of innate differences of talent. For in different ways, these movements all drew attention to the environmental factors that could determine an individual's social status. And in their efforts to conceive of an alternative social order that could serve their values, they eschewed the utilitarian impulses that had often accompanied the meritocratic arguments of 1960s planners.

As the New Left railed against Wilson's project, the forces of the right mounted their own challenge to meritocratic reasoning. According to Thatcher and her colleagues in the New Right, the concept of merit could not be located at the centre of a successful project of social and economic renewal. For while they regarded equality of opportunity as a desirable objective, they discounted the notion that rewards should be distributed on the basis of merit. Not only did they claim that such an arrangement would require an external authority to make unjust interventions in the operation of the market, but they also challenged the professional ethic that had legitimated meritocratic reasoning.

By placing the logic of the market at the core of her discourse, Thatcher awarded new meanings to the declinist sentiments that

---

91 In 1979, the Penguin edition of Michael Young's *The Rise of the Meritocracy* was allowed to go out of print. The impetus behind the decision is not revealed by the archival record. It seems likely, however, that falling sales were a contributing factor. These falling sales reflected a sense that, as Barker has noted, 'the book's political message had had its day'. Paul Barker, 'A Tract for the Times', *Political Quarterly*, Vol. 77 (2006), p. 43.

had proliferated in the early 1960s. Like the technocratic writers whose arguments Penguin popularised, she placed emphasis on the need for social order and individual enterprise. But while the former had sought to realise these objectives by removing barriers to opportunity and uniting different social groups behind the common objective of growth, Thatcher identified the discipline of the market as the solution to Britain's malaise.[92] At a time when many voters were losing faith in the ability of the state to modify the social order, such arguments were able to gain considerable resonance.

These changes shifted the boundaries of political contestation. Not only was the centre ground hollowed out as intellectuals and policy-makers abandoned social democratic assumptions, but those that remained committed to 'middle way' strategies found themselves allied with different institutions and movements. Many of the centre-left authors of the 1960s, for instance, found themselves aligned with the forces of the right on a number of key political questions.[93] And Penguin, which had been regarded as a benign national institution for much of its history, came to be understood by some as an organ of ideas that were inimical to the national interest.

Two arguments follow from the story that this chapter has told. The first argument concerns the nature of the change that took place in the 1970s. Thatcher's New Right project is often understood as a counter-revolution against the social democratic consensus of the post-war decades. But this notion diverts attention from the way in which Thatcherism drew upon the ideas and arguments that had been employed to prop up the post-war political

---

92 Margaret Thatcher, speech to the Institute of Directors, 7 November 1974. MTF/102434.

93 Ortolano has drawn attention to the way in which writers like C. P. Snow became allied with the forces of the right over the course of the 1970s. Ortolano, *Two Cultures*, pp. 233–237.

settlement. If we accept that this settlement was, above all else, meritocratic, we begin to see how Thatcherism emerged out of it. In many ways, Thatcher pushed at an open door. Centre-left declinists has already broken decisively with the more egalitarian ideas that had made the political weather in the wartime period, and the concepts and ideas that they had popularised were ripe for reinterpretation.

The second argument relates to the first. Although the vibrant political debates of the 1970s followed from real economic and social changes, we should be suspicious of the idea that Thatcherism was the 'natural' outcome of these changes.[94] Ideas played an important role in shaping the way changes were understood, and we must recognise that there were other bodies of ideas that were competing for attention.[95] Penguin's progressive authors engaged in a war of position in their efforts to frame popular understandings of the context that they operated within. This battle for ideas took place in what Hay and others have termed a 'strategically selective context': that is, a context in which some strategies were favoured over others. But its outcomes were not determined by this context. Thatcher's vision of 'regressive modernisation' may have triumphed in May 1979. It was not, however, the only vision that was made available as actors searched for alternatives to the meritocratic logic that had sustained the prevailing political settlement. If we are to understand the ascendency of Thatcherism, it is necessary to acknowledge the way in which it operated upon the conceptual terrain that this settlement had left behind.

---

94 Colin Hay, 'Chronicles of a Death Foretold: The Winter of Discontent and Construction of the Crisis of British Keynesianism', *Parliamentary Affairs*, Vol. 63, No. 3 (2010), pp. 446–470.

95 Guy Ortolano, *Thatcher's Progress: From Social Democracy to Market Liberalism through an English New Town* (Cambridge: Cambridge University Press, 2019), pp. 17–22.

6

FREE TO CHOOSE

Seven months before Margaret Thatcher won her first election victory in May 1979, Penguin Books appointed Peter Mayer, an American publisher who had been the director of Avon Books, as its chief executive.[1] The appointment had significant consequences. In the subsequent decade, Mayer substantially changed Penguin's organisational structure and editorial policies. As well as introducing more aggressive marketing strategies, he also established a more vertical publishing model, whereby Penguin published a greater number of original hardback titles in order to reduce its expenditure on reprint rights.[2] These reforms were designed to reconcile Penguin with the changes that had taken place in the book trade in the preceding decade. Having observed the rapid expansion of major publishing corporations, Mayer arrived at the conclusion that Penguin could only remain viable if it was able to acquire best-selling books and market them to a global audience of readers.

---

1   In a recent essay, Mayer reflected on his experience at Penguin Books. Peter Mayer, 'Penguin Books in the Long-1970s: A Company Not a Sacred Institution' in Lawrence Black, Hugh Pemberton and Pat Thane (eds), *Reassessing 1970s Britain* (Manchester: Manchester University Press, 2013), pp. 212–223.
2   Bellaigue, 'Wingless Bird', p. 132.

Progressive commentators regarded Penguin's transformation as one symptom of a broader cultural change. Under Mayer's leadership, they argued, it had become indistinguishable from other trade publishers and had abandoned its commitment to the progressive ideas that had informed Allen Lane's approach to publishing. The social historian Ken Worpole wrote that 'the political impulse that went into earlier forms of mass publishing is currently in abeyance … Penguins, now part of Pearson, a multinational conglomerate, have become completely market-orientated.'[3] A similar observation was made by Richard Gott, a Marxist historian who had been the editor of the Pelican Latin America Library. 'Penguin,' he wrote, had become a 'pretty tacky conservative publisher, owned by a large and multi-faceted public company, and run by an overly rich low-brow American … its trajectory is an excellent example of the way in which serious English culture has become distorted and trivialised'.[4] Both Worpole and Gott located Penguin within a broader political and cultural transformation. The publisher's trajectory, they argued, signalled the proliferation of commercial and individualist values championed by Margaret Thatcher and her colleagues.

Some accounts of post-1979 British politics have reproduced the basic features of Gott and Worpole's narratives. According to their authors, the 1979 election was a decisive moment in Britain's political development, for it marked the moment when the ideas that had informed the social democratic post-war settlement were displaced by the acquisitive, individualist ideas associated with the New Right. These accounts tend employ a particular description of the political settlement that had been established in the immediate post-war period. After 1945, they argue, Britain acquired a state regime that was distinctly social democratic in character. In turn, they tend to identify the

---

3   Worpole, 'Penguin's Progress?'. Also see Valentine Cunningham, 'Orange, Green, Blue and Read', *Observer*, 2 July 1995.

4   Richard Gott, 'Pick Up a Penguin?', *Guardian*, 19 September 1985.

Thatcherite project as a counter-revolution that imposed a very different set of assumptions and beliefs.

Recent studies have begun to revise this familiar narrative of social democratic retreat and neo-liberal advance. By drawing attention to narratives that are concealed by a focus on Thatcher and her governments, Stephen Brooke has challenged the notion that the 1980s was a decade in which one political settlement was seamlessly replaced by another. Returning to themes explored by Stuart Hall's influential work on the period, he has sketched an alternative story about the 1980s that accommodates the period's peculiar contradictions. The decade, he argues, may have brought about legislative changes that institutionalised a more neo-liberal state regime. But it also witnessed the emergence of social movements and initiatives that sought to preserve the key achievements of Britain's social democratic experiment. It is thus necessary, as Brooke suggests, to 'think about how, in different ways and at different points, social democracy persisted against or even alongside neo-liberalism'.[5] Elsewhere, Emily Robinson, Camilla Schofield, Florence Sutcliffe-Braithwaite and Natalie Thomlinson and have explored the multiple trajectories of what they term 'popular individualism'. It has often been assumed that Thatcherism was the chief beneficiary of the individualist attitudes that seemed to follow from the economic and social changes of the 1960s and 1970s. Yet Thatcherism, they argue, did not exhaust the range of meanings that individualist beliefs could acquire. And in many instances, the demands for greater individual autonomy that marked the politics of the period were incompatible with its ideological assumptions.[6]

This chapter contributes to this reassessment of the changes that are often associated with Thatcherism. By exploring Penguin's texts

---

5   Stephen Brooke, 'Living in "New Times": Historicizing 1980s Britain', *History Compass*, Vol. 12, No. 1 (2013), pp. 20–32.
6   Robinson, Schofield, Sutcliffe-Braithwaite and Thomlinson, 'Telling Stories about Post-war Britain'.

and their reception, it suggests that the political and social changes of the 1980s cannot be accommodated within a linear narrative of social democratic decline and Thatcherite advance. Although certain assumptions of a Thatcherite character obtained a hegemonic status in the 1980s, the period also witnessed the emergence of new oppositional movements that challenged Thatcherism's authority and awarded alternative meanings to the values and concepts that it had placed at the centre of its discourse. Many of these movements could trace their origins to earlier moments, and they operated upon the contradictions of Thatcherism to create space for new political projects to challenge its authority.

The chapter also challenges the notion that Thatcherism was the natural beneficiary of structural changes that reshaped the social order. Significant social and economic forces certainly reshaped the political landscape in the 1980s. But they did not generate their own meanings, and in the battle for ideas that ensued in the decade, Thatcherism struggled to resolve many of the contradictions that it had inherited. By seizing upon the market as a criterion for determining the distribution of rewards and status, Thatcherites had constructed one alternative to the meritocratic consensus that had been forged during the wartime period. But this alternative was fraught with its own tensions, which were ripe for exploitation by oppositional forces.

In many cases, these oppositional forces held Thatcherism to account for its failure to resolve the antagonisms that had contributed to the dissolution of the meritocratic settlement. This meritocratic settlement had dissolved, in part, because the argument that the talented would use their disproportionate status and rewards for the benefit of all wore thin in the wake of the perceived crises of the 1970s. But Thatcherism's alternative justification for inequality was not always better equipped to quell the discontent that had followed from these crises. By defining liberty in negative terms and regarding the pursuit of economic equality as an affront to freedom, Thatcher did shift the responsibility for inequality to the impersonal forces of the market. But she also generated opposition from those individuals and groups who did not possess the resources or opportunities necessary to operate within an increasingly competitive market system. One striking conclusion that emerges from a study of Penguin's texts from this period is the extent to which they expose trajectories that cut across the 1979 election. Many of its authors drew upon arguments that had emerged from the social movements of the preceding decade and employed them to make arguments and claims that could not be accommodated by Thatcherite logic.

It may be necessary to 'decentre' the category of Thatcherism from our narratives of the 1980s and begin the difficult work of untangling the multiple and divergent responses to the eclipse of Britain's meritocratic moment. Describing the political order that succeeded it as 'Thatcherite' may even be problematic. It may have been Thatcherism that seized the ideological initiative in the late 1970s, but many of the developments that we might associate with its advance – the deregulation of markets, the decline of the professional ideal and the rise of individualism – could be anchored to different ideological positions. Moreover, the hegemony of the market was often dependent on its ability to deliver outcomes that Thatcherism found difficult to accommodate.

Before we explore the patterns that emerge when we employ Penguin as a lens through which to view the 1980s, it is instructive to consider the publisher's own trajectory. In doing so, we can observe some of the broader economic and cultural changes that were reshaping both the political landscape and the conditions in which Penguin was operating.

Peter Mayer's revolution and the eclipse of left-culturism

As preceding chapters have noted, the Penguin enterprise had been one manifestation of what Alan Sinfield termed 'left-culturism'. This ideology sought to reconcile an egalitarian commitment with a Leavisite conception of culture, and it exerted considerable influence upon the cultural politics of post-war Britain. But from the late 1960s, it became increasingly marginalised. Its demise can, in part, be attributed to the slow dissolution of the structures of deference that punctuated mid-century social attitudes.[7] But of equal significance was the rapid expansion of private consumption and the concomitant fragmentation of cultural taste.[8] Penguin was implicated in these shifts, and it is possible to locate Mayer's project of reorganisation within them.

In economic terms, the late 1970s was a difficult period for Penguin. Volume sales fell by 5 million between 1974 and 1979, eroding the firm's profit margin to just 1.2 per cent. And while the firm acquired the American publisher Viking in an attempt to expand its overseas markets, its export sales remained fragile.[9] These problems could, in part, be attributed to the cyclical economic crises of the period. But some of the publisher's managers also identified a structural frailty within Penguin's business model. They began to suggest that if the firm was to secure its long-term future, it would need to significantly amend its practices and organisation, and to this end, they appointed Peter Mayer in September 1978. Upon his arrival, Mayer raised concerns about Penguin's extensive backlist of titles. Because a large proportion of Penguin's capital was absorbed by purchasing reprint rights for older titles, it was difficult, Mayer argued, for it to bid for those new titles that were capable of achieving high volume sales. He advocated a more vertical model, whereby Penguin would publish original hardbacks in order to obtain rights to their respective paperback editions. Mayer also expressed dissatisfaction with Penguin's marketing strategies. Deep within the Penguin culture, he remarked, 'was a feeling that because Penguin was what it was, the world owed it a living'.[10]

7   Florence Sutcliffe-Braithwaite, *Class, Politics and the Decline of Deference in England, 1968–2000* (Oxford: Oxford University Press, 2018).
8   Jeremy Aynsley, 'Fifty Years of Penguin Design' in *Fifty Penguin Years*, p. 130.
9   Bellaigue, 'Wingless Bird', pp. 129–30.
10 BBC interview with Peter Mayer, 1984. PA: DM1294/6/2/27.

Mayer argued that in the increasingly competitive environment of the global book trade, such assumptions were untenable. Increasingly, readers' behaviour was determined by marketing and pricing rather than brand loyalty.

Mayer was also critical of the aesthetic and cultural assumptions that had informed Penguin's earlier approaches to publishing. Reflecting on his tenure at Penguin, he later stated that 'there ha[d] always been a hidden bias, even a snobbery, in the presumption of some mythical Penguin "reader" whose elevated tastes, on the one hand, or grateful hunger for enlightenment, on the other, determined our list'.[11] According to Mayer, good literature could take different forms and perform different functions. As he put it in an interview with *The Times*, 'Not everything has to be self-consciously noble. People read books to relax, not just to learn. All I ask is that whatever we publish should be good of its kind.'[12] Mayer also questioned whether the pursuit of cultural improvement was necessarily a democratic aspiration. Too often, he argued, Penguin had failed to meet the needs of readers whose tastes and interests did not correspond with its own. This was rooted in an argument about the nature of good literature. Whereas Lane and his editors had believed that good literature was that which possessed superior aesthetic qualities, Mayer offered a different view: 'the distinction between up-market and down-market is not known in the US. It's a symptom of a class society. All I see are either good books or bad books.'[13]

But if Mayer was critical of some of the ideas that Penguin had been wedded to, he also expressed a desire to 're-dedicate Penguin to many of Allen Lane's principles'.[14] He shared Lane's belief that

---

11   Mayer, 'Penguin Books', p. 219.
12   *The Times*, 27 September 1978. The 'good of its kind' argument was explicitly rejected by cultural commentators like Richard Hoggart. See Jim McGuigan, 'Richard Hoggart: Public Intellectual', *International Journal of Social Policy*, Vol. 12, No. 2 (2006), p. 205.
13   Quoted in 'Can Penguin's Book Balance?', *Marketing*, 9 July 1980.
14   Interview on the BBC Saturday Review, 20 July 1985.

the book trade should be concerned, in the last instance, with 'the idea of the book'. And while he believed that the market could provide a form of 'democratic protection' for readers, he also acknowledged that it could also stimulate a vicious competition for shelf space that encouraged publishers to lose sight of their moral and educative objectives:

> Much has been lost by universal business becoming the touchstone; if *everything* is current figures, it is a nasty industry that will burst out of the egg … perhaps we might consider whether we are losing sight of the book, or whether various over-emphases, stimulated by a necessity for us to be competitive, is healthy for ourselves as individuals, for the book we publish, and those who wrote them.[15]

During his tenure at Penguin, Mayer was reluctant to state his political convictions. In a recent reflection, however, he acknowledged that he was a 'left-leaning publisher with an editorial background who had made his career in the cut and thrust of the marketplace.'[16] Like Allen Lane, then, he believed that it was possible to reconcile commercial success with progressive publishing values.

As we have seen, Penguin's editors had often been suspicious of aggressive marketing strategies. Although they did not have a 'conscientious objection to advertising', they were often critical of those publishers that employed lurid covers and expensive advertising campaigns to cajole readers into purchasing books that were of inferior quality.[17] Nor did they believe that such strategies would be commercially advantageous. On the contrary, they had believed that because most readers bought Penguins because they trusted the publisher to provide them with the best works of literature, aggressive marketing would harm, rather than enhance, Penguin's

---

15 Peter Mayer, 'A Longer View of the Current Account', *Bookseller*, 13 January 1979.

16 Peter Mayer, 'Penguin Books in the Long-1970s', p. 215.

17 *The Penguin Story*, pp. 42–44.

commercial prospects. Mayer was suspicious of these paternalistic convictions. In his view, it was not the publisher's duty to operate as a cultural gatekeeper. Rather, its role was to publish books 'that readers were interested in reading'.[18]

Unsurprisingly, proponents of left-culturism were critical of Penguin's trajectory. Richard's Hoggart lamented the company's willingness to publish tawdry fiction: 'whilst it still produces some very good titles, [it] is also willing to produce some quite awful bestsellers. The *Boule de Suif* argument, that the whores can protect the virtuous women, doesn't suit artistic matters.'[19] Ken Worpole suggested that Penguin had capitulated to the demands of the market:

> Large sums of money have been paid in advances, and spent on promotion campaigns for novels of indifferent worth such as *The Far Pavilions* and the new Stephen King and Peter Straub horror novel *The Talisman*.[20]

In a sense, Mayer's reorganisation of the Penguin enterprise and the response it provoked reveals much about the cultural politics that followed from the eclipse of Britain's meritocratic moment. When they had defined 'good' culture in the post-war period, left-culturist commentators adhered to a certain kind of meritocratic logic. Richard Hoggart and other leading proponents of left-culturism had claimed that by expanding access to higher forms of cultural production, agencies like Penguin could construct a common culture that would erode class distinctions.[21]

18 Mayer, 'Penguin Books', p. 221.
19 Richard Hoggart, *An Imagined Life: Life and Times 1959–91* (Chatto and Windus, 1992), p. 50.
20 Worpole, 'Penguin's Progress?', p. 43.
21 In his study, Laing drew attention to the way in which Hoggart's most notable work, *The Uses of Literacy*, viewed social change through the lens of adult education. Stuart Laing, *Representation of Working-Class Life, 1957–64* (London: Macmillan, 1986), p. 196. We can observe a similar approach in Hoggart's later writings. See, for instance, Richard Hoggart, *The Way We Live Now* (London: Pimlico, 1995), pp. 297–299.

Yet their reasoning had been informed by a particular definition of cultural value that was undermined by many of the social and cultural changes of the 1970s, and when they reproduced it to construct critiques of Mayer's reorientation of Penguin, they exposed some of its tensions. On the one hand, its advocates had defended the egalitarian notion that all individuals and groups deserved access to the best kinds of culture. On the other, they defended the elitist notion that certain forms of cultural authority could be defended if they reflected 'educated' taste.[22]

When Mayer rejected the cultural distinctions that had informed Penguin's original vision, he both subverted the logic of left-culturism and gestured towards an alternative conception of cultural democracy. Because it was informed by a hostility to those hierarchies of cultural taste that had been bound up with Britain's class system, this version of cultural democracy was, in a sense, egalitarian. But by creating space for a relativist conception of cultural value, it broke decisively with the aesthetic judgements that informed the thought of Matthew Arnold, F. R. Leavis and the chief patron of Penguin's vision, Richard Hoggart.[23]

It is tempting to regard Penguin's trajectory as evidence of social democracy's retreat and Thatcherite advance. After all, it seemed to reflect the broader success of market values and the demise of those egalitarian ideas that Lane embodied. But such a reading of Penguin's development would conceal the complexity of Penguin's journey. The arguments made by Mayer and his critics cut across the boundary that separated these ideological traditions. Nor is it appropriate to read the eclipse of left-culturism as a symptom of Thatcherism's advance. The 'enterprise culture' of the 1970s that displaced this formation may have overlapped with

---

22 Ortolano has noted the elitism of meritocratic logic. Ortolano, *Two Cultures*, p. 251.
23 Many progressives in the 1980s sought to reconceptualise the market as a democratic instrument.

Thatcher's entrepreneurial agenda, yet we encounter substantial difficulties when we attempt to locate the complex social and cultural forces of the period within the parameters of Thatcher's vision. This point was acknowledged by Hoggart, who identified relativism, not Thatcherism, as the guiding force of the 1980s. In his view, the 'underlying process' that brought about the 'Market Driven Mentality ... preceded [Thatcher's acolytes] and will, more's the pity, outlast them'.[24] This is not the appropriate place to make aesthetic or moral judgements about the cultural changes of the 1980s. Yet Hoggart was correct to suggest that these changes are difficult to map on to a chronology of Thatcherism's development. They took root long before Thatcher entered Downing Street, and in many respects they were susceptible to appropriation by a range of ideological forces.

The above point can inform a reassessment of the intellectual politics of the 1980s. Although it is difficult to tell a story about the 1980s without attending to the phenomenon of Thatcherism and the corresponding fortunes of social democracy, these categories can obscure some of the changes that Thatcher's government oversaw. Adopting alternative starting points may help us to construct alternative narratives of the period that illuminate significant features of this moment.

From merit to the market? Thatcherism and the intellectual politics of the 1980s

As Mayer restructured Penguin's business model, Margaret Thatcher was launching her own project of reform as she sought to reconstitute Britain's state regime. This project was outlined in the preceding chapter, but it is useful to reiterate that it represented a counter-revolution against the meritocratic aspirations of the post-war political settlement. According to the monetarist ideas

---

24 Hoggart, *The Way We Live Now*, pp. 10–11.

that informed the thinking of Keith Joseph, Thatcher and other architects of Thatcherism, the market was the supreme criterion for determining the distribution of rewards and status. The market, it was argued, could aggregate the aspirations and demands of consumers and, in doing so, generate prosperity and social justice by rewarding entrepreneurial activity and discouraging restrictive practices. Thatcher often employed the language of meritocracy to legitimate her programme of reform, and the principle of equality of opportunity was not irreconcilable with her entrepreneurial vision. But in the last instance, Thatcherites could not endorse meritocratic reasoning. In their view, the value of ability and merit, like all human qualities, could only be determined adequately by the impersonal forces of the market.

By identifying the market as the best tool for allocating resources, Thatcherism relocated the burden of responsibility for inequality. It was no longer the state that was responsible for defending or resolving inequities; it was now the decisions and actions of consumers and producers that were accountable for the distribution of wealth and rewards. This way of thinking about the distribution of rewards had significant consequences. Most importantly, it shielded the Thatcherite state from the full burden of explaining inequality. If inequalities were the product of the choices and actions of ordinary individuals, it was difficult to blame the agencies of the state for their persistence. Yet we should not assume that Thatcherite logic was any less contradictory than that which informed the meritocratic reasoning that it displaced. It may have provided a clear explanation of inequality, but it was not necessarily well placed to resolve the antagonisms that emerged in response to the crises of the preceding decade. Nor did its constituent parts always hold together. As Hugh Pemberton, Aled Davies and James Freeman have noted, it was an ideology that struggled to reconcile its vision of the market with a coherent understanding of the individual. Its advocates sought to construct a community of ruthless capitalists who were able to make rational decisions about their economic investments. Yet they also privileged values of thrift and acknowledged that actors would not necessarily be able to navigate the complex economic contexts within which they were located.[25]

Thatcherism represented one attempt to channel the collapse of cultural and political authority that followed from the crisis of the meritocratic settlement and its concomitant professional ideal. Yet it was by no means the only one, and when we observe the discourses of the 1980s, we can observe movements that were able to give alternative meanings to its themes of enterprise and individualism.

Although Mayer was committed to reviving Penguin's political list, he believed that the publisher's task was to make available topical ideas from across the political spectrum. He was thus critical of the kinds of books that Penguin had published since the early 1970s. In a private letter to senior editors, he wrote that:

> The received wisdom is that Penguin Specials became ever more parochial and polemical i.e. they didn't necessarily expose an issue which the world should know about but increasingly presented a minority point of view of what *should be done* and over time lost creditability.[26]

In turn, Mayer sought to reorientate Penguin's political list. Writing in 1984, he stated that:

> Penguin's role ought to be the continued engagement with the major issues: with unemployment; with the health service; with diet perhaps; with growth or non-growth of the British economy ... with issues like proportional representation. We should be publishing on all of those issues, but perhaps not to any prescriptive pattern.[27]

---

25   Aled Davies, James Freeman and Hugh Pemberton, '"Everyman a Capitalist" or "Free to Choose"? Exploring the Tensions within Thatcherite Individualism', *The Historical Journal*, Vol. 61, No. 2 (2018), pp. 477–501.
26   Peter Mayer to Joy Chamberlain, Peter Carson and John Rolfe, 12 July 1984. PA: DM1294/3/6/7/3.
27   BBC interview with Peter Mayer, 1984. PA: DM1294/6/2/27.

Because he was reluctant to align Penguin with a clear ideological agenda, Mayer was often prepared to publish titles authored by figures who situated themselves on the right of the political spectrum. A notable example was Milton and Rose Friedman's *Free to Choose*, a book that identified markets as conduits to freedom. Despite being critical of the book's arguments, Mayer concluded that Penguin should attempt to acquire the reprint rights:

> It really is an in inaudible right-wing document. However, different in many respects I feel about it, I'm sure we should be bidding [for], and getting, this book. We publish for all markets and he is 'credentialised' and his views of things are part of debate … We need this book [if we] are to be contentious, alive and kicking.[28]

Free to Choose was not the only statement of neo-classical economic thought that Penguin published in the 1980s. In 1985, George Gilder's *The Spirit of Enterprise* was published under its Viking imprint. Gilder, who was then the director of the International Centre for Economic Policy Studies in Manhattan, claimed that it was entrepreneurs who were the principal source of technological and economic progress. To support his thesis, Gilder constructed a reading of the entrepreneur that ran counter to meritocratic reasoning. Challenging the association that had often been made between merit and expertise, Gilder situated enterprise in opposition to the 'suave voices of expertise'. Here he challenged the idea that expertise was the engine of political progress: 'the entrepreneur', he wrote, 'finds a higher source of hope than reason, a deeper well of faith than science, a farther reach of charity than welfare'.[29]

---

28 Peter Mayer to Peter Carson, undated memo. PA: DM1952/Box 238. Also see Bob Woffindon, 'Penguin's Progress', *New Statesman*, 31 December 1982. Milton Friedman and Rose Friedman, *Free to Choose* (Penguin, 1980).

29 George Gilder, *The Spirit of Enterprise* (Harmondsworth: Viking, 1985), p. 258.

If Mayer was willing to acquire titles from the right, it must be noted that his tenure coincided with a renewal of Penguin's tradition of progressive publishing. As Mayer stated in 1984, Penguin continued to publish 'rather more material from the left side than from the right', and many of these texts were authored by centre-left figures who were attempting to revitalise Britain's social democratic tradition in response to the ascendency of Thatcher.[30] Shirley Williams and David Owen, who had co-founded the Social Democratic Party (SDP) in March 1981, authored books that sought to reconcile their social democratic values with the social and economic conditions of the 1980s; William Keegan, a Keynesian economist, wrote a critique of the first Thatcher government's economic policy; and Malcolm Wicks, a parliamentary candidate for the Labour party, published a book on welfare policy.[31] These books invite a reading of post-1979 intellectual politics that cuts across some of the fault lines of the existing historiography. On the one hand, they expose the way in which Britain's political terrain had been reshaped by the crises of the preceding decade. But on the other, they demonstrate that the hegemony of Thatcher's political project was remarkably contingent.

Penguin's centre-left authors were certainly willing to suggest that the authority of social democratic ideas had been eroded by recent social and economic change. In *Politics Is for People*, Shirley Williams suggested that 'the balance of opinion has moved against the typical product of social democratic government ... The

---

30 BBC *Saturday Review*: 'Penguin Books', 20 July 1985.
31 Shirley Williams, *Politics Is for People* (Penguin, 1981). Shirley Williams, *A Job to Live: The Impact of Today's Technology on Work and Society* (Penguin, 1985). David Owen, *A Future That Will Work* (Penguin, 1984). David Owen, *A United Kingdom* (Penguin, 1986). William Keegan, *Mrs Thatcher's Economic Experiment* (Penguin, 1984). Malcolm Wicks, *A Future for All: Do We Need a Welfare State?* (Penguin, 1987). David Owen was also invited to write a book on the National Health Service but declined due to time constraints. David Owen to Martin Soames, 30 August 1984. PA: DM1292/148/7785.

intellectual winds now blow from a different quarter.'[32] The economist William Keegan offered a similar view. After tracing the way
in which Thatcher and her colleagues had 'devalued the level of
public economic debate', he concluded that many voters were failing to recognise an alternative to a monetarist agenda.[33]

Some of Penguin's advisory editors also believed that social attitudes had shifted to the right. In 1981, when Malcolm Wicks sub-
mitted a draft of his book on the welfare state, the sociologist
Anthony Rees suggested that many of its arguments were moribund. Rees devoted attention to its preoccupation with direct taxation, a policy instrument which he believed was unsuited to the
social conditions of the 1980s:

> The crucial point here is whether it is any longer a feasible strategy
> to extend the process of taking large sums of money through taxa-
> tion ... it seems that very many working-class people no longer sub-
> scribe to the beliefs in question ... this draft is fatally old-fashioned.[34]

Rees' suspicion of older social democratic ideas was shared by
David Owen, who became the leader of the Social Democratic
Party following the 1983 General Election. Writing in *A Future That
Will Work*, which Penguin published in 1984, Owen outlined an
alternative to the model of social democracy that had informed
the Labour party's thinking in the preceding decades. One of the
book's central argument concerned the way in which socialists had
conceptualised the objective of social equality. Too often, Owen
argued, it had been assumed that all redistributive practices were
conducive to social justice. But in the conditions of the 1980s, he
argued, some forms of redistributive taxation could impair economic efficiency and, in turn, harm the conditions of the poorest
members of the community. Owen buttressed this argument by

---

32 Williams, *Politics Is for People*, p. 28.
33 Keegan, *Mrs Thatcher's Economic Experiment*, p. 208.
34 PA: DM1952/Box238.

making reference to the work of the American philosopher John Rawls. A just society, Rawls had argued, was one in which the least advantaged were as well off as they could be. It followed that differentials of income could be justified if they benefited the poorest members of the community.[35] Owen endorsed this way of thinking about justice. As he put it, maximum justice and equal rights are 'more inspiring than advocating equality of income, a goal which few believe in and even fewer are prepared to work for'.[36] By arriving at such a conception of social justice, Owen had reconfigured social democracy's conceptual architecture. Traditionally, social democrats had regarded equality as their central objective, and although they had sought to enhance individual liberty, they had tended to define this freedom in positive, rather than negative, terms. For Owen, by contrast, the task of social democracy was to create a society in which the principle of equal liberty was privileged.[37] This feature of his thought was most evident when he discussed the role of the state. 'In Britain,' he wrote, 'reliance on the state had gone too far, and the result has been a loss of drive and dynamism and a playing-down of the importance of market forces as the progenitor of change and progress.'[38]

Owen advocated an economic strategy that he termed the 'social market'. Within such a system, a competitive market economy would be reconciled with social justice by introducing a system of industrial democracy that could repair the vagaries of the price mechanism. Rather than being understood as an instrument that could intervene in the allocation of resources, the state was imagined as a body that could ensure the efficient function of the market by discouraging restrictive practices and funding competitive public enterprises. Owen anchored this strategy to an argument about social values: 'we

---

35 Samuel Freeman, *Rawls* (London: Routledge, 2007), pp. 99–120.
36 Owen, *A Future That Will Work*, p. 108.
37 Owen, *A United Kingdom*, p. 125.
38 Owen, *A Future That Will Work*, p. 103.

cannot reverse our relative economic decline by arguing whether competitiveness should take second place to compassion or compassion second place to competitiveness. We need them both.'[39]

Owen's reassessment of social democracy can be read as an attempt to reconcile a conception of social justice with market imperatives.[40] He did not reproduce the moral themes of the New Right project, and in many respects he attempted to award new meanings to the values that Thatcher and her colleagues had attempted to popularise. But in his efforts to resolve the apparent tension between individual enterprise and communal obligation, Owen broke decisively with the assumptions and beliefs that had informed the egalitarian ideas of Hobhouse, Tawney and Marshall. As we have seen, these writers had tended to believe that the individual possessed no moral rights that could not be reconciled with the common good. And, in turn, they had tended to regard competition between individuals as unnecessary and disruptive.[41] Owen, by contrast, seemed to assume that there was a necessary tension between communal and private interests that needed to be reconciled by a contractarian arrangement. Indeed the 'social market' was, in many respects at least, an attempt to forge a new kind of social contract that was commensurable with the individualist and acquisitive values that Thatcher had celebrated. In his review of *A Future That Will* Work, the Conservative Ferdinand Mount suggested that Owen had abandoned the pursuit of equality, and he questioned whether his Rawlsian turn had led him away from the social democratic tradition.[42] If the mark of an ideology's hegemony is its ability to impose limits on the arguments of oppositional forces, then Owen's book does suggest that in some spheres at least, Thatcherism had gained considerable salience.[43]

---

39 Owen, *A Future That Will Work*, p. 29.
40 Hewison, *Culture and Consensus*, p. 216.
41 Freeden, *Liberalism Divided*, pp. 224–225.
42 Ferdinand Mount, 'The Flying Doctor', *Spectator*, 8 September 1984.
43 Hewison, *Culture and Consensus*, p. 216.

Those social democrats that had remained in the Labour party were critical of Owen's formulations. In their view, Owen had capitulated to the right's argument by substituting the politics of enterprise for the politics of equality. But it must be noted that many of these figures also adjusted their thinking in response to Thatcher's advance. Consider Roy Hattersley's *Choose Freedom*, which was published in Penguin's main list in 1987. Hattersley was then Shadow Chancellor, and his book's principal objective was to challenge the assumptions that informed the New Right's political thinking. One of the New Right's central claims was that equality and freedom existed in an inverse relationship, such that the pursuit of the former necessarily constrained the latter. Invoking Tawney, Hattersley took issue with this argument. Freedom, he argued, was a corollary of equality, for individuals could not be free unless they possessed an equal share of the goods and opportunities that were conducive to its realisation. But if Hattersley firmly opposed the conception of liberty that had been advanced by the New Right, he also made an attempt to reconcile his egalitarianism with the market forces that its advocates were so anxious to liberate.[44] In contrast to those socialists who had regarded the market as anathema, Hattersley argued that in some spheres, competitive private enterprise could enhance productive capacity and guard against monopolistic practices that produced concentrations of wealth.[45] And although he awarded the state an important role in regulating the market, he suggested that socialism did not possess an adequate theory for planning human need.[46] Nor did Hattersley oppose David Owen's distributive logic. Like Owen, he endorsed Rawls' difference principle and suggested that some inequalities could contribute to the wealth available to all.[47] In one sense, there

---

44 Ellison, *Egalitarian Thought and Labour Politics*, p. 208.
45 Roy Hattersley, *Choose Freedom: The Future for Democratic Socialism* (Penguin, 1987), p. 150.
46 Hattersley, *Choose Freedom*, p. 165.
47 Hattersley, *Choose Freedom*, p. 98.

was little that was novel about such principles. In the 1950s, Crosland and other social democrats had accepted that some inequalities would be needed to provide incentives for productive activity. But Rawls' principle seemed to place greater emphasis on the attainment of equal liberty rather than the extension of social citizenship. And by endorsing Rawls, Hattersley seemed to accept that the objective of equality could only be achieved if it was paired with the pursuit of efficiency. It would be problematic to suggest that Hattersley's Penguin signalled the centre-left's capitulation to monetarist doctrine. But the book does suggest that opponents of Thatcherism were operating within new intellectual constraints. Not only did they assume the presence of a more individualist electorate that was less receptive to the communitarian appeals of the past; they also regarded the task of undoing market relationships as impractical and undesirable.

Penguin's publishing also exposes some of the ways in which ideas that we associate with Thatcherism began to punctuate the vernacular languages that were employed to describe economic activity.[48] Thatcher and her colleagues often celebrated the virtues of 'popular capitalism'. By providing opportunities for ordinary citizens to intervene in the financial sector, it would be possible, they argued, to 'enfranchise the many'.[49] Individuals would be liberated from the authority of the state, and they would also develop the sort of entrepreneurial values that had been impaired by postwar collectivism. To realise this vision, the second Thatcher government introduced a range of legislative reforms that were designed to promote share ownership and deregulate the financial sector. These reforms, despite having some contradictory consequences, did create new opportunities for ordinary consumers to

---

48 Amy Edwards, '"Financial Consumerism": Citizenship, Consumerism and Capital Ownership in the 1980s', *Contemporary British History*, Vol. 31, No. 2 (2017), pp. 210–299.

49 Margaret Thatcher's speech to the Conservative Party Conference, 10 October 1986. MTF/106498.

manage their own financial affairs. In turn, they generated a demand for information about stock markets, tax arrangements and investment schemes. From 1986, Penguin began to meet this demand by publishing tax guides that were produced by Lloyd's Bank. As an advertisement for the first edition stated, their objective was to provide readers with the knowledge that they required to reduce their tax burden:

> Cut through the complexities! Work the system in *your* favour! Don't pay a penny more than you have to! Written for anyone who has to deal with personal tax, this up-to-date and concise new handbook includes all the important changes in this year's budget.[50]

But if these texts reveal the emergence of a certain kind of popular capitalism that might have had some resonance with Thatcherism's social logic, there were others that demonstrated valences of individualism that rubbed against the grain of this project. We should not assume that the proliferation of claims for individual autonomy were always commensurable with the particular social and moral arguments that we might associate with Thatcherism, and in what follows attention will be drawn to some of the ways in which Penguin gave voice to alternative visions of the future that constrained the frontiers of Thatcherism's advance.

The limits of Thatcherism's advance

Although Thatcherism offered a potent critique of the Keynesian assumptions that had been hegemonic in the 1950s and 1960s, its own ideological contradictions rendered it vulnerable to challenges from a rejuvenated centre-left. And by the mid-1980s, when the social consequences of Thatcher's economic policies were

---

50 The advert was featured in Keith Thompson, *Under Siege: Racial Violence in Britain Today* (London: Penguin, 1988).

becoming increasingly visible, a number of texts were published that challenged its legitimising ideology. William Keegan's aforementioned study of the Thatcher government's economic policy was particularly influential. First published in the Allen Lane imprint, the book offered a Keynesian critique of the deflationary strategy that had been pursued from 1980. This strategy, Keegan argued, had been a failure. Not only had it exacerbated the problem of underinvestment, but it had also contributed to further increases in unemployment.[51] Elsewhere, the economics editor of the *Sunday Times*, David Smith, drew attention to the concentration of power and wealth that had followed from Thatcher's economic policies. While investment and job opportunities had expanded for the middle classes in the south of England, the north had experienced relative stagnation. This growing regional divide, Smith argued, threatened the overall objective of economic growth,[52] for it both exacerbated inflationary pressures and contributed to labour-market inefficiency. To repair the malaise that he described, Smith advocated a regional policy that would redistribute wealth and disperse political authority. Some of Thatcher's followers acknowledged the potential force of these centre-left arguments. Jock Bruce-Gardyne, despite being critical of the conclusions of Keegan's book, acknowledged that 'Mr Keegan writes lucidly and carries us along with him'.[53]

Keegan and Smith's arguments were broadly commensurable with those that Galbraith had offered in the late 1950s. Their respective books sought to reconcile the mixed economy with a reformed system of Keynesian management that could revitalise the public sector. As it has done in the 1960s, this aspiration gained support from a wide range of political opinion. The SDP, in its efforts to reconcile private enterprise with a social democratic

---

51 Keegan, *Mrs Thatcher's Economic Experiment*, pp. 131–183.
52 David Smith, *North and South: A Growing Divide* (London: Penguin, 1984).
53 Jock Bruce-Gardyne, 'Clouds Over Lombard St.', *Spectator*, 10 March 1984.

social policy, advocated a policy of decentralisation in line with Smith's enthusiasm for devolved decision-making.

Other studies reconfigured these ideas in order to explain the peculiar social problems of the 1980s. Paul Harrison's *Inside the Inner City*, which was published as a Pelican in 1983, was one of the most influential examples. Revising the conventional Galbraithian formulation, he made reference to 'private squalor and public squalor'.[54] There was, Harrison argued, an inverse relationship between private need and public provision. Areas with a high concentration of poor residents were more likely to receive low levels of public spending because such areas tended to have a low rate base and were less politically powerful. Harrison traced the origins of this problem to the economic crises of the preceding decade, but he suggested that the Thatcher government's policies had exacerbated its social consequences. By increasing the cost of public goods and services, the government, he argued, had allowed the poor to bear the burden of the slump: 'The conclusion is inescapable: the Thatcher government, which sacrificed the jobs and hopes of millions of people in the battle against inflation, was itself a major source of inflation for the power-paid and council tenants.'[55] According to Harrison, then, the government's economic strategy was fraught with contradiction. One of its central objectives had been to expand private choice. Yet in its efforts to reduce public expenditure, it had compelled poorer individuals and families to devote a greater share of their private wealth to public services.

From 1983 to 1985, Penguin published a series of books in association with the Socialist Society, a campaign group that had been established by leading members of the New Left. Each title engaged with a different social problem, and their authors

---

54   Paul Harrison, *Inside the Inner City: Life under the Cutting Edge* (Penguin, 1983), p. 179.
55   Harrison, *Inside the Inner City*, p. 178.

challenged many of the assumptions that informed Thatcherite thinking.[56] In their contribution, *What Is to Be Done about Law and Order?*, John Lea and Jock Young offered a left realist reading of crime. Their principal argument was that incidents of working-class crime were often a secondary consequence of relative deprivation and unemployment. Until the 1970s, they argued, most workers had been able to exert influence upon the political system by participating in union activity. But the collapse of corporatism, combined with the increase in economic inequality that had followed from the Thatcher government's monetarist experiments, had led many individuals to become excluded from the communities in which they lived. One consequence of this social exclusion, Lea and Young maintained, was an increase in criminal activity, since individuals who were denied access to conventional forms of negotiation and compromise were more likely to engage in illegal practices to redress their grievances.[57]

Other books in the series exposed the Thatcher government's failure to resolve the new forms of social conflict that had emerged in the 1970s. *What Is to Be Done about the Family?* was one such title. Edited by Lynne Segal, it identified substantial inconsistencies in the government's social policies. One the one hand, Thatcher and her colleagues had committed themselves to restoring traditional family life. Yet on the other, they had introduced cuts in public spending that had exacerbated family problems:

> with friends like Mrs Thatcher, who needs to 'smash the family'? Tory pro-family sentiments relate to pro-family policies (ones which might assist those caring for dependents) like the expression of love relates to the act of murder.[58]

---

56 The books were intended to 'be for the 80s what our series "Britain in the 60s" was for that decade'. PA: DM1952/Box 132.

57 John Lea and Jock Young, *What Is to Be Done about Law and Order?* (London: Penguin, 1984), pp. 211.

58 Lynne Segal (ed.), *What Is to Be Done about the Family?* (Penguin, 1983), p. 223.

It is difficult to trace the influence of these books. What can be established, however, is the way they operated upon Thatcherism's contradictions to award alternative meanings to the concepts and themes that it sought to colonise. Thatcherism did not exhaust the demands that were being made for individual autonomy and that had helped to discredit the structures of authority associated with the meritocratic moment. The institution that it celebrated – the market – may have been best placed to meet some of the demands for individual liberation. But there were initiatives and movements that channelled individualism into progressive causes. Matthew Hilton, Chris Moores and Florence Sutcliffe-Braithwaite have drawn attention to the way in which institutions like the Greater London Council and publications such as *Marxism Today* forged new kinds of progressive politics by drawing upon the aspirations that had been released by the social and cultural changes of the 1970s.[59] Similarly, Robinson, Sutcliffe-Braithwaite and Schofield have shown how anti-racist movements in the 1970s drew upon the language of individual entitlement to hold the state to account for failing to deliver equality of opportunity.[60] A study of Penguin's texts from the 1980s adds weight to these readings of the period. These texts expose aspirations, antagonisms and arguments that ran against the political and moral agenda that Thatcherism had forged, and they reveal trajectories that cut across the 1979 election.

1997

Two arguments have been outlined above. First, it has been suggested that the meritocratic settlement of the post-war period was not displaced by a monolithic and omnipotent Thatcherite project. The market may have disposed merit as the hegemonic

59 Matthew Hilton, Chris Moores and Florence Sutcliffe-Braithwaite, 'New Times Revisited: Britain in the 1980s', *Contemporary British History*, Vol. 31, No. 2 (2017), p. 155.
60 Robinson, Schofield and Sutcliffe-Braithwaite, 'Telling Stories', pp. 297–302.

justification for inequality. But in many respects, the progressive critiques of the meritocratic discourses of the post-war period continued to obtain resonance in 'Thatcher's decade'. Second, it has been argued that the political developments we associate with Thatcherism were more fragile than older narratives suggested. Thatcher's electoral victories were not overdetermined by structural forces whose consequences were fixed, and not all of the trajectories we can trace through the 1980s complemented Thatcherism's ideology.

Both of these arguments can be brought into relief by carrying our story forward to 1997, a moment which has been described as both Thatcherism's zenith and its nadir.[61] In advance of the General Election of that year, Penguin, as they had done in 1947, 1959 and 1964, invited members of Britain's main political parties to author books that summarised their party's beliefs. When read together, these titles reveal the emergence of a post-Thatcherite political landscape. For while they expose the resilience of some Thatcherite economic assumptions, they also reveal the advance of 'third way' ideas that ran counter to its logic. In his book, David Willetts, who was then Paymaster General, in John Major's final government, conceded that his party had allowed progressive forces to reconfigure the terms of political debate:

> The power of free-market thinking, the drive of technology, the collapse of Marxism, the moral authority of the appeal to personal freedom, all mean that modern Conservatives ought to feel that the tide of ideas and events is in our favour ... But in other ways Conservatives can still feel like an embattled minority ... Despite all the advances we have made since 1979, the collapse of the socialist Left

---

61 For an account that regards New Labour as the apotheosis of Thatcherism, see Richard Heffernan, *New Labour and Thatcherism* (Basingstoke: Palgrave, 2001). For an account that places emphasis on the decline of Thatcherism in the 1990s, see Robert Saunders, 'Crisis? What Crisis? Thatcherism and the Seventies' in Jackson and Saunders (eds), *Making Thatcher's Britain*, pp. 25–42.

has not given Conservatives the intellectual dominance which we deserve ... [Labour's] language may have shifted from Fabian socialism to stakeholding and social cohesion but they are still exploiting misconceptions and misunderstandings about the free market'.[62]

Willetts' analysis bore some resemblance to that which Hogg had offered in *The Case for Conservatism*. In response to the defeat of 1945, Hogg had argued that Conservatives needed to respond to the moral argument that had been made by their socialist opponents. Willetts endorsed a similar approach. Too often, he argued, his party had failed to recognise the moral appeal of socialism.

Tony's Wright's *Why Vote Labour?* outlined a conception of social democracy that could reconcile individual liberty and market economics with the values of community and social justice. In doing so, the book reproduced one tenet of the agenda that David Owen had outlined in *A Future That Will Work*. As we have seen, Owen had attempted to break with the false dichotomies of the past by advocating a 'new synthesis ... a combination of what are too often wrongly assumed to be incompatible objectives',[63] and Wright advocated a 'politics of synthesis' that could reconcile private enterprise with civic responsibility.[64] This 'third way' logic had struggled to take root when Owen was writing in the mid-1980s. But by the mid-1990s, when it had been given new impetus by the sociological analyses of Anthony Giddens and others, it was able to sustain a vibrant alternative to the perceived dogmatism of Thatcherism.

In some respects, then, the origins of New Labour's ascendency can be traced to the mid-1970s. One of the central aspirations of Blair and his colleagues was to reconcile monetarist economics with a social policy that could restore the kind of civic values associated with earlier bodies of progressive thought. In the conditions of the 1980s, the latter had been crowded out by the former, but by

62 David Willetts, *Why Vote Conservative?* (London: Penguin, 1997), pp. 2–3.
63 Owen, *A Future That Will Work*, front cover.
64 Tony Wright, *Why Vote Labour?* (London: Penguin, 1997), p. 43.

the early 1990s, the oppositional forces that had gathered pace in the 1970s had become more influential. That is not to say, of course, that Blair and other architects of New Labour reproduced their arguments in an unmediated form. When they drew upon the arguments and concepts that had been developed by progressive forces in the preceding decades, the architects of New Labour often awarded them new meanings. Yet we can read it as an attempt to channel the popular individualism that had marked the intellectual politics of the 1970s.

Conclusion

It would be tempting to locate Penguin's post-war political publishing within a linear narrative of social democratic advance and decline. Such a narrative would identify Penguin as one beneficiary of the collectivist and egalitarian aspirations that took root in the middle of the twentieth century, and it would regard Mayer's reforms of the 1980s as symptoms of a broader social and political shift that displaced the post-war consensus and allowed Thatcher's project to gain resonance. But such a narrative would fail to accommodate the complexity of the political and social change that took place in the post-war period. The eclipse of a meritocratic justification of inequality with a market-orientated one cannot be mapped neatly on to a story of social democratic decay and Thatcherite dominance. The categories of social democracy and Thatcherism still have value for students of post-war British politics. But by locating other concepts and categories at the centre of our analyses, we can expose alternative readings of the social and political turbulence of the 1970s and 1980s. These readings might place less emphasis on the notion that the 1979 election was a critical juncture in which the political landscape was reshaped, and they might also expose some of the complex legacies of the social movements and political campaigns that had helped to displace the meritocratic settlement of the post-war period.

CONCLUSION

By telling a story about the books that were produced by of one of Britain's leading publishers, this study has traced the ideas and narratives that shaped political thinking in the post-war period. The empirical base of the study is not sufficient to expose the full range of ideas and social movements that determined the ideological shifts of the three decades that succeeded the Second World War. But the corpus of texts that Penguin published do invite us to conceptualise the intellectual politics of the period in new terms. In particular, they open up the possibility of constructing a new metanarrative. As Ortolano has argued, the politics of the period can be mapped on to a story about the emergence and eclipse of what might be termed Britain's 'meritocratic moment'.[1] This distinctive epoch in Britain's political development can trace its origins to the late inter-war period, when social antagonisms and political turbulence placed existing orthodoxies under considerable strain. As they cast around for new ideas that could inform a new political settlement, intellectuals, commentators and policymakers arrived at different positions. But out of their debates emerged a hegemonic set of ideas that would form the basis for a new political consensus. These ideas cut across Britain's major ideological traditions, but they were all commensurate with a

---

1   Ortolano, *Two Cultures*, p. 251.

certain kind of meritocratic logic. Ability and expertise were considered to be important qualifications for the acquisition of status and rewards, and equality of opportunity became an objective that was almost universally endorsed.

In one sense, the authority of this meritocratic settlement rested on its ability to reconcile the principles of equality and liberty. Yet in another, it only deferred the question of the relationship that should exist between these concepts, and as the relative prosperity of the 1950s and 1960s gave way to the economic and social turbulence of the 1970s, many contemporaries began to advocate principles and ideas that ran counter to its logic. Not only did many actors return to class-based conceptions of justice; they also reconfigured the meanings of concepts that had legitimated the preceding political settlement. The outcome was the emergence of a more polarised ideological landscape in which old forms of political conflict were reawakened. The forces of the right were not destined to win this battle for ideas, but Margaret Thatcher's project of regressive modernisation was able to rework the conceptual architecture of the prevailing political settlement and displace merit as the hegemonic criterion for determining the distribution of rewards and status.[2] This hegemony was always contingent, and as the final chapter of the book noted, it co-existed with tendencies that worked against the grain of Thatcherite logic. Yet as Ortolano observed, the market was to the 1980s what merit had been to the post-war period: an organising principle for political thinking that was hegemonic.

This narrative has some implications for our broader understanding of post-war British politics. In one sense, it is a story that decentres some of the categories that have often been employed to understand post-war intellectual politics. Of these, perhaps the most prominent are those of social democracy and Thatcherism. When many accounts have sought to tell a story about ideological

---

2   Stuart Hall, 'Gramsci and Us', *Marxism Today*, June 1987.

change, these categories have been employed to distinguish between two political settlements that were separated by the crises of the 1970s.[3] The former, it is argued, was ascendant until the mid-1970s and was then rapidly usurped by the latter. This study has complicated this narrative by offering a different sense of what was at stake when intellectuals and policy-makers engaged in ideological debate. If the three decades that followed the 1945 election were characterised not by a common commitment to social democratic objectives but a contingent agreement on the need for meritocratic arrangements, we are compelled to reassess our sense of what was at stake in the 1970s. Indeed by acknowledging the dominant meanings that were awarded to the concept of merit in the post-war decades, we can construct a different account of the political change that took place in the late 1970s. Often this moment has been understood as a counter-revolution against the egalitarianism and collectivism of the post-war period. But although Thatcherism did offer a fervent critique of social democratic ideology, this study has cautioned against the notion that its principal achievement was to reverse a collectivist trajectory. As Chapter 5 demonstrated, Thatcherism operated upon an intellectual landscape that had legitimated certain individualist assumptions long before the crises of the 1970s took root. The trajectories of Penguin authors like John Vaizey are revealing here. After being a Labour member who supported Wilson's technocratic conception of social democracy in the early 1960s, he came to endorse Thatcher's project in the late 1970s. This change of allegiance did not reflect Vaizey's own ideological transformation. Rather, it reflected the changing political and cultural context in which actors like Vaizey were operating. Vaizey's earlier enthusiasm for equality was predicated upon his belief that freedom and equality could be reconciled through the advance of social mobility. But when the crises

---

3   This point has been made in a recent intervention. See Hilton, Moores and Sutcliffe-Braithwaite, 'New Times Revisited'.

of the 1970s appeared to render the meritocratic ideal unattainable, Vaizey gravitated towards Thatcher's individualist and anti-statist project. We might conclude that while the late 1970s was a moment when one intellectual settlement was replaced by another, it is problematic to describe this shift in terms of a transition from social democracy to Thatcherism. The latter operated upon the tensions and contradictions of an intellectual settlement that had deferred, rather than resolved, the question of the appropriate relationship between equality and liberty. It is perhaps unsurprising, then, that when Thatcher attempted to construct an alternative to its social logic, she was able to award new meanings to the concepts of social mobility, efficiency and merit that were so central to its legitimising ideology.

A related point can be made about the concepts of merit and the market. Although the findings of this study are not a sufficient basis for constructing an adequate metanarrative of post-war British politics, they do encourage us to consider these concepts as potential starting points for doing so, for the story that has been told suggests that these concepts might be able to accommodate some of the continuities and changes that marked the period. We can consider, for instance, the way in which the objective of equal opportunity gained political meanings over time. If we understand this objective as the exclusive property of social democratic thinking, then we run into significant problems when we attempt to understand the political upheavals of the late 1970s. After all, Thatcher and her colleagues possessed their own positive conception of the term. It might be more appropriate to tell a story about the way in which a meritocratic conception of equal opportunity was displaced by a market-orientated one. Such a story would help us to trace the way in which distributive questions were framed in new ways in the wake of the crises of the 1970s. It would also compel us to recognise that Thatcher operated within a long tradition of political thinking that had enshrined the principle of equal opportunity.

As well as destabilising the conceptual architecture of some established accounts, the book's narrative also invites us to take up new methodologies when we study intellectual politics. First, it suggests that a more conceptual approach to the study of ideas could be profitable. Most existing accounts of the post-war period employ Britain's major ideological traditions as the starting point of their analyses. One consequence is that they tend to regard intellectual politics as a contest between relatively coherent formations of thought with distinctive ideological objectives. But while this approach can tell us much, it can also conceal some of the ways in which these formations overlapped and developed as they came into contact with new social and cultural contexts. As Michael Freeden and others have demonstrated, political ideologies attempt to contest common meanings in a cultural environment that structures the semantic terrain of politics.[4] Once we acknowledge this, it becomes necessary to identify research strategies that are diachronic in nature. Taking concepts as the starting point for studying ideological change is one such strategy. Not only does it allow us to trace the way in which concepts acquired and shed meanings over time, but it can also help us to identify ideological developments that cannot be situated neatly within a story about Britain's major ideological traditions.

Second, the study encourages students of twentieth-century Britain to employ a broader frame of reference when we study intellectual politics. Typically, accounts have been preoccupied with a narrow range of elite thinkers, such as Beveridge and Keynes, who were deemed to be the architects of the ideas that framed political activity. But while these actors were influential, it was not necessarily their ideas that formed the basis of vernacular discussions about social and political problems. If we want to access these discussions, we need to broaden our field of vision. The Penguin book provides one tool for doing so, for it was a

---

4   Michael Freeden, 'Political Concepts and Ideological Morphology', *Journal of Political Philosophy*, Vol. 2, No. 2 (1994), pp. 140–164.

mass-produced vehicle for ideas that was a point of contact between the intelligentsia and ordinary readers. But it is possible to imagine a range of other sources that could be equally valuable.

Third, the study has placed emphasis on the way in which narratives of historical change informed ideological contestation. For several decades, social scientists have been drawing attention to the way in which history mediates political thought and behaviour.[5] This tradition of scholarship has done much to aid the study of political ideas. It has been attentive, for instance, to the way in which an actor's location in a sequence of events may determine their receptivity to new ideas. But actors' thinking about temporality is not solely determined by the movement of objective, biological time. Their thought practices are also determined by the stories that are told about the past, present and future.[6] This study has revealed the importance of this insight by illustrating the way in which historical narratives allowed particular ideas to obtain legitimacy. One of the reasons that broadly meritocratic ideas were upheld by a wide range of elite actors in the 1950s is because many of them viewed these ideas in relation to a narrative of social and economic progress. Progressives could regard the attainment of equality of opportunity as the first stage in a longer trajectory of egalitarian progress, while Conservatives could regard it as an engine of social harmony that legitimated inequality. When the narratives of progress that had been forged in the 1950s came under threat, this fragile consensus dissolved. Those on the left began to observe inequalities that could not be resolved by social mobility, while those on the right began to identify the market as a more effective criterion for determining rewards than merit. Moreover, the thinking of actors across the political spectrum tended to

5   Pierson, *Politics in Time*.
6   Emily Robinson, *History, Heritage and Tradition in Contemporary British Politics: Past Politics and Present Histories* (Manchester: Manchester University Press, 2012).

243

be informed by shorter time horizons and a corresponding enthusiasm for abrupt change.

Significantly, the ability of narratives to inform political thinking was not determined by objective material conditions. That is not to say that there was no relationship between such conditions and the ability of certain narratives to become hegemonic. Narratives needed to account for concrete changes in the social environment if they were to be adopted by actors. Yet as Hay and others have argued, ideas must, in the last instance, be conceived as constitutive causal forces.[7] Until an actor draws upon ideas about the social environment in which they are situated, they cannot acquire a sense of their interests. It follows that if we are to reconstruct the ideational environment of the post-war period, we need to uncover the stories that actors told themselves about the social environments that they inhabited.

If we should be sensitive to the agency of ideas, we should also place these ideas within their conditions of production. This study has reminded us of the way in which the production and transmission of ideas are implicated within material, social processes.[8] Books and other material vehicles for ideas are not the unmediated expressions of their authors' beliefs and values; they are products of selection, negotiation and revision, and each of these processes is implicated within a commercial and cultural environment that structures the behaviour of both editors and authors.[9] Once we

---

7   Colin Hay, 'Narrating Crisis: The Discursive Construction of the "Winter of Discontent"', *Sociology*, 30(2), pp. 253–277. Andreas Gofas and Colin Hay, 'Varieties of Ideational Explanation' in Andreas Gofas and Colin Hay (eds), *The Role of Ideas in Political Analysis* (London: Routledge, 2010), p. 50. Lawrence and Sutcliffe-Braithwaite, 'Margaret Thatcher and the Decline of Class Politics', p. 147.

8   Here I draw upon Raymond Williams' cultural materialism. Williams, *Marxism and Literature*, p. 94.

9   Gavin Miller, 'Psychiatric Penguins: Writing on Psychiatry for Penguin Books, c. 1950–c. 1980', *History of the Human Sciences*, Vol. 28, No. 4 (2015), pp. 76–101.

acknowledge this, we are compelled to problematise the notion that ideas can be separated, at an analytical level, from the whole social process that they belong to. Nor should we ignore the materiality of the book itself when we explore the ideas that it contained.[10] The invention of the political paperback did not just make political ideas more accessible; it also made ideas more mobile. In comparison to their hardback equivalents, the compact and distinctive Penguin Specials and Pelicans could be purchased, transported and exchanged much more easily. They were also material signifiers of certain dispositions and identities. When an individual was in possession of a non-fiction Penguin, they were often located within an imagined community of readers.[11]

A related point can be made here. Although it has made reference to the way in which social identities were bound up with political ideas, this study has not employed Penguin as a lens through which to view what we might term the sociology of political knowledge. That is, it has not sought to trace the way in which social relations mediated the production and transmission of ideas about politics. But some of its findings do suggest that if we want to better understand this aspect of political change, tracing the activities of publishers and other producers of ideas might be a very useful exercise. It has demonstrated, for instance, that the ascendency of meritocratic ideas from the 1930s was facilitated by the emergence of new social identities and that the bearers of these identities were often the kinds of individuals who purchased Penguin's non-fiction books. It follows that if we understand the way in which Penguin addressed this audience and framed its needs, we will, in turn, develop a better understanding of the social forces that made ideological change possible. It is also the case that while

---

10 Contemporaries often drew attention to the material qualities of the paperback. Richard Hoggart, 'Report on Paperbacks', *Listener*, 13 October 1960.

11 Richard Hoggart, 'A Penguin Parade' in *Pelican Books: A Sixtieth Anniversary Celebration*, p. 41.

Penguin aspired to democratise knowledge, the vast majority of its authors were white and male. This reflected broader structures of power and had consequences for the kinds of political knowledge that Penguin popularised. Future research on publishers and their relationships with both authors and audiences might illuminate some of these consequences.[12]

Epilogue: Social class in the twenty-first century

In 1988, Penguin terminated the Specials series. The reasoning that informed the decision is not revealed by the Penguin archive. It is possible, however, to identify a number of developments that had eroded the profitability of the imprint. Of particular significance was the expansion of commercial television. As early as 1968, Dieter Pevsner had suggested that television posed challenges to the Pelican tradition: 'the audience, being only human, will demand books so presented that they can at least bear comparison to the vividness and painlessness of television communication'.[13] By the late 1980s, when Channel Four had begun to broadcast current-affairs programmes, television had become an alternative source of political information, and the Specials, whose profitability continued to depend on high volume sales, were particularly threatened by this development.[14]

It is also possible to detect an erosion of the Specials' identity. Prior to the 1970s, Penguin had employed distinctive cover designs to distinguish Specials from their counterparts in other lists. Changes in the way non-fiction books were marketed and sold,

12 The field of book history is becoming attentive to these concerns. See Trysh Travis, 'The Women in Print Movement: History and Implications', *Book History*, Vol. 11 (2008), pp. 275–300.

13 Pevsner, 'The Demands of Another 30 Years'.

14 Ian Savage, who was one of Penguin's marketing managers in the 1970s, has suggested that the proliferation of television coverage served to erode the audience for the Specials series. Author interview with Ian Savage, 9 March 2011.

however, made such practices less effective. One of the most significant developments concerned the way in which bookshops organised their displays. It had once been common for books to be organised by imprint. But an increasing number of retailers began to organise their displays by subject, and it was thus necessary for individual titles to compete for shelf space on the basis of their covers and contents. Mayer acknowledged these changed conditions in 1985. 'The subscription figures for E. P. Thompson's *Protest and Survive*', he wrote, 'will be no greater for being on a Penguin Special than published as a Penguin, as it is E. P. Thompson and the subject that will do the job ... What we need,' he concluded, 'is a commitment to Penguin Specials.'[15] But when subsequent books failed to sell in significant quantities, this commitment quickly dissipated. Of the Specials that were produced in the 1980s, few obtained sales figures in excess of 15,000, and many struggled to sell sufficient copies to return a profit. William Keegan's *Britain without Oil*, for instance, sold only 4,037 copies in the six months after its publication.[16]

It is possible to claim that the commercial decline of the Specials was one symptom of Thatcherite hegemony and a corresponding decline of serious British political thought. Some commentators arrived at such a conclusion. Bernard Crick, who, as we have seen, had been an advisor to Penguin in the 1970s, suggested that the political book had been in decline throughout the post-war period. To support his argument, he drew particular attention to the aforementioned 'Why Vote...?' books that Penguin had published in advance of the 1997 General Election. His chief complaint was that their authors had suppressed their own views in order to reproduce the sterile arguments endorsed by their party leaders. In his view, Penguin's pre-election books had

15 Peter Mayer to Alan Wherry, Peter Carson and Patrick Hutchinson, 28 October 1985. PA: DM1952/618.
16 PA: DM1952/385.

exposed a greater interest in personalities rather than ideas. Crick regarded the decline of the political book as one consequence of the social changes that had taken place in the post-war period. In the 1930s and 1940s, it had been possible for writers like H. G. Wells and Harold Laski to conceptualise a 'common reader' who their books should speak to. By the early 1970s, however, this imagined individual had been replaced by a 'general educated reader' whose identity was more difficult to align with notions of the common good:

> In the 1930s good political books were common, today they are few ... if the proof of the pudding has to be in the eating, then consider Penguin's list of books in print. They used to be the leading non-academic political publisher. Currently there are two and three-quarter columns of books listed under 'Politics' (the majority of them primarily for the university market) and nineteen columns under 'New Age', nearly all written to be accessible to the general reader![17]

This is not the appropriate place to intervene in the debate about the impact that social and economic change has had upon the quality of political debate in Britain. What can be noted, however, is that when Crick identified a decline in the quality of political thinking, his analysis was informed by assumptions that can be contested. He not only assumed that there was a correlation between the abstraction of a political argument and its quality, but he also privileged a conception of citizenship that can be associated with a particular tradition of left-liberal thought. If we were to reject these kinds of prejudices, we might arrive at a different reading of political publishing's trajectory in the late twentieth century.

It is certainly true that many of the social and cultural assumptions that informed non-fiction publishing in the post-war period had been rendered redundant by the 1980s. As one

---

17 Crick, *Essays on Citizenship*, p. 182.

of the final Specials editors noted, 'the old-style Penguin self-help, self-education sort of centre-left publishing has really gone out of fashion'.[18] But it does not necessarily follow that the outcome was a victory for the forces of the right or a sign of an irreversible decline in political publishing. In the period since 1988, a number of independent publishers have successful committed themselves to ambitious programmes of political publishing. And in the last decade, Penguin has re-entered the political fray by re-establishing the Specials as an ebook imprint. The impetus for this decision appeared to be the financial crash of 2008. As the social and economic consequences of this seismic event became apparent, many of the political ideas that had been hegemonic in the preceding decades were brought under scrutiny, and Penguin, alongside other publishers, sought to meet the demand for new ideas that followed.

This is not the place to offer a detailed description of the ideas and arguments that Penguin has helped to popularise in recent years. But it is instructive to consider the way in which its authors have engaged with some of the concepts and themes to which this book has devoted attention. In particular, it is notable how they have intervened in debates about social mobility, class and the role of merit in determining the distribution of rewards.

Of the Pelicans that have been published in recent years, perhaps the most influential has been Mike Savage's *Social Class in the 21st Century*. Based upon the most extensive survey of social attitudes ever to be conducted, the book offers an introduction to the nature of social relations in post-2008 Britain. Savage challenges the view that class has become a less pervasive feature of social life and makes the claim that new forms of inequality have emerged in recent decades. One of the drivers of these inequalities has been the reproduction of neo-liberal ideas about the relationship between markets and the concept of merit. By arguing that the

---

18   Interview with Neil Middleton, September 1984. PA: DM1294/6/2/27.

market is capable of determining the 'merit' of particular forms of labour, advocates of these ideas have concealed both the extent and consequences of the social divisions that continue to mark British society. But, as Savage claims, these kinds of arguments are coming under threat. During the period that coincided with Tony Blair's Labour governments, when relatively high levels of economic growth were able to militate against the social consequences of inequality, it was possible to argue that disparities of reward were commensurable with the improvement of living standards among the poorest sections of the community. In the post-crash environment, however, this argument has worn increasingly thin, and the contradictions of neo-liberalism's distributive logic have been more visible.

To describe neo-liberal conceptions of distributive justice as 'meritocratic' is rather problematic. Their advocates, echoing Margaret Thatcher, tend to employ the concept of merit to prop up claims about the virtues of outcomes that are determined by the operation of the market, and, as we have seen, the market is not necessarily sensitive to the criterion of merit. Nonetheless, neo-liberal discourses do tend to equate freedom with equality of opportunity, and in doing so, they necessarily marginalise conceptions of distributive justice that place emphasis on equality of outcomes. It is this aspect of neo-liberalism's ideological repertoire that is now particularly vulnerable. Evidence is accumulating that inequalities, far from facilitating equal opportunity and social mobility, create a wealthy elite that pulls up the ladder of opportunity behind it. As Savage's study has revealed, 'a highly competitive education system and labour market, it is those who can maximise every possible advantage and who start from the most advantaged positions who are best able to succeed within this meritocratic structure'.[19] If neo-liberal arrangements are increasingly regarded as a threat to, rather than a facilitator of, equality of

---

19   Mike Savage, *Social Class in the 21st Century* (London: Penguin, 2015), p. 400.

opportunity and freedom, it is likely that redistributive policies will become much more acceptable.

But if space is opening up for a politics of equality, it is far from certain what ideas will fill it. In their efforts to construct a basis for such a project, some recent Penguin authors have sought to reimagine the objective of social mobility by shedding it of its neo-liberal logic. Lee Major and Stephen Machin, for instance, have advocated a new model of social mobility that could 'develop all talents, not just academic, but vocational and creative'.[20] Although they address the tensions in neo-liberalism's distributive logic, Major and Machin's arguments are, at times, reminiscent of those that legitimated the post-war meritocratic settlement. They appear to argue that social mobility is a useful ideological objective in itself and, in doing so, presume the need for both a social elite and significant inequities of rewards.

Other advocates for change have embraced a more expansive conception of inequality. In another Pelican, the economist Guy Standing has advocated a system of universal basic income to resolve some of the extreme inequalities that have been produced by the slow erosion of social security budgets and the proliferation of means-tested benefits. The universalism that informs Standing's conception of distributive justice is more reminiscent of the kinds of egalitarian arguments that were advanced by socialists in inter-war Britain. Put simply, he anchors the idea of equality to a communitarian argument about the way in which rewards are distributed: 'Wanting others to have what you want takes courage.'[21]

Whether any of the above arguments can form the basis for a new progressive politics is difficult to anticipate. What is certain,

20 Lee Eliot Major and Stephen Machin, *Social Mobility and Its Enemies* (London: Penguin, 2018), p. 220.
21 Guy Standing, *Basic Income and How We Can Make It Happen* (London: Penguin Random House, 2017), p. 94.

however, is that a battle for ideas is now being waged to determine the nature of a new political settlement, and if this book's arguments about the past have any bearing on the present, then it is likely that any resolution will be determined by the way in which recent history is understood. If an absence of social mobility is understood as the main cause of the social and economic problems of the last decade, it is likely that the existing political settlement will be able to weather the storm without radically modifying the distribution of wealth. But if these problems are understood as a product of structural inequities that have followed from neo-liberal capitalism, it may well be that a different ideology could obtain hegemony. This logic will have to find ways of uniting different social groups behind common objectives, and it will have to overcome resistance from the beneficiaries of inequality. But as Penguin's rich history of non-fiction publishing demonstrates, ideas that are marginalised at one historical moment can quickly become the nodal points around which new political forces can coalesce.

BIBLIOGRAPHY

Archives

Penguin Books Archive, University of Bristol

DM1107
DM1107: Editorial correspondence relating to Penguin Specials and Pelican titles

DM1294
DM1294/1/1: Scrapbook of early press cuttings
DM1819/1/2: General correspondence of Allen Lane
DM1294/3/2/9: Correspondence between Allen Lane and W. E. Williams
DM1294/3/4/3: Papers relating to Anthony Godwin's resignation
DM1294/3/4/4: 'General Research File'
DM1294/3/4/5: Press cuttings and articles, 1960–1969
DM1294/3/5: '1970s General Research File'
DM1294/3/5/3: Penguin Education research file
DM1294/3/6: '1980s General Research File'
DM1294/4/1/20: Copies of *Penguins Progress*, 1950
DM1294/5: Files of correspondence and papers relating Penguin's fiftieth anniversary
DM1294/6/2/27: VHS recording of the BBC's *Penguin Books* programme (1985)
DM1294/10/2: New titles and stock lists of all books published by Penguin

DM1613
DM1613/5/3: Papers relating to Penguin's finances in the 1970s
DM1613/5/7: Peter Mayer's papers relating to Penguin's educational publishing

BIBLIOGRAPHY

DM1819/3/2: Allen Lane's letters
DM1819/3/7: Correspondence relating to *Film Review*
DM1819/11/7: Correspondence relating to *Russia Review*
DM1819/27/10: Papers relating to Anthony Godwin
DM1819/24/2: Correspondence concerning staff members, 1952–1968

DM1843
DM1843/8: Correspondence relating to Richard Hoggart's *The Uses of Literacy*
DM1843/17: Transcripts of interviews with Richard Hoggart, September 1992

DM1952
DM1952/64: List of rejected and unpublished titles
DM1952/612: Pelican and Penguin Education editorial files
DM1952/613: 'General Editorial File'
DM1952/617: Press cuttings, 1954–1974

DM22
DM22/21: Chris Dolley papers
DM22/98: Ian Savage papers (deposited by the author, March 2011)

Churchill Archives Centre, Cambridge University
Quintin Hogg Papers

Modern Records Centre, University of Warwick
Victor Gollancz Papers
Socialist Union records

Nuffield College, University of Oxford
G. D. H. Cole Papers

Albert Sloman Library, University of Sussex
Papers of the Social Democratic Party's Political Philosophy Forum

University College London
Hugh Gaitskell Papers

Newspapers and periodicals

The Bookseller
Encounter

BIBLIOGRAPHY

The Guardian
Horizon
The Listener
London Review of Books
Marxism Today
New Left Review
The New Reasoner
New Society
New Statesman
Penguin News
Picture Post
The Observer
Socialist Commentary
The Spectator
The Times
Universities and Left Review

Personal interviews

Correspondence with Robin Blackburn, 9 October 2010.
Interview with Dieter Pevsner, 19 November 2010.
Interview with Ian Savage, 19 February 2011.

Books published by Penguin Books (place of publication is Harmondsworth unless otherwise stated)

A Blueprint for Survival (1972).
Britain by Mass-Observation (1939).
Hornsey Affair (1969).
May Day Manifesto 1968 (1968).
Science and the Nation (1947).
Science in War (1940).
Twentieth Century Socialism (1956).
Abel-Smith, Brian and Stevens, Robert, *In Search of Justice* (1968).
Acland, Richard, *Unser Kampf* (1940).
Ackroyd, Carol, Margolis, Karen, Rosenhead, Jonathan and Shallice, Tim, *The Technology of Political Control* (1977).
Alderson, Stanley, *Britain in the Sixties: Housing* (1964).
Angell, Norman, *The Great Illusion – Now* (1939).
Angell, Norman, *Why Freedom Matters* (1940).
Bailey, Ron, *The Homeless and the Empty Houses* (1977).

255

Bannock, Graham, *How to Survive the Slump* (1975).

Beattie, Alan, *Who's in Charge Here? How Governments are Failing the World Economy* (London: 2012).

Benn, Tony, *Arguments for Socialism* (1980)

Beteille, Andre, *Social Inequality* (1969).

Bishop, Matthew, *The Future of Jobs* (London: 2012).

Blackburn, Robin and Cockburn, Alexander, *The Incompatibles: Trade Union Militancy and the Consensus* (1967).

Blackburn, Robin and Cockburn, Alexander, *Student Power: Problems, Diagnosis, Action* (1969).

Bottome, Phyllis (ed.), *Our New Order or Hitler's?* (1943).

Burgess, Tyrell (ed.), *Matters of Principle: Labour's Last Chance* (1968).

Calvocoressi, Peter and Wint, Guy, *Middle East Crisis* (1956).

Chapman, Leslie, *Your Disobedient Servant* (1978).

Cobler, Sebastian, *Law, Order and Politics in West Germany* (1978).

Cohen, Gerda, *What's Wrong with Hospitals?* (1964).

Cohn-Bendit, Daniel and Cohn-Bendit, Gabriel, *Obsolete Communism: The Left-wing Alternative* (1968).

Cole, G. D. H., *Practical Economics* (1937).

Cole, G. D. H., *Socialism in Evolution* (1938).

Coombes, B. L., *Miner's Day* (1945).

Coote, Anna and Grant, Lawrence, *Civil Liberty: The NCCL Guide* (1972).

Cox, Barry, *Civil Liberties in Britain* (1975).

Cowie, Harry, *Why Liberal?* (1964).

Crosland, Anthony, Boyle, Edward and Kogan, Maurice, *The Politics of Education* (1971).

Dalton, Hugh, *Hitler's War* (1940).

Darke, Bob, *The Communist Technique in Britain* (1952).

Earle, Nick, *What's Wrong with the Church?* (1961).

Evans, A. J., *Why Not Prosperity?* (1943).

Ferris, Paul, *The New Militants: Crisis in the Trade Unions* (1972).

Fletcher, Ronald, *Britain in the Sixties: The Family and Marriage* (1962).

Foot, Paul, *The Politics of Harold Wilson* (1968).

Fromm, Erich (ed.), *Socialist Humanism* (1967).

Fromm, Erich and Illich, Ivan D., *Celebration of Awareness: A Call for Institutional Revolution* (1973).

Fulford, Roger, *The Liberal Case* (1959)

Galbraith, J. K., *The Affluent Society* (1953)

Garratt, G. T., *Mussolini's Roman Empire* (1938).

Garsia, Clive, *Planning the War* (1939).

Gilder, George, *The Spirit of Enterprise* (Viking, 1985).

Gloag, John, *What about Business?* (1942).

BIBLIOGRAPHY

Glyn, Andrew and Sutcliffe, Bob, *British Capitalism: Workers and the Profits Squeeze* (1972).

Grant Duff, Sheila, *Europe and the Czechs* (1938).

Hadam, John, *Good God* (1940).

Haldane, J. B. S., *The Inequality of Man* (1937).

Haldane, J. B. S., *Science and Everyday Life* (1941).

Hall, Andrew and Wichelow, Anthony, *What's Wrong with Parliament?* (1964).

Harrington, Michael, *The Other America; Poverty in the United States* (1963).

Harrison, Paul, *Inside the Inner City: Life under the Cutting Edge* (1983).

Hattersley, Roy, *Choose Freedom: The Future for Democratic Socialism* (1987).

Head, David (ed.), *Free Way to Learning: Educational Alternatives in Action* (London: Penguin Education, 1974).

Herbert, Mervyn, *Britain's Health* (1939).

Hill, Christopher, *Rights and Wrongs: Some Essays on Human Rights* (1969).

Hogg, Quintin, *The Case for Conservatism* (1947).

Hogg, Quintin (Viscount Hailsham), *The Conservative Case* (1959)

Hoggart, Richard, *The Uses of Literacy* (1958).

Horabin, Tom, *Politics Made Plain* (1944).

Horsefield, J. K, *The Real Cost of War* (1940).

Jay, Douglas, *After the Common Market* (1968).

Jenkins, Roy, *The Labour Case* (1959).

Joll, James, *Antonio Gramsci* (1978).

Kaufman, Gerald (ed.), *Renewal: Labour's Britain in the 1980s* (1983).

Keegan, William, *Mrs Thatcher's Economic Experiment* (1984).

Lapping, Brian, *The Labour Government, 1964–70* (1970).

Laski, Harold, *Liberty in the Modern State* (1938).

Laski, Harold, *Where Do We Go from Here?* (1940).

Lea, John and Young, Jock, *What Is to Be Done about Law and Order?* (London: 1984).

Lewis, Roy and Maude, Angus, *The English Middle Classes* (1949).

Lilienthal, David, *TVA: Democracy on the March* (1944).

Lloyd-Jones, Linda, *Fifty Penguin Years* (London: 1985).

Mackenzie, R. F., *State School* (1970).

Major, Lee Elliot and Machin, Stephen, *Social Mobility and its Enemies* (London: Pelican, 2018).

Malik, Rex, *What's Wrong with British Industry?* (1964).

Marsh, David, *The Future of the Welfare State* (1964).

Martin, Kingsley, *The Crown and the Establishment* (1964).

Mayer, Martin, *Madison Avenue USA* (1961).

McConville, Maureen and Searle, Patrick, *French Revolution 1968* (1968).

Mishan, E. J., *The Costs of Economic Growth* (1971).

Mitchell, Jeanette, *What Is to Be Done about Illness and Health?* (London: 1984).

Mitchell, Juliet and Oakley, Ann (eds), *The Rights and Wrongs of Women* (1976).

Moorhouse, Geoffrey, *Britain in the Sixties: The Other England* (1964).

Mowrer, Edgar, *Germany Puts the Clock Back* (1937).

Nicolson, Harold, *Why Britain Is at War* (1939).

Northcott, Jim, *Why Labour?* (1964).

Oakley, Ann, *Housewife* (1976).

O'Conner, Philip, *Britain in the Sixties: Vagrancy* (1963).

Owen, David, *A Future That Will Work* (London: 1984).

Owen, David, *A United Kingdom* (London: 1986).

Packard, Vance, *The Status Seekers* (1960).

Packard, Vance, *The Waste Makers* (1964).

Parker, John, *Labour Marches On* (1947).

Price, John, *Organised Labour in the War* (1944).

Pritt, D. N., *Light on Moscow* (1939).

Raison, Timothy, *Why Conservative?* (1964).

Reimer, Everett, *School is Dead: An Essay on Alternatives in Education* (1971).

Rogaly, Joe, *Grunwick* (1977).

Rowbotham, Sheila, *Women, the Resistance and the Revolution* (1974).

Rowland, Jon, *Community Decay* (1973).

Rubinstein, David and Stoneman, Colin, *Education for Democracy* (1972).

Russell, Bertrand, *Has Man a Future?* (1961).

Savage, Mike, *Social Class in the 21st Century* (Pelican, 2015).

Segal, Lynee, *What Is to Be Done about the Family?* (London: 1983).

Shanks, Michael, *The Stagnant Society* (1961).

Shaw, Jack, *On Our Conscience: The Plight of the Elderly* (1971).

Shonfield, Andrew, *British Economic Policy since the War* (1958).

Smith, David, *The Rise and Fall of Monetarism: The Theory and Politics of an Economic Experiment* (1987).

Smith, David, *North and South: Britain's Economic, Social and Political Divide* (London: 1989).

Snow, C. P., *Corridors of Power* (1966).

Standing, Guy, *Basic Income: And How We Can Make It Happen* (London: 2017).

Steed, Wickham, *The Press* (1938).

Steward, Michael, *Keynes and after* (1967).

Tabouis, Genevieve, *Blackmail or War?* (1938).

Temple, William, *Christianity and Social Order* (1942).

Thompson, E. P., *Warwick University Ltd* (1970).

Thompson, E. P., *Star Wars* (London: 1985).

Thompson, E. P. and Smith, Dan, *Protest and Survive* (London: 1980).

Thompson, Keith, *Under Siege: Racial Violence in Britain Today* (London: 1988).

Vaizey, John, *Britain in the Sixties: Education for Tomorrow* (1962).

Waddington, C. H., *The Scientific Attitude* (1941).

Wallace, William, *Why Vote Liberal Democrat?* (1997).

Ward, Barbara, *A Policy for the West* (1952).
Wedgwood, Josiah, *The Economics of Inheritance* (1939).
Wells, H. G., *Travels of a Republican Radical in Search of Hot Water* (1939).
Wells, H. G., *The Common Sense of War and Peace* (1940).
Wells, H. G., *The Rights of Man* (1940).
Whitaker, Ben, *The Police* (1964).
Whyte, William, *The Organisation Man* (1960).
Wicks, Malcolm, *A Future for All: Do We Need a Welfare State?* (1987).
Wickham, Henry Steed, *The Press* (1938).
Wigham, Eric, *What's Wrong with the Unions?* (1961).
Willetts, David, *Why Vote Conservative?* (London: 1997).
Williams, Juliette Rhys, *A New Look at Britain's Economic Policy* (1965).
Williams, Raymond, *Britain in the Sixties: Communications* (1962).
Williams, Raymond, *The Long Revolution* (1965).
Williams, Raymond, *Communications* (1970).
Williams, Shirley, *Politics Is for People* (London: 1980).
Williams, Shirley, *A Job to Live* (London: 1985).
Wintringham, Tom, *People's War* (1942).
Wilson, Harold, *The New Britain: Labour's Plan* (1964).
Wright, Tony, *Why Vote Labour?* (1997).
Young, George, *Country and Town* (1943).
Young, Michael, *The Rise of the Meritocracy* (1961)
Young, Wayland, *Strategy for Survival* (1959).

Other published sources

Acland, Richard, *What It Will Be Like in the New Britain* (Gollancz: London, 1942).
Anderson, Perry and Blackburn, Robin (eds), *Towards Socialism* (London: Fontana, 1965).
Beales, H. L., 'Has Labour Come to Stay?', *Political Quarterly*, Vol. 18, No. 1 (1947).
Bell, Daniel, *The End of Ideology* (Glencoe: Free Press, 1960).
Beveridge, William, *Why I Am a Liberal* (London: Herbert Jenkins, 1945).
Bradley, Ian, *The Strange Rebirth of Liberal Britain* (London: Chatto & Windus, 1985).
Brailsford, Henry, *Why Capitalism Means War* (London: Gollancz, 1938).
Butler, David and King, Anthony, *The British General Election of 1964* (London: Macmillan, 1965).
Can Planning Be Democratic? (London: Labour Book Service, 1944).
Cole, G. D. H., 'Chants of Progress', *Political Quarterly*, Vol. 6 (1935) pp. 534–535.
Cole, G. D. H., 'A British People's Front: Why and How?' *Political Quarterly*, Vol. 7 (1936) pp. 490–498.

Cole, G. D. H., *People's Front* (Gollancz: London, 1937).

Cole, G. D. H., *Great Britain in the Post-War World* (London: Gollancz, 1942).

Cole, G. D. H., *Labour's Second Term* (London: Fabian Society, 1949).

Cole, Margaret, *The General Election of 1945 and after* (London, 1945).

Crick, Bernard, *Essays on Citizenship* (London: Continuum, 2004).

Critcher, Chas, Clarke, John, Hall, Stuart and Jefferson, Tony, *Policing the Crisis* (London: Macmillan, 1978).

Crosland, Anthony, *The Future of Socialism* (London: Cape, 1956).

Crosland, Anthony, *Can Labour Win?* (London: Fabian Society, 1960).

Crosland, Anthony, *Socialism Now and Other Essays* (London: Cape, 1974).

Crossman, Richard, *Socialist Values in a Changing Civilisation* (London: Fabian Society, 1951).

Crossman, Richard, *Labour in the Affluent Society* (London: Fabian Society, 1960).

Cox, C. B. and Dyson, A. E., *Black Paper Two: The Crisis in Education* (London, 1969).

Glass, David (ed.), *Social Mobility in Britain* (London: Routledge, 1953).

Green, T. H, *Lectures on the Principles of Political Obligation* (London: Longmans, 1901).

Hall, Stuart, *The Hard Road to Renewal: Thatcherism and Crisis of the Left* (London: Verso, 1988).

Hall, Stuart and Jefferson, Tony, *Resistance through Rituals* (London: Hutchinson, 1976).

Haseler, Stephen, *The Death of British Democracy* (London: Prometheus, 1976).

Hobsbawn, Eric, *The Forward March of Labour Halted* (London: Verso, 1981).

Hobson, J. A., *Wealth and Life: A Study in Values* (London: Macmillan, 1929).

Hoggart, Richard, *An English Temper* (London: Chatto & Windus, 1982).

Hoggart, Richard, *The Way We Live Now* (London: Pimlico, 1995).

Howell, David, *A New Style Emerges* (London: Conservative Political Centre, 1971).

Jewkes, John, *The New Ordeal by Planning* (London: Macmillan, 1968).

Kramnick, Isaac (ed.), *Is Britain Dying? Perspectives on the Current Crisis* (Cornell: Cornell University Press, 1979).

Lane, Allen, 'Books for the Million', *Left Review*, May 1938.

Laski, Harold, *Democracy in Crisis* (London: Allen & Unwin, 1933).

Laski, Harold, *Parliamentary Government in England* (New York: Viking, 1938).

Laski, Harold, *The Decline of Liberalism* (New York: Viking, 1940).

Laski, Harold, *Faith, Reason and Civilisation* (New York: Viking, 1944).

Laski, Harold, *The Rise of European Liberalism* (London: Allen & Unwin, 1947).

Lippmann, Walter, *Public Opinion* (New York: Brace, 1922).

Macmillan, Harold, *The Middle Way* (London: Macmillan & Co., 1938).

Mallock, W. H., *Aristocracy and Evolution: A Study of the Rights, the Origin, and the Social Functions of the Wealthier Classes* (London: Adam and Charles, 1898).

Marshall, T. H. and Bottomore, Tom, *Citizenship and Social Class* (London: Pluto, 1992).

Maschler, Tom (ed.), *Declaration* (London: Macgibbon & Key 1957).

Maude, Angus, *The Common Problem* (London: Constable, 1969).

Miliband, Ralph, *Parliamentary Socialism: A Study in the Politics of Labour* (London: Merlin, 1973).

Millar, Robert, *The New Classes* (London: Longmans, 1966).

Moss, Robert, *The Collapse of Democracy* (London: Sphere, 1977).

Muir, Ramsay, *The Faith of a Liberal* (London: Lovat Dickson, 1933).

Oakeshott, Michael, *Rationalism in Politics and Other Essays* (London: Methuen, 1962).

Owen, David, *Face the Future* (London: Cape, 1981).

Popper, Karl, *The Open Society and Its Enemies* (London: Routledge, 1945).

Priestley, J. B., *English Journey* (London: Gollancz, 1934).

Russell, Bertrand, *Education and the Social Order* (London: Unwin, 1932).

Seldon, Arthur (ed.), *The Rebirth of Britain* (London: Pan, 1964).

Shanks, Michael, *Planning and Politics: The British Experience, 1960–76* (London: Allen & Unwin, 1977).

Snow, C. P., *The Two Cultures* (Cambridge: Cambridge University Press, 1959).

Spender, Stephen, *Forward to Liberalism* (London: Gollancz, 1937).

Strachey, John, *The Coming Struggle for Power* (London: Gollancz, 1937).

Strachey, John, *A Programme for Progress* (London: Gollancz, 1940).

Tawney, R. H., *Equality* (London: Allen & Unwin, 1931).

Tawney, R. H., *The Acquisitive Society* (London: Fontana, 1961).

Thompson, E. P., *Out of Apathy* (London: New Left Books, 1960).

Titmuss, Richard, *The Irresponsible Society* (London: Fabian Society, 1960).

Tribe, David, *The Rise of the Mediocracy* (London: Allen & Unwin, 1975).

Tyrell, R. E. (ed.), *The Future That Doesn't Work: Social Democracy's Failures in Britain* (Doubleday & Co.: New York, 1977).

Unwin, Stanley, *The Truth about Publishing* (London: George Allen & Unwin, 1976).

Vaizey, John, *Education in a Class Society* (London: Fabian Society, 1962).

Vaizey, John, *In Breach of Promise* (London: Littlehampton, 1983).

Williams, W. E. (ed.), *Adult Education in Great Britain and the United States of America* (London: British Institute for Adult Education, 1938).

Williams, W. E., *The Penguin Story* (Harmondsworth: Penguin, 1956).

Zweig, Ferdynand, *The Worker in an Affluent Society: Family Life and Industry* (London: Heinemann, 1962).

Biography

Blackburn, Dean, 'Young, Edward Preston', *Oxford Dictionary of National Biography* (Oxford: Oxford University Press, 2012).

Carpenter, L. P., *G. D. H. Cole* (Cambridge: Cambridge University Press, 1973).

Cockett, Richard, *David Astor and* The Observer (London: Andre Deutsch, 1991).

Crosland, Susan, *Tony Crosland* (London: Cape, 1982).

BIBLIOGRAPHY

Dudley Edwards, Ruth, *Victor Gollancz: A Biography* (London: Gollancz, 1987).
Gold, Ann (ed.), *Edward Boyle* (London: Macmillan, 1991).
Gollancz, Victor, *More for Timothy* (Gollancz: London, 1953), pp. 357–377.
Grant Duff, Sheila, *The Parting of Ways* (London: Owen, 1982).
Jefferys, Kevin, *Anthony Crosland* (London: Politicos, 2008).
Kramnick, Isaac and Sheerman, Barry, *Harold Laski: A Life on the Left* (London: Hamish Hamilton, 1993).
Lehmann, John, *The Whispering Gallery* (London: Longmans, 1955).
Martin, Kingsley, *Harold Laski* (London: Cape, 1969).
Meredeen, Sander, *The Man Who Made Penguins: The Life of William Emrys Williams* (Stroud: Darien-Jones, 2007).
Morpurgo, J. E., *Allen Lane: King Penguin* (London: Hutchinson, 1979).
Newman, Michael, *John Strachey* (Manchester: Manchester University Press, 1989).
Lewis, Geoffrey, *Lord Hailsham* (London: Cape, 1997).
Lewis, Jeremy, *Penguin Special: The Life and Times of Allen Lane* (London: Penguin, 2005).
Storer, Richard, *F. R. Leavis* (London: Routledge, 2009).
Thomas, Hugh, *John Strachey* (New York: Harper & Row, 1973).
Tracey, Michael, *A Variety of Lives: A Biography of Sir Hugh Greene* (London: The Bodley Head, 1983).
Williams, Phillip, *Hugh Gaitskell: A Political Biography* (Oxford: Oxford Paperbacks, 1982).
Williams, W. E., *Allen Lane: A Personal Portrait* (London: The Bodley Head, 1973).

Secondary sources

Abercrombie, Nicholas and Warde, Alan (eds), *Social Change in Contemporary Britain* (Cambridge: Polity Press, 1999).
Addison, Paul, *The Road to 1945* (London: Jonathan Cape, 1975).
Addison, Paul, *Now the War is Over* (London: Jonathan Cape, 1985).
Addison, Paul, 'Consensus Revisited', *Twentieth Century British History*, Vol. 4, No. 1 (1993), p. 91–94.
Addison, Paul, *No Turning Back: The Peaceful Revolutions of Post-war Britain* (Oxford: Oxford University Press, 2010).
Altbach, Philip, 'Publishing and the Intellectual System', *Annals of the American Academy of Political and Social Science*, Vol. 421 (1975), pp. 1–13.
Andrews, Geoff, Cockett, Richard, Hooper, Alan and Williams, Michael (eds), *New Left, New Right and Beyond* (London: Macmillan, 1999).
Apter, David (ed.), *Ideology and Discontent* (New York: Free Press, 1964).
Armstrong, Gary and Gray, Tim, *The Authentic Tawney: A New Interpretation of the Political Thought of R. H. Tawney* (Exeter: Imprint, 2011).

262

BIBLIOGRAPHY

Bailey, Michael, Clarke, Ben and Walton, John K., *Understanding Richard Hoggart* (London: Wiley-Blackwell, 2012).

Baldwin, Peter, *The Politics of Social Solidarity* (Cambridge: Cambridge University Press, 1993).

Ball, Stuart and Seldon, Anthony (eds)., *Recovering Power: The Conservatives in Power since 1867* (Basingstoke: Palgrave, 2005).

Barberis, Peter, 'The Labour Party and Mr Keynes in the 1930s', *Labour History Review*, Vol. 71, No. 2. (2006), p. 153.

Barker, Paul, 'A Tract for the Times', *Political Quarterly*, Vol. 77 (2006), pp. 36–44.

Bates, T. R., 'Gramsci and the Theory of Hegemony', *Journal of the History of Ideas*, Vol. 36, No. 2 (1975), pp. 351–366.

Beach, Abigail and Weight, Richard (eds), *The Right to Belong: Citizenship and National Identity in Britain, 1930–1960* (London: I.B. Tauris, 1998).

Béland, Daniel, *How Ideas and Institutions Shape the Politics of Public Policy* (Cambridge: Cambridge University Press, 2019).

Bellaigue, Eric de, 'The Extraordinary Flight of Book Publishing's Wingless Bird', *Logos*, Vol. 12, No. 3 (2001), p. 75.

Bellaigue, Eric de, *British Book Publishing as a Business since the 1960s* (London: British Library, 2004).

Bentley, Michael, 'Liberal Toryism in the Twentieth Century', *Transactions of the Royal Historical Society*, Vol. 4 (1994), pp. 177–201.

Berthèzene, Clarisse, *Training Minds for the War of Ideas: Ashridge College, the Conservative Party and the Cultural Politics of Britain, 1929–54* (Manchester: Manchester University Press, 2015).

Blaazer, David, *The Popular Front and the Progressive Tradition* (Cambridge: Cambridge University Press, 1992).

Black, Lawrence, 'Social Democracy as a Way of Life: fellowship and the Socialist Union, 1951–59', *Twentieth Century British History*, Vol. 10, No. 4 (1999), pp. 499–539.

Black, Lawrence, *The Political Culture of the Left in Affluent Britain, 1951–64* (Basingstoke: Palgrave, 2003).

Black, Lawrence and Pemberton, Hugh (eds), *An Affluent Society? Britain's Postwar 'Golden Age' Revisited* (London: Ashgate, 2004).

Black, Lawrence et al., *Consensus or Coercion? The State, the People and Social Cohesion in Post-war Britain* (Cheltenham: New Clarion Press, 2001).

Blackledge, Paul, *Perry Anderson, Marxism and the New Left* (London: Marlin, 2004).

Blake, Lord and Patten, John (eds), *The Conservative Opportunity* (London: Macmillan, 1976).

Blyth, Mark, *Great Transformations* (Cambridge: Cambridge University Press, 2002).

Bochel, Hugh, 'One Nation Conservatism and Social Policy, 1951–64', *Journal of Poverty and Social Justice*, Vol. 18, No. 2 (2010), pp. 123–134.

Bogdanor, Vernon and Skidelsky, Robert (eds), *The Age of Affluence* (London: Macmillan, 1970).

Bonham-Carter, Victor, *Dartington Hall: The Formative Years, 1927–1957* (Clarendon: Oxford University Press, 1971).

Bor, Michael, *The Socialist League* (Twickenham: Athena, 2005).

Brooke, Stephen (ed.), *Reform and Reconstruction: Britain after the War, 1945–51* (Manchester: Manchester University Press, 1995).

Brooke, Stephen, 'Living in "New Times": Historicizing 1980s Britain', *History Compass*, Vol. 12, No. 1 (2013), pp. 20–32.

Brown, Kenneth (ed.), *Essays in Anti-Labour History: Responses to the Rise of Labour in Britain* (London: Palgrave, 1994).

Buckler, Steve and Dolowitcz, David, 'Ideology, Party Identity and Renewal', *Journal of Political Ideologies*, Vol. 14, No. 1 (2009), pp. 11–30.

Budge, Ian, 'Relative Decline as a Political Issue', *Contemporary British History*, Vol. 7, No. 1 (1993), pp. 1–23.

Calder, Angus, *The People's War* (London: Pimlico, 1992).

Callaghan, John, *Socialism in Britain* (Blackwell: Oxford, 1990).

Callaghan, John, 'British Labour's Turn to Socialism in 1931', *Journal of Political Ideologies*, Vol. 14, No. 2 (2009), pp. 115–132.

Callaghan, John, Fishman, Nina, Jackson, Ben and McIvor, Martin (eds), *In Search of Social Democracy* (Manchester: Manchester University Press, 2009).

Caute, David, *The Fellow-Travellers* (Yale: Yale University Press, 1988).

Clarke, John and Newman, Janet, *The Managerial State* (London: Sage, 1997).

Clarke, Peter, 'The Progressive Movement', *Transactions of the Royal Historical Society*, Vol. 24 (1974), pp. 166–181.

Clarke, Peter, *Liberals and Social Democrats* (Cambridge: Cambridge University Press, 1981).

Clarke, Peter and Trebilock, Clive (eds), *Understanding Decline: Perceptions and Realities of British Economic Performance* (Cambridge: Cambridge University Press, 1997).

Colander, David and Coates, A. W. (eds), *The Spread of Economic Ideas* (Cambridge: Cambridge University Press, 1989).

Collini, Stefan, *Absent Minds: Intellectual in Britain* (Oxford: Oxford University Press, 2007).

Collini, Stefan, *Common Reading* (Oxford: Oxford University Press, 2008).

Conekin, Becky, Mort, Frank and Waters, Chris (eds), *Moments of Modernity: Reconstructing Britain, 1945–64* (London: Rivers Oram, 1999).

Copsey, Nigel and Olechnowicz, Andrzej (eds), *Varieties of Anti-Fascism* (Basingstoke: Palgrave, 2011).

Cronin, James, *New Labour's Pasts* (London: Longman, 2004).

Cunningham, Valentine, *British Writers of the Thirties* (London: Clarendon, 1989).

BIBLIOGRAPHY

Cutler, Tony, Williams, John and Williams, Karel, *Keynes, Beveridge and Beyond* (London: Routledge, 1986).

Davies, Aled, Freeman, James and Pemberton, Hugh, "'Everyman a Capitalist" or "Free to Choose"? Exploring the Tensions within Thatcherite Individualism', *The Historical Journal*, Vol. 61, No. 2 (2018), pp. 477–501.

Davis, Madeleine, 'Arguing Affluence: New Left Contributions to the Socialist Debate, 1957–63', *Twentieth Century British History*, Vol. 23, No. 4 (2012), pp. 496–528.

Deakin, Nicholas, 'In Search of the Post-war Consensus' (Working Paper: Suntory Toyota Centre for Economics and Related Disciplines, 1987).

Dean, Jodi (ed.), *Cultural Studies and Political Theory* (Ithaca: Cornell University Press, 2000).

Dench, Geoff (ed.), *The Rise and Rise of Meritocracy* (Oxford: Blackwell, 2006).

Dolowitz, David, 'Thatcherism and the Three "Rs": Radicalism, Realism and Rhetoric in the Third Term of the Thatcher Government', *Parliamentary Affairs*, Vol. 49 (1996), pp. 455–470.

Dorey, Peter, *British Conservatism and Trade Unionism, 1945–1964* (Farnham: Ashgate, 2009).

Dutton, David, *British Politics since 1945* (London: Blackwell, 1991).

Dworkin, Dennis, *Cultural Marxism in Postwar Britain* (North Carolina: Duke University Press, 1997).

Dworkin, Dennis, *Class Struggles* (London: Pearson, 2007).

Eatwell, Roger, *The 1945–1951 Labour Governments* (London: Batsford, 1979).

Edgerton, David, 'The Decline of Declinism', *The Business History Review*, Vol. 71, No. 2 (1997), pp. 201–206.

Edgerton, David, *Warfare State: Britain, 1920–70* (Cambridge: Cambridge University Press, 2006).

Edgerton, David, *Britain's War Machine: Weapons, Resources and Experts in the Second World War* (London: Allen Lane, 2011).

Edwards, Amy, '"Financial Consumerism": Citizenship, Consumerism and Capital Ownership in the 1980s', *Contemporary British History*, Vol. 31, No. 2 (2017), pp. 210–299.

Ekrich, Arthur, 'Harold Laski: The Liberal Manque or Lost Libertarian?', *Journal of Libertarian Studies*, Vol. 4, No. 2 (Spring 1980), p. 147.

English, Richard and Kenny, Michael (eds), *Rethinking British Decline* (London: Palgrave, 1999).

Evans, Stephen, 'The Not So Odd Couple: Margaret Thatcher and One Nation Conservatism', *Contemporary British History*, Vol. 23, No. 1 (2009), pp. 101–121.

Favretto, Ilaria, '"Wilsonism" Reconsidered: Labour Party Revisionism, 1952–64', *Contemporary British History*, Vol. 14, No. 4 (2000), pp. 54–80.

Fawcett, Helen, 'The Beveridge Strait-jacket: Policy Formation and the Problem of Poverty in Old Age', *Contemporary British History*, Vol. 10, No. 1 (1996), pp. 20–42.

Feather, John, *A History of British Publishing* (London: Routledge, 2005).

Fielding, Steven, 'Labourism in the 1940s', *Twentieth Century British History*, Vol. 3, No. 2 (1992), pp. 138–153.

Fielding, Steven, 'What Did "the People" Want?: The Meaning of the 1945 General Election', *The Historical Journal*, Vol. 35, No. 3 (1992), pp. 623–639.

Fielding, Steven, 'The Second World War and Popular Radicalism: The Significance of the "Movement Away from Party"', *History*, Vol. 8, No. 258 (1995), pp. 38–58.

Fielding, Steven, Thompson, Peter and Tiratsoo, Nick, *England Arise! The Labour Party and Popular Politics in 1940s Britain* (Manchester: Manchester University Press, 1996).

Foote, Geoffrey, *The Labour Party's Political Thought* (London: Croom Helm, 1985).

Francis, Martin, '"Economics and Ethics": The Nature of Labour's Socialism, 1945–51', *Twentieth Century British History*, Vol. 6, No. 2 (1995), pp. 220–245.

Francis, Martin, *Ideas and Policies under Labour, 1945–51: Building a New Britain* (Manchester: Manchester University Press, 1997).

Francis, Martin and Zweiniger-Bargielowska, Ina (eds), *The Conservative Party and British Society, 1880–1999* (Cardiff: University of Wales Press, 1996).

Fraser, Duncan, 'The Postwar Consensus: A Debate Not Long Enough?', *Parliamentary Affairs*, Vol. 53 (2000), pp. 352–355.

Freeden, Michael, *Liberalism Divided* (Oxford: Oxford University Press, 1986).

Freeden, Michael, 'The Stranger at the Feast: Ideology and Public Policy in Twentieth Century Britain', *Twentieth Century British History*, Vol. 1, No. 1 (1990), pp. 9–34.

Freeden, Michael, *Ideologies and Political Theory: A Conceptual Approach* (London: Clarendon, 1996).

Freeden, Michael, *Liberal Languages* (Princeton: Princeton University Press, 2005).

Garnett, Mark and Hickson, Kevin, *Conservative Thinkers* (Manchester: Manchester University Press, 2009).

George, Vic and Wilding, Paul, *Welfare and Ideology* (Hemel Hempstead: Harvester, 1994).

Goldthorpe, J., 'Social Class Mobility in Modern Britain: Changing Structure, Constant Process', *Journal of the British Academy*, Vol. 4 (2018), pp. 89–111.

Gottlieb, Julie V. and Toye, Richard (eds), *The Aftermath of Suffrage: Women, Gender and Politics in Britain, 1918–1939* (Basingstoke: Palgrave, 2013).

Grant, Matthew, 'Historians, the Penguin Specials and the "State-of-the-Nation" Literature, 1958–1964', *Contemporary British History*, Vol. 17, No. 3 (2003), pp. 23–54.

Green, E. H. H., *Ideologies of Conservatism* (Oxford: Oxford University Press, 2002).

Green, E. H. H. and Tanner, Duncan, *The Strange Survival of Liberal England* (Cambridge: Cambridge University Press, 2007).

Hall, Peter, *The Political Power of Economic Ideas* (Princeton: Princeton University Press, 1989).

Hall, Peter, 'Policy Paradigms, Social Learning and the State', *Comparative Politics*, Vol. 25, No. 3 (1993), pp. 275–296.

Hall, Stuart and Jacques, Martin (eds), *New Times: The Changing Face of Politics in the 1990s* (London: Lawrence & Wishart, 1989).

Hampton, Mark, *Vision of the Press in Britain, 1859–1950* (Champaign: University of Illinois Press, 2005).

Hare, Steve, *Penguin Portrait: Allen Lane and the Penguin Editors, 1935–1970* (London: Penguin, 1995).

Harker, Ben, '"Communism is English": Edgell Rickword, Jack Lindsay and the Cultural Politics of the Popular Front', *Literature & History*, Vol. 16, No. 2 (2011), pp. 16–34.

Harris, Jose, 'Political Ideas and the Debate on State Welfare, 1940–45' in Smith, H. L. (ed.), *War and Social Change* (Manchester: Manchester University Press, 1986), pp. 233–263.

Harris, Jose, 'War and Social History: Britain and the Home Front during the Second World War', *Contemporary European History*, Vol. 1, No. 1 (1992), p. 25.

Harris, Jose, 'War Socialism and Its Aftermath: Debates about a New Social and Economic Order in Britain, 1945–50' in Dominik Geppert (ed.), *The Postwar Challenge* (Oxford: Oxford University Press, 2003), pp. 179–186.

Harrison, Brian, *Peaceable Kingdom* (Oxford: Clarendon, 1992).

Harrison, Brian, 'The Rise, Fall and Rise of Political Consensus in Britain since 1940', *History*, Vol. 84 (1999), pp. 301–324.

Harrison, Rodney, 'Observing, Collecting and Governing "Ourselves" and "Others": Mass-Observation's Fieldwork Agencements', *History and Anthropology*, Vol. 25, No. 2 (2014), pp. 227–245.

Harrison, Tom and Madge, Charles, *Mass Observation Series: Number One* (London: Fredrick Miller, 1937).

Haseler, Stephen, *The Gaitskellites: Revisionism in the British Labour Party, 1951–64* (London: Macmillan, 1969).

Haseler, Stephen, *The Battle for Britain* (London: Taurus, 1989).

Hawkins, Carrol, 'Laski: A Preliminary Analysis', *Political Science Quarterly*, Vol. 65, No. 3 (1950), pp. 376–392.

Hay, Colin, *Re-stating Social and Political Change* (London: Open University Press, 1996).

Hay, Colin, 'Crisis and the Structural Transformation of the State: Interrogating the Process of Change', *British Journal of Politics and International Relations*, Vol. 1, No. 3 (1999), pp. 317–344.

Hay, Colin, *The Political Economy of New Labour* (Manchester: Manchester University Press, 1999).

BIBLIOGRAPHY

Hay, Colin, *Political Analysis* (Basingstoke: Palgrave, 2002).

Hay, Colin and Gofas, Andreas (eds), *The Role of Ideas in Political Analysis* (London: Routledge, 2009).

Heffernan, Richard, *New Labour and Thatcherism* (Basingstoke: Palgrave, 2001).

Hennessy, Peter, *Establishment and Meritocracy* (London: Haus, 2013).

Hewison, Robert, *Culture and Consensus: England, Art and Politics since 1940* (London: Methuen, 1995).

Hickson, Kevin, 'Post-war Consensus Re-visited', *Political Quarterly*, Vol. 75, No. 2 (2004), pp. 142–154.

Hilliard, Christopher, *To Exercise Our Talents: The Democratization of Writing in Britain* (Harvard: Harvard University Press, 2006).

Hilliard, Christopher, 'Producers by Hand and by Brain: Working-Class Writers and Left-Wing Publishers in 1930s Britain', *Journal of Modern History*, Vol. 78, No. 1 (2006), pp. 37–64.

Hills, J., Ditch, J. and Glennerster, H. (eds), *Beveridge and Social Security: An International Perspective* (Oxford: Oxford University Press, 1994).

Hilson, Mary and Melling, Joseph, 'Public Gifts and Political Identities: Sir Richard Acland, Common Wealth and the Moral Politics of Land Ownership in the 1940s', *Twentieth Century British History*, Vol. 11, No. 2 (2000), pp. 156–182.

Hilton, Matthew, Moores, Chris and Sutcliffe-Braithwaite, Florence, 'New Times Revisited: Britain in the 1980s', *Contemporary British History*, Vol. 31, No. 2 (2017), pp. 145–165.

Hoefferle, Caroline, *British Student Activism in the Long Sixties* (London: Routledge, 2013).

Holman, Valerie, *Print for Victory: Book Publishing in England, 1939–45* (London: British Library, 2008).

Hoover, Kenneth, 'Ideologizing Institutions: Laski, Hayek, Keynes and the Creation of Contemporary Politics', *Journal of Political Ideologies*, Vol. 4, No. 1 (1999), pp. 87–115.

Hopkinson, Tom, *Picture Post, 1938–50* (London: Allen Lane, 1970).

Hornsey, Richard, '"The Penguins Are Coming": Brand Mascots and Utopian Mass Consumption in Interwar Britain', *Journal of British Studies*, Vol. 57 (October 2018), pp. 812–839.

Horowitz, Daniel, *Vance Packard and American Social Criticism* (Chapel Hill: University of North Carolina, 1994).

Howell, David, *British Social Democracy* (London: Croom Helm, 1980).

Howell, David, 'Wilson and History: "1966 and All That"', *Twentieth Century British History*, Vol. 4, No. 2 (1993), pp. 174–187.

Hubble, Nick, *Mass Observation and Everyday Life* (Basingstoke: Palgrave, 2005).

Hunter, Ian and Reynolds, Jaime, 'Liberal Class Warrior', *Journal of Liberal History*, Vol. 28 (2000), pp. 17–21.

BIBLIOGRAPHY

Hutton, Alexander, "'A Repository, a Switchboard, a Dynamo'": H. L. Beales, a Historian in a Mass Media Age', *Contemporary British History*, Vol. 30, No. 3 (2016), pp. 407–426.

Ironside, Philip, *The Social and Political Thought of Bertrand Russell: The Development of an Aristocratic Liberalism* (Cambridge: Cambridge University Press, 1996).

Jackson, Ben, 'Revisionism Reconsidered: "The Property-owning Democracy" and Egalitarian Strategy in Post-war Britain', *Twentieth Century British History*, Vol. 16, No. 4 (2005), pp. 416–440.

Jackson, Ben, *Equality and the British Left* (Manchester: Manchester University Press, 2007).

Jackson, Ben and Saunders, Robert (eds), *Making Thatcher's Britain* (Cambridge: Cambridge University Press, 2012).

Jackson, Ben and Stears, Marc (eds), *Liberalism as Ideology: Essays in Honour of Michael Freeden* (Oxford: Oxford University Press, 2012).

Jacques, Martin and Mulhern, Francis (eds), *The Forward March of Labour Halted?* (London: Verso, 1981).

James, Simon and Preston, Virginia (eds), *British Politics since 1945* (Palgrave: London, 2001).

Jarvis, Mark, *Conservative Governments, Morality and Social Change in Affluent Britain, 1957–64* (Manchester: Manchester University Press, 2005).

Jefferys, Kevin, 'British Politics and Social Change during the Second World War', *The Historical Journal*, Vol. 30 (1987), pp. 123–144.

Jefferys, Kevin, *Retreat from New Jerusalem: British Politics 1951–64* (Basingstoke: Macmillan, 1997).

Jefferys, Kevin, *Politics and the People* (London: Atlantic, 2007).

Joicey, Nicholas, 'A Paperback Guide to Progress: Penguin Books, 1935–c.1951', *Twentieth Century British History*, Vol. 4, No. 1 (1993), p. 55.

Jones, H. and Brivati, Brian (eds), *What Difference Did the War Make?* (Leicester: Leicester University Press, 1993).

Jones, Tudor, *Remaking the Labour Party: From Gaitskell to Blair* (London: Routledge, 1996).

Joyce, Peter, 'The Liberal Party and the Popular Front', *Journal of Liberal History*, Vol. 28 (2000), pp. 10–16.

Jupp, James, *The Radical Left in Britain, 1931–1941* (London: Frank Cass, 1982).

Kandiah, Michael and Jones, Harriet (eds), *The Myth of Consensus* (London: Macmillan, 1996).

Kandiah, Michael, Hopkins, Michael and Staerck, Gillian (eds), *Cold War Britain, 1951–64* (London: Palgrave, 2003).

Kavanagh, Dennis, *Thatcherism and British Politics: The End of Consensus?* (Oxford: Oxford University Press, 1997).

Kavanagh, Dennis and Morris, Peter, *Consensus Politics from Attlee to Thatcher* (London: Blackwell, 1994).

Kelly, Richard (ed.), *Changing Party Policy in Britain: An Introduction* (Oxford: Blackwell, 1999).

Kenny, Michael, *The First New Left* (London: Lawrence & Wishart, 1995).

Kent, John, *William Temple: Church, State and Society in Britain, 1890–1944* (Cambridge: Cambridge University Press, 1992).

Kerr, Peter, *Post-war British Politics: From Conflict to Consensus* (London: Routledge, 2001).

King, Anthony and Wyman, Robert, *British Political Opinion, 1937–2000* (London: Politicos, 2001).

Kingsford, R. J. L., *The Publishers Association, 1896–1946* (Cambridge: Cambridge University Press, 1970).

Kynaston, David, *Austerity Britain, 1945–51* (London: Bloomsbury, 2007).

Laing, Stuart, *Representation of Working Class Life, 1957–1964* (London: Macmillan, 1986).

Lamb, Peter, 'Laski's Ideological Metamorphosis', *Journal of Political Ideologies*, Vol. 4, No. 2 (1999), pp. 239–260.

Lamb, Peter and Morrice, David, 'Ideological Reconciliation in the Thought of Harold Laski and C. B. Macpherson', *Canadian Journal of Political Science*, Vol. 35, No. 4 (2002), pp. 795–810.

Lawrence, Jon, 'Class, "Affluence" and the Study of Everyday Life in Britain, c. 1930–64', *Cultural and Social History*, Vol. 10, No. 2 (2013), pp. 273–299.

Laybourn, Keith, *Marxism in Great Britain* (London: Routledge, 2006).

Lee, Richard, *Life and Times of Cultural Studies* (North Carolina: Duke, 2003).

LeMahieu, D. L., *A Culture for Democracy: Mass Communication and the Cultivated Mind in Britain Between the Wars* (Oxford: Clarendon, 1998).

Littler, Jo, *Against Meritocracy: Culture, Power and Myths of Mobility* (Oxford: Routledge, 2018).

Long, David, *Towards a New Liberal Internationalism: The International Theory of J. A. Hobson* (Cambridge: Cambridge University Press, 2008).

Lowe, Rodney, 'The Second World War, Consensus, and the Foundation of the Welfare State', *Twentieth Century British History*, Vol. 1, No. 2 (1990), pp. 152–182.

Lowe, Rodney, 'The Replanning of the Welfare State' in M. Francis and I. Zweiniger-Bargielowska (eds), *The Conservatives and British Society 1880–1990* (Cardiff: University of Wales Press, 1996), pp. 255–273.

Maddison, Angus, *Economic Growth in the West* (London: Allen & Unwin, 1964).

Mandler, Peter, '"Good Reading for the Million": The "Paperback Revolution" and the Diffusion of Academic Knowledge in Mid-20th Century Britain and America', Eugene Lunn Memorial Lecture, UC Davis, 3 April 2015, https://video.ucdavis.edu/media/0_mcuv32lu (accessed 18 September 2020).

Marquand, David, *The Progressive Dilemma* (London: Weidenfeld & Nicolson, 1999).

Marquand, David and Seldon, Anthony (eds), *The Ideas That Shaped Post-War Britain* (London: Fontana, 1996).

Marsh, David et al., *British Postwar Politics in Perspective* (Cambridge: Polity Press, 1999).

Marwick, Arthur, 'Middle Opinion in the Thirties: Planning, Progress and Political "Agreement"', *English Historical Review*, Vol. 79 (1964), pp. 285–298.

Matthijs, Matthias, *Ideas and Economic Crises in Britain from Attlee to Blair* (London: Routledge, 2011).

McCleery, Alistair, 'The Return of the Book Publisher to Book History: The Case of Allen Lane', *Book History*, No. 5 (2002), pp. 164–165.

McCleery, Alistair, 'The Paperback Evolution: Tauchnitz, Albatross and Penguin' in Nickianne Matthews and Nicole Moody, Judging a Book by Its Cover (London: Ashgate, 2007), pp. 3–18.

McCulloch, Gary, '"Teachers and Missionaries": The Left Book Club as an Educational Agency', *Journal of the History of Education Society*, Vol. 14, No. 2 (1985), pp. 137–153.

McKibbin, Ross, *Classes and Cultures: England: 1918–1951* (Oxford: Oxford University Press, 1998).

McKibbin, Ross, *Parties and People* (Oxford: Oxford University Press, 2010).

Mercer, Neil, 'Mass Observation 1937–40: The Range of Research Methods' (Working Papers in Applied Social Research: Manchester University Press, 1989).

Meseguer, Covadonga, 'Policy Learning, Policy Diffusion and the Making of a New Order', *The Annals of the American Academy of Political and Social Science*, Vol. 598, No. 1 (2005), pp. 67–82.

Mitchell, Stuart, *The Brief and Turbulent Life of Modernising Conservatism* (Newcastle: Cambridge Scholars, 2006).

Moores, Christopher, 'From Civil Liberties to Human Rights? British Civil Liberties Activism and Universal Human Rights', *Contemporary European History*, Vol. 21, No. 2 (2012), pp. 169–192.

Morgan, David and Evans, Mary, *The Battle for Britain: Citizenship and Ideology in the Second World War* (London: Routledge, 2002).

Morgan, K. O., *The People's Peace* (Oxford: Oxford University Press, 1999).

Morgan, K. O., *Ages of Reform* (London: I.B. Tauris, 2010).

Negrine, Ralph, *Politics and the Mass Media in Britain* (London: Routledge, 1994).

Nevin, Michael, *The Age of Illusions: The Political Economy of Britain, 1968–1982* (London: Gollancz, 1983).

Norrie, Ian, *Publishing and Bookselling: 1870–1970* (London: Cape, 1974).

Nuttall, Jeremy, *Psychological Socialism* (Manchester: Manchester University Press, 2006).

Nuttall, Jeremy, 'Equality and Freedom: The Single, Multiple and Synthesis in Labour Party Thought since the 1930s', *Journal of Political Ideologies*, Vol. 13 (2008), pp. 11–36.

O'Hara, Glen, *From Dreams to Disillusionment: Economic and Social Planning in 1960s Britain* (London: Macmillan, 2007).

O'Hara, Glen, 'This Is What Growth Does': British Views of the European Economies in the Prosperous 'Golden Age' of 1951–73', *Journal of Contemporary History* Vol. 44, No. 4 (October 2009), pp. 697–718.

Oliver, Michael and Pemberton, Hugh, 'Learning and Change in Twentieth Century British Economic Policy', *Governance*, Vol. 17, No. 3 (2004), pp. 415–441.

Ortolano, Guy, 'Decline as a Weapon in Cultural Politics' in Wm. Roger Louis (ed.), *Penultimate Adventures with Britannia: Personalities, Politics and Culture in Britain* (London: I.B. Tauris, 2005), pp. 201–211.

Ortolano, Guy, *The Two Cultures Controversy: Science, Literature and Cultural Politics in Postwar Britain* (Cambridge: Cambridge University Press, 2009).

Ortolano, Guy, *Thatcher's Progress: From Social Democracy to Market Liberalism through an English New Town* (Cambridge: Cambridge University Press, 2019).

Overy, Richard, *The Morbid Age: Britain and the Crisis of Civilisation, 1919–1939* (London: Penguin, 2010).

Owen, Sue (ed.), *Richard Hoggart and Cultural Studies* (London: Macmillan, 2008).

Parsons, Wayne, *The Power of the Financial Press: Journalism and Economic Opinion in Britain and America* (Aldershot: Edgar, 1989).

Peden, G. C., *British Economic and Social Policy: From Lloyd George to Margaret Thatcher* (Oxford: Philip Allen, 1985).

Peden, G. C., *The Treasury and British Public Policy, 1906–1959* (Oxford: Oxford University Press, 2000).

Pelling, Henry, 'The 1945 General Election Reconsidered', *The Historical Journal*, Vol. 23 (1980), pp. 399–314.

Pemberton, Hugh, *Policy Learning and British Governance in the 1960s* (Basingstoke: Palgrave, 2004).

Pemberton, Hugh, 'Relative Decline and British Economic Policy in the 1960s', *The Historical Journal*, Vol. 47, No. 4 (2004), pp. 989–1013.

Pennybacker, Susan D., 'Mass Observation Redux', History Workshop Journal, Vol. 64, No. 1 (2007), pp. 411–419.

Perkin, Harold, *The Rise of Professional Society: England since 1880* (London: Routledge, 1989).

Pickering, Jeffrey, *Britain's Withdrawal from East of Suez* (London: Palgrave, 1998).

Pimlott, Ben, *Labour and the Left in the 1930s* (Cambridge: Cambridge University Press, 1977).

Pollard, Sidney, *The Development of the British Economy, 1914–1990* (London: Edward Arnold, 1992).

Pugh, Martin, 'The Liberal Party and the Popular Front', *English Historical Review*, Vol. 494 (2006), pp. 1327–1350.

Raison, Timothy, *Tories and the Welfare State* (London: Macmillan, 1990).

Renwick, Chris 'Eugenics, Population Research, and Social Mobility Studies in Early and Mid-Twentieth Century Britain', *The Historical Journal*, Vol. 59, No. 3 (2015), pp. 845–867.

Renwick, Chris, *Bread for All: The Origins of the Welfare State* (London: Allen Lane, 2017).

Renwick, Chris 'Movement, Space and Social Mobility in Early and Mid-Twentieth-Century Britain' in *Cultural and Social History*, Vol. 16, No. 1 (2019), p. 24.

Ritschel, Daniel, 'The Making of Consensus: The Nuffield College Conferences during the Second World War', *Twentieth Century British History*, Vol. 6, No. 3 (1995), pp. 267–301.

Ritschel, Daniel, *The Politics of Planning* (Oxford: Clarendon, 1997).

Robinson, Emily, Schofield, Camilla, Sutcliffe-Braithwaite, Florence and Thomlinson, Natalie, 'Telling Stories about Post-War Britain: Popular Individualism and the "Crisis" of the 1970s', *Twentieth Century British History*, Vol. 28, No. 2 (2017), pp. 268–304.

Rodgers, Terence, 'The Right Book Club: Text Wars, Modernity and Cultural Politics in the Late Thirties', *Literature & History*, Vol. 12, No. 2 (2003), pp. 1–15.

Rose, Hilary, 'Rereading Titmuss', *Journal of Social Policy*, Vol. 10, No. 4 (1981).

Rose, Jonathan, *The Intellectual Life of the British Working Classes* (London: Yale University Press, 2010).

Rose, Sonya, *Which People's War? National Identity and Citizenship in Wartime Britain 1939–1945* (Oxford: Oxford University Press, 2004).

Rylance, Rick, 'Reading with a Mission: The Public Sphere of Penguin Books', *Critical Quarterly*, Vol. 47, No. 4 (2005), pp. 48–66.

Samuels, Stuart, 'The Left Book Club', *Journal of Contemporary History*, Vol. 1, No. 2 (1966), pp. 65–86.

Savage, Mike, *Identities and Social Change in Britain since 1940: The Politics of Method* (Oxford: Oxford University Press, 2010).

Savage, Mike and Majima, Shinobu, 'Contesting Affluence: An Introduction', *Contemporary British History*, Vol. 22, No. 4 (2008), pp. 445–455.

Savage, Mike, Barlow, James, Dickens, Paul and Fielding, Tom, *Property, Bureaucracy and Culture: Middle-Class Formation in Contemporary Britain* (London: Routledge, 1992)

Scarbrough, Elinor, *Political Ideology and Voting* (Oxford: Clarendon, 1984).

Searle, G. R., *The Quest for National Efficiency: A Study in British Politics and Political Thought, 1899–1914* (London: Blackwell, 1971).

Seldon, Anthony, 'Consensus: A Debate Too Long?', *Parliamentary Affairs*, Vol. 47, No. 4 (1994), pp. 501–514.

Seymour-Ure, Colin., *The Political Impact of Mass Media* (London: Constable, 1994).

Shaw, Tony, 'Britain and the Cultural Cold War', *Contemporary British History*, Vol. 19, No. 2 (2005), pp. 109–115.

Sinfield, Alan, *Literature, Politics and Culture in Postwar Britain* (London: Continuum, 2004).

Skinner, Quentin, *Visions of Politics: Volume One* (Cambridge: Cambridge University Press, 2010).

Sloman, Peter, 'Rethinking a Progressive Moment: The Liberal and Labour Parties in the 1945 General Election', *Historical Research*, Vol. 84, No. 226 (2011), pp. 722–744.

Smith, L. M. (ed.), *The Making of Britain: Echoes of Greatness* (London: Macmillan, 1988).

Stanley, Nick, 'The Extra Dimension: A Study and Assessment of the Methods Employed by Mass-Observation in Its First Period 1937–40' (PhD thesis, Birmingham Polytechnic, 1981).

Stapleton, Julia, 'Resisting the Centre at the Extremes: "English" Liberalism in the Political Thought of Inter-war Britain', *British Journal of Politics and International Relations*, Vol. 1, No. 3 (1999), pp. 270–292.

Stapleton, Julia, *Political Intellectuals and Public Identities* (Manchester: Manchester University Press, 2001).

Stark, G., *Entrepreneurs of Ideology: Neoconservative Publishers in Germany, 1890–1933* (Chapel Hill: University of North Carolina Press, 1981).

Steele, Tom, *The Emergence of Cultural Studies, 1945–65* (London: Lawrence & Wishart, 1997).

Stephenson, Hugh, *Mrs Thatcher's First Year* (London: Jill Norman, 1980).

Stephenson, Hugh, *Claret and Chips: The Rise of the SPD* (London: Michael Joseph, 1982).

Stevenson, Ian, *Book Makers: British Publishing in the Twentieth Century* (London: British Library, 2010).

Stone, Dan, *Responses to Nazism in Britain, 1933–39* (Basingstoke: Palgrave, 2003).

Summerfield, Penny, 'Mass-Observation: Social Research or Social Movement?', *Journal of Contemporary History*, Vol. 20, No. 3 (1985), pp. 439–452.

Sutcliffe-Braithwaite, Florence, *Class, Politics and the Decline of Deference in England, 1968–2000* (Oxford: Oxford University Press, 2018).

Sutherland, John, *Bestsellers: Popular Fiction of the 1970s* (London: Routledge, 1981).

Swann, Brenda and Aprahamian, Francis (eds), *J. D. Bernal: A Life in Science and Politics* (London: Verso, 1999), p. 172.

Symons, Julian, *The Thirties* (Faber and Faber: London, 1975).

274

Taylor, Richard, *Against the Bomb: The British Peace Movement, 1958–1965* (Oxford: Clarendon, 1998).

Themelis, Spyros, 'Meritocracy through Education and Social Mobility in Postwar Britain: A Critical Examination', *British Journal of Sociology of Education*, Vol. 29, No. 5 (2007), pp. 427–438.

Thomas, James, *Popular Newspapers, the Labour Party and British Politics* (London: Routledge, 2005).

Thompson, Denys, (ed.), *The Leavises* (Cambridge: Cambridge University Press, 1984).

Thompson, Duncan, *Pessimism of the Intellect? A History of the* New Left Review (Monmouth: Merlin, 2007).

Thompson, James, '"Pictorial lies"? Posters and Politics in Britain, 1880–1914', *Past and Present*, Vol. 197 (November 2007), pp. 177–210.

Thompson, John, *Merchants of Culture: The Publishing Business in the Twenty-First Century* (London: Polity Press, 2010).

Thompson, Noel, *Left in the Wilderness* (Acumen: Chesham, 2002).

Thompson, Noel, 'Socialist Political Economy in an Age of Affluence: The Reception of J. K. Galbraith by the British Social Democratic Left in the 1950s and 1960s', *Twentieth Century British History*, Vol. 21, No. 1 (2010), pp. 50–79.

Thorpe, Andrew, 'Reasons for "Progressive" Disunity: Labour and Liberal Politics in Britain, 1918–45', *Socialist History*, Vol. 27 (2005), pp. 21–42.

Tichelar, Michael, 'The Labour Party, Agricultural Policy and the Retreat from Rural Land Nationalisation during the Second World War', *Agricultural History Review*, Vol. 52, No. 2 (2003), pp. 209–225.

Tichelar, Michael, *The Failure of Land Reform in Twentieth-Century England: The Triumph of Private Property* (London: Routledge, 2018).

Tiratsoo, Nick, *Reconstruction, Affluence and Labour Politics: Coventry, 1945–60* (London: Routledge, 1990).

Tiratsoo, Nick (ed.), *The Attlee Years* (London: Pinter, 1991).

Tomlinson, Jim, 'Inventing "Decline": The Falling Behind of the British Economy in the Postwar Years', *Economic History Review*, Vol. 49, No. 4 (1996), pp. 731–757.

Tomlinson, Jim, *The Politics of Decline* (London: Longman, 2000).

Tomlinson, Jim, 'The Decline of the Empire and the Economic "Decline" of Britain', *Twentieth Century British History*, Vol. 14, No. 3 (2003), pp. 201–221.

Tomlinson, Jim, *The Labour Governments, 1964–70: Economic Policy* (Manchester: Manchester University Press, 2004).

Tomlinson, Jim, 'Thrice Denied: "Declinism" as a Recurrent Theme in British History in the Long Twentieth Century', *Twentieth Century British History*, Vol. 20, No. 2 (2009), pp. 227–251.

Tomlinson, Jim, 'Deindustrialization not Decline: A New Metanarrative for Post-War British History', *Twentieth Century British History*, Vol. 27, No. 1 (2016), pp. 76–99.

Toye, Richard, 'Keynes, the Labour Movement and "How to Pay for the War"', *Twentieth Century British History*, Vol. 10, No. 9 (1999), pp. 255–281.

Toye, Richard, *The Labour Party and the Planned Economy, 1931–51* (London: Royal Historical Society, 2003).

Toye, Richard, 'H. G. Wells and the New Liberalism', *Twentieth Century British History*, Vol. 18, No. 2 (2008), pp. 156–185.

Toye, Richard, 'From "Consensus" to "Common Ground": The Rhetoric of the Post-war Settlement and Its Collapse', *Journal of Contemporary History*, Vol. 41, No. 1 (2013), pp. 3–23.

Underhill, F. H., 'Philosophy and Politics', *International Journal*, Vol. 4, No. 1 (1948), pp. 60–66.

Walsha, Robert, 'The One Nation Group and One Nation Conservatism', *Contemporary British History*, Vol. 17. No. 2 (2003), pp. 69–120.

Warde, Alan, *Consensus and Beyond: The Development of Labour Party Strategy since the Second World War* (Manchester: Manchester University Press, 1982).

Waxman, Chaim I. (ed.), *The End of Ideology Debate* (New York: Clarion, 1969).

Webber, G. C., *The Ideology of the British Right, 1918–39* (London: Croom Helm, 1986).

Wickham-Jones, Mark, 'Monetarism and Its Critics: The University Economists' Protest of 1981', *Political Quarterly*, Vol. 63, No. 2 (1992), pp. 171–185.

Wild, Jonathan, '"Insects in Letters": John O' London's Weekly and the New Reading Public', *Literature & History*, Vol. 15, No. 2 (2006), pp. 50–62.

Winter, Jay (ed.), *The Working Class in Modern British History* (Cambridge: Cambridge University Press, 1983).

Wright, A. W., *G. D. H. Cole and Socialist Democracy* (Oxford: Clarendon Press, 1979).

Zweiniger-Bargielowska, Ina, 'Rationing, Austerity and the Conservative Party Recovery after 1945', *The Historical Journal*, Vol. 37, No. 1 (1994), pp. 173–197.

Zweiniger-Bargielowska, Ina, *Austerity in Britain* (Oxford: Oxford University Press, 2000).

INDEX

Abrams, Mark 113–114, 160
Acland, Richard 24, 44, 47, 91
affluence 106, 107, 125, 129–132,
    149–158, 172, 179, 188
Alderson, Stanley 154, 155,
    160–161
Alvarez, Al 136
Ambrose, Peter 184
Angell, Norman 43, 44–45, 46, 72
Arblaster, Anthony 192
Arvill, Robert 193–194
Attlee, Clement 102, 109, 143
    see also Labour party

BBC 17, 140
Beales, H. L. 22, 108
Bell, Clive 56–57
Bell, Daniel 125, 126
Beveridge, William 5, 70, 72, 100,
    187, 203, 242
Blair, Tony 236–237
Bodley Head, The 11
Bottome, Phyllis 80, 81, 89,
    99–100
Boyle, Edward 199–201
Boyson, Rhodes 200
Burgess, Tyrell 180
Burnham, James 114–115

Campaign for Nuclear
    Disarmament 139
Chalmers-Mitchell, Peter 40
Churchill, Winston 79, 81, 108
citizenship 19, 27, 32, 35–37,
    46–48, 55–60, 86–96,
    100–102, 147, 150, 187–190,
    196, 229, 248
    see also professionalism
class,
    and cultural politics 129–131,
        170, 216, 218–229
    and Penguin Books 3, 11–14,
        17–22, 34, 36–37, 68
    and political thought 40, 42,
        46–49, 54–57, 72, 78, 82, 96,
        100–102, 106–109, 112–122,
        125–127, 152–153, 155,
        158–163, 167–168, 179, 184,
        185–191, 198, 206, 239,
        246–252
Coates, Ken 186–187
Cold War 126, 128, 139–140
Cole, G. D. H. 38–40, 72, 97–98
Cole, Margaret 33–34, 60
Colenutt, Bob 184
Communist Party of Great Britain
    49, 127

consensus, post-war 4–8, 15, 48,
    76–78, 94, 101–103, 106,
    108–112, 134, 162, 169,
    202–204, 212–214, 240–242
Conservative party 81, 145, 196,
    200–204
Cox, Caroline 200
Crankshaw, Edward 128
Crick, Bernard 205–206, 247–248
crisis 2–3, 37–45, 65, 177, 181–185,
    222
Crosland, Anthony 9, 113–114, 116,
    150–151, 171, 229
Crossman, Richard 147, 151, 156
Curry, W. B. 61, 71

decline 133–135, 139–149,
    158–163, 181–183

Eden, Anthony 140
education 12–15, 18–19, 52–61, 81,
    86, 90–92, 100–102, 110–112,
    116–117, 120, 125, 131, 153,
    164, 168, 189, 191–192, 199, 250
elections 108, 113, 166–170, 178,
    210, 234
embourgeoisement 113
entrepreneurialism 144, 146,
    162–163, 166, 172, 196,
    219–220, 222
environmental politics 193–195
equality 41–42, 56, 69–74, 81–82,
    86–87, 89–91, 102, 106,
    109–111, 116–118, 145–147,
    158–163, 169, 174, 180, 193,
    203, 213–214, 227–228,
    239–241
    see also meritocracy
Evans, A. J. 88–89
expertise 6, 31, 52–59, 61, 63,
    64, 67–68, 83, 92, 107, 119,
    198, 223
    see also professionalism

Fanti, Giorgio 157
fascism 40, 42–48, 50, 73, 79
feminism 137, 192–193
Flanders, Allan 115
Fletcher, Ronald 163
Foot, Paul 179
Friedman, Milton 223

Gaitskell, Hugh 116
Galbraith, J. K. 120, 150–151,
    187
Gallacher, William 127–128
Glass, David 124
Gloag, John 80, 89–91, 98
Glover, Alan 128, 136
Glyn, Andrew 184
Godwin, Anthony 136–139,
    141, 155
Gollancz, Victor 60, 97, 105
Gott, Richard 211
Gramsci, Antonio 25
    see also hegemony
Gregory, Richard 84
Grieve Smith, John 180
Griffiths, Eldon 157–158

Haldane, J. B. S. 41–42, 57
Hall, Stuart 132, 178, 212
Harrison, Paul 232
Harrison, Tom 34, 45, 65
Haseler, Stephen 181
Hattersley, Roy 228–229
Hayek, Friedrich 172, 197
hegemony 24–26, 148, 150, 173,
    195, 214, 224
Hinden, Rita 114–116
Hogg, Quintin 109–112, 147, 203
Hoggart, Richard 1, 13–14, 19,
    20, 104, 129–130, 135,
    218–220
Horabin, Tom 91, 100–101
Hucker, Elroy 156
Hutchison, Robert 103

individualism 153, 212, 214, 222, 230
industrial relations 143, 152, 165, 198, 233

Jackson, Brian 188–189
Jenkins, Roy 116, 121
Joad, C. E. M. 43
Jones, Aubrey 204
Joseph, Keith 221
justice 68, 74, 78, 89–90, 99–100, 111, 127, 146, 174, 225, 236, 250–252
  see also meritocracy

Keynes, J. M. 9, 72, 151, 176, 196
Kramnick, Isaac 181

Labour party 27, 82, 87, 97, 113–114, 121, 156, 161, 179, 237
Lane, Allen 1, 11–14, 16, 18, 22–23, 27, 33–37, 53, 60, 66, 67, 75, 85, 104–107, 127–130, 135–137, 211, 216, 219
Lane, Richard 105
Laski, Harold 24, 39–40, 42, 55, 70–71, 79, 97, 101, 248
Laski, Marghanita 18, 20
Leavis, F. R. 18, 214, 219
Left Book Club 47, 60
  see also Gollancz, Victor
Lehmann, John 49–50, 130, 131
Lessing, Doris 140
Lewis, Roy 117–119
liberalism 43, 46–49, 71, 85, 182

Machin, Stephen 251
Macmillan, Harold 72, 82, 147
Madge, Charles 34, 45–46, 66, 68
Major, Lee 251
Malik, Rex 148–149, 163
Mallock, W. H. 110

  see also Conservative party
Mander, John 141
Mannheim, Karl 125
market forces 143, 146, 163, 186–187, 196–97, 207–208, 213–214, 219–220
  see also monetarism
Marquand, David 140
Marsden, Dennis 188–189
Marsh, David 163
Marshall, T. H. 150, 187
Marxism 25, 39, 46–47, 184–185, 201, 205–206
Mass Observation 20–21, 34, 45, 59, 64–68, 93, 105
Maude, Angus 117–118, 198–200
May Day Manifesto 1968 178
Mayer, Peter 210–211, 214–220, 222–224
meritocracy 4–11, 52–53, 57, 58–59, 68, 72, 74, 77–78, 82, 88–95, 99, 102, 106–108, 110, 116–117, 119, 122–129, 131–132, 134, 145–147, 152, 157–163, 169, 171, 188–196, 207–209, 213, 220–222, 237, 238–239, 241
  see also sociology
Middleton, Neil 184
Mishan, E. J. 194–195
Mitchell, Juliet 193
monetarism 202
Moorhouse, Geoffrey 154
Mount, Ferdinand 227
Mowrer, Edgar 43

New Labour 236–237
  see also Labour party
New Left 137, 155, 170–173
New Right 170–173, 176–177, 196–199, 207, 208, 211, 228
  see also Thatcherism
Northcott, Jim 166–168

Oakley, Ann 193
Orwell, George 23, 34–35
Owen, David 224–228

Packard, Vance 152
Park, Trevor 183
Parker, John 109–112
Penguin Books
    and publishing 11–15, 136–138,
        214–220
    and readers 16–22, 59–60,
        93–94, 132, 205
    and social change 20–21, 53–54,
        55–57, 59–60, 129–131,
        218–220
    Specials 2–3, 23–24, 27, 104–105,
        135, 138, 183–184, 222, 245
Penguin Education 190–191
Penguin New Writing 48–40,
    130–131
    see also Lehmann, John
Perkin, Harold 6, 51, 94, 95
Pevsner, Dieter 137, 246
Picture Post 105
planning 41, 61–64, 69–72, 85,
    142–149, 177
Popper, Karl 121
Pritt, D. N. 22
professionalism 52–53, 58–59, 61,
    72, 91, 101, 120, 161–162,
    172–173, 198, 207, 222
    see also expertise
Profumo, John 157
property 46, 71, 95–96, 184
public ownership 95, 98, 101, 146

Raison, Timothy 167–169
Rawls, John 226
Rose, Richard 113
Rowbotham, Sheila 193
    see also feminism
Russia Review 128
    see also Cold War

Russel, Trevor 204
Russell, Bertrand 52, 55, 139

Sampson, Anthony 171
Savage, Mike 60, 67, 249–250
Second World War 5–6, 27,
    77, 85
Seers, Dudley 179–180
Segal, Lynne 233
Seldon, Arthur 172
Shanks, Michael 144–148, 159–160,
    164, 181
Shaw, George Bernard 38
Shaw, Jack 187–188
Shonfield, Anthony 142–144, 148,
    161–162, 171
Silburn, Richard 186
social democracy 4–5, 70, 72, 76,
    92, 102–103, 109, 132, 176,
    179–180, 208–212, 219–220,
    223–225, 237, 240
Social Democratic Party (SDP) 224,
    231–232
Socialist Society 232
sociology, 31, 64–69, 112–114,
    182, 245
    see also Mass Observation
Smith, David 231
Snow, C. P. 182
Spender, Stephen 47–48, 139
Standing, Guy 251
Stedman Jones, Gareth 191
student protest 190–191
Suez crisis 140–141, 173

Tawney, R. H. 56, 57, 72, 90,
    95, 116, 123, 159, 165, 227,
    228
television 130, 138, 140, 155, 246
Temple, William 92, 98
Thatcher, Margaret 29, 176,
    196–197, 199, 204, 207, 209,
    210–211, 220

Thatcherism 176, 177, 208–209, 212–213, 221–222, 229, 230–237, 239–241
see also Conservative party
Thompson, E. P. 178, 247
see also May Day Manifesto 1968
time horizons 243
Tribe, David 182–183

Unwin, Stanley 12

Vaizey, John 155, 159–161, 186, 201–203, 240–241

Wedgwood, Josiah 56, 68–69
welfare state 5, 28, 31, 131, 165, 187, 196, 203, 225
see also Beveridge, William
Wells, H. G. 79, 81, 96, 248

Weybright, Victor 130
Whyte, William 152–154
Willetts, David 235–236
Williams, Raymond 25, 154–155, 170, 178, 206
Williams, Shirley 224–225
Williams, W. E. 17, 22, 130, 135–136, 142, 144
Wilson, Harold 134, 147, 148, 155–156, 165, 177–181, 183, 240
Worpole, Ken 211
Wright, Tony 236

Young, Edward 13
Young, Michael 10, 122–124, 145, 158, 182

Zuckerman, Solly 85

a Pelican Book 3/6

The Stagnant Society

Michael Shanks